D1538906

For Reference

Not to be taken from this room

The Shaping of the Point

THE SHAPING OF THE POINT

Pittsburgh's
Renaissance Park

Robert C. Alberts

R
917.4886
AL14s

University of Pittsburgh Press

Published by the
University of Pittsburgh Press, Pittsburgh, Pa. 15260
Copyright © 1980, University of Pittsburgh Press
All rights reserved
Feffer and Simons, Inc., London
Manufactured in the United States of America

Library of Congress Cataloging in Publication Data

Alberts, Robert C
  The shaping of the Point.

  Includes bibliographical references and index.
  1. Pittsburgh—Parks—Point State Park.
2. Urban renewal—Pennsylvania—Pittsburgh. I. Title.
F159.P67P643   974.8′86   79-26885

The John J. Wright Library
LA ROCHE COLLEGE
9000 Babcock Boulevard
Pittsburgh, Pa. 15237

*The writing and publication
of this book were made possible by grants from
the A. W. Mellon Educational and Charitable Trust,
the Buhl Foundation,
the Pittsburgh Foundation,
and the Allegheny Conference on
Community Development.*

This book is dedicated to
WALLACE RICHARDS
1904–1959

His active work in Pittsburgh began in 1937
and ended on January 25, 1953—
fewer than fifteen years.
In that time he conceived great ideas for Pittsburgh,
influenced people who had the power to put them into effect,
and so set in motion forces that remade the city.
He is now almost a legend in Pittsburgh:
the stranger who came into the community,
stayed a while,
worked a miracle,
and died for his work.

(Page 146)

Books by Robert C. Alberts

The Most Extraordinary Adventures of Major Robert Stobo
The Golden Voyage: The Life and Times of William Bingham 1752–1804
The Good Provider: H. J. Heinz and His 57 Varieties
Benjamin West: A Biography
The Shaping of the Point

Contents

Illustrations

Preface

I knew, when I began to research this book, that Point State Park was a landmark of city planning in the United States. I knew that it was the spearhead of the country's earliest large downtown renewal program after World War II, and that this was the first (and the last) such program conceived, directed, and largely paid for with private capital by corporate business. I knew, too, that a towering commercial development came to the city simply because the park was being built, and that the development was a testing ground for a radical new legal concept in city planning. And I knew that during its building, the park and the development drew national, even international, attention from city planners and the press, with some seventy-eight delegations traveling to Pittsburgh—one from Australia—to study what was being done there, and how.

What I had forgotten, or had never known, was the extent to which this was also a story of human interest, with elements of controversy, conflict, suspense and, in two instances, of comedy. After a smooth beginning, Point State Park became a battleground where civic leaders, politicians, city planners, architects, artists, landscape architects, traffic engineers, academic historians, and several motivated interest groups fought for their theories, their aesthetic principles, and their claimed rights. Which concepts of city planning would prevail? Would Pittsburgh end up with a real park or with a landscaped traffic interchange? Would the two old bridges be used or dismantled? Would the 1764 Blockhouse be retained, or moved, or torn down? Would there be red, white, and blue park benches in the park? A complex of public buildings? A lighthouse at the Point? An immense stainless steel statue of Joe Magarac? A carillon bell tower?

I wrote this book at the suggestion of Theodore L. Hazlett, Jr., who was president of the A. W. Mellon Educational and Charitable Trust and the last chairman of the Point Park Committee of the Allegheny Conference on Community Development—the group of businessmen who had managed Pittsburgh's postwar "renaissance" program. I had lunch on January 8, 1975, with Hazlett and Joseph G. Smith, director of the Historical Society of Western Pennsylvania. Hazlett asked me: Would I consider working on a history of Point State Park?

He proposed that the work be done in two phases. First, I would research the whole story thoroughly over the next year or two, interviewing all the surviving principals. Second, we would then study the research and decide what kind of book, if any, should be written. The Educational and Charitable Trust, the Buhl Foundation, and the Pittsburgh Foundation would join the Allegheny Conference to pay the costs of research, writing, and publication. The Historical Society would administer the funds and accept all the research material in its permanent archives.

I gathered that key Allegheny Conference people had discussed the need for a history at a luncheon held several months earlier, on the day the park was dedicated. They were convinced that they had participated in a historically significant event. They were distressed by the recent deaths of several of their colleagues, whose recollections of their work had not been recorded and so were lost forever. They wished to see that credit was given to those who had worked the hardest, longest, and most effectively in building what was now being hailed as an outstanding success. And they realized that when the facts are not on record, the uninformed may move to fill the void, with the possibility of error and misapplied credit. This, in fact, had already been happening on Point State Park.

I was heavily committed at the beginning of 1975 to a good many works in progress or promised. A biography of the American artist Benjamin West for Houghton Mifflin. An article on General Matthew B. Ridgway for *American Heritage*. A short book on George Rogers Clark, and another on the Mount Washington Tavern, for the National Park Service. A bicentennial map and pamphlet on western Pennsylvania history for Pittsburgh National Bank. Final work on a two-year effort to edit and put a manuscript on Pittsburgh glass into publishable form. Book reviews for the Sunday New York *Times* and a continuing burden of correspondence following a recent *Times Magazine* cover story. Despite these commitments, I wanted very much to do the Point Park history, for reasons that will become apparent. Writers are optimists: They will take on any project they like that does not need to be started immediately and finished on a deadline. I accepted the Point Park commission with the stipulation that I would have a free hand in the research, without editorial control, and in the writing of the book, if I wrote it.

Over the next year and a half, at places as far away as Williamsburg, Virginia, and New York City, I interviewed sixteen men who had played leading roles in designing and building Point State Park. Some of them gave me drawers and boxes filled with records on the park. One person, who seemed to be in good health when I interviewed him at his farm at Newtown, Pa., died shortly afterward.

Researching the history of Point State Park

was an odd and fascinating experience, a long step backward in time into a partly forgotten past. During four years on the staff of a Pittsburgh newsmagazine, the *Bulletin-Index* (1938–1942), the last two years as editor, I had written weekly articles about Pittsburgh affairs and had interviewed many of the people who were later to initiate and carry out the city's postwar redevelopment program. In reading Roy Lubove's *Twentieth Century Pittsburgh* (1969), I dutifully looked up certain articles he gave as sources and was surprised (and somewhat pleased) to find that I had written them myself. As a writer and as editor of the magazine, I had a working relationship with Wallace Richards, then executive director of the Pittsburgh Regional Planning Association, who later became the prime mover in the Pittsburgh Renaissance. I called on Richards for information on stories, and he sometimes, I realized, fed me material he wanted to see in print. On one occasion he wished to rebuke Richard King Mellon for a mistake in judgment. The Pittsburgh Chamber of Commerce had formed a committee in 1939 for civic betterment, and Richards was disturbed that Mr. Mellon, the committee's chairman, held the organizational meeting in the Duquesne Club and invited only a narrow cross-section of interested persons, all Republican. Mr. Mellon was rebuked in the issue of November 2, 1939.

I left Pittsburgh in 1943 for what was to be a five-year absence, returning from a twenty-eight month stay in West Germany in June, 1948, and so I was not familiar with the early developments of the postwar renewal program. I was required to learn them on my return, however, in my work for Ketchum, MacLeod and Grove. For ten years (1960–1969) I watched the progress at the Point from my twentieth-floor office window in Gateway Four. I met Richard K. Mellon in October 1963, when I managed a press conference for him at 525 William Penn Place on behalf of his unsuccessful attempt to give Pennsylvania a new constitution. The worry of press conferences is always that no one may show up, but Mellon's were quite rare, and the array of television cameras was such that the fuses for the thirty-ninth floor blew out the moment the general made his entrance. He chatted amiably with the reporters until a building engineer restored light and power.

I finished my research on Point State Park in April 1976, and turned over a report to Ted Hazlett and the Historical Society. It was accompanied by the cassettes of my sixteen interviews, some hundreds of pages of typed transcriptions, a list of documents entrusted to me, a recommendation that a history of the park be written, and an outline of how I thought it should be done. At a meeting two days later with Hazlett, Smith, and John J. Grove, assistant director of the Allegheny Conference, I agreed to write the history. The arrangements were confirmed at a meeting six weeks later with Hazlett, Smith, Louis R. Fosner, Robert B. Pease, William G. Swain, and Alfred W. Wishart, Jr.

I delivered a completed first draft of the history, eighteen chapters, some two hundred fifty manuscript pages, in January 1978. Hazlett asked for a stronger ending, which I gave him, and he requested that there be less copy about himself, which change I declined to make, citing his promise of editorial independence. I had broadened the book to encompass a history of the Pittsburgh "Renaissance," and this change was accepted. I wrote three more drafts of the book in 1978 and 1979.

My sources for this work, and the names of those who were interviewed, who read all or parts of the manuscript, and who otherwise helped on the research and writing of this book, appear, with my grateful thanks, on pages 225–32.

The Shaping of the Point

1

"A Clear View
to the West"

August 30, 1974. People begin to stream into Point State Park around eleven o'clock, gathering in the area of the new fountain. It is a happy crowd. The rain had stopped that morning, the sun is shining, it is Friday, and the Pittsburgh Pirates are in first place by a game and a half. Everyone is prepared to take part in a moment of history—to witness something Pittsburghers have been working and waiting for since October 1945, almost thirty years earlier.

The dedication ceremonies begin at 12:15, after the arrival of throngs from the nearby office buildings. Theodore L. Hazlett, Jr., chairman of the citizens' committee that directed the design and construction of the park, is master of ceremonies. He speaks the required words of welcome and calls for a prayer. He then delivers the opening remarks, for which he has allowed himself eight minutes.

There are not many occasions in a lifetime that afford the opportunity—even the compelling necessity—of looking both backward and forward at the same time. I believe this to be one. . . .

We cannot forget the historical importance of this hallowed ground. The Point symbolizes a milepost in early American history—the planting of Anglo-Saxon civilization on the American frontier. . . . Men for decades had dreamed of this site as a monument to our historical past. . . . The last element of the park—the fountain—is completed today.

A fountain at the apex of the Point is most appropriate. It not only signifies the meeting of the three rivers, the role the rivers have played in the growth and development of our city, but also from time immemorial fountains and water have been the symbols of everlasting life, the eternal renewal of life itself. It is a fitting symbol for this great and beautiful city in which we all take pride.

And in a reference to a lull in Pittsburgh's "Renaissance" program and to certain difficulties with a new and unfriendly administration in city hall:

Now we must look to the future. Sustained in heart by this example from the past, the community must find the ways and means to recapture its lost faith and forward progress, its ability to resolve differences, restore trust between private and public leadership and march resolutely forward to develop an even greater city for ourselves and our children.

Distinguished guests and important personages are introduced, and as is inevitable on such occasions, the list is long. First, Dr. Maurice K. Goddard, the secretary of the Pennsylvania Department of Environmental Resources (known in earlier, simpler days as Forests and Waters), who had directed the building of the park for the past twenty years, through the administrations of four governors. He calls the park "a springboard for the resurgence of Downtown Pittsburgh," on which the state has expended $17 million. He is followed by eight other state officials. Then the chairman of the insurance company that provided the capital to transform twenty-three acres of commercial slum adjoining Point State Park into Gateway Center, a shining development with its nine towering new buildings. "Renewal, regeneration and rebirth," he says, "ought to be a continuous process, not spasmodic, not dictated by dire necessity, but carefully planned. . . . We should resolve that never again shall we require a phoenix to be raised out of the kind of agony which Pittsburgh suffered."

The introductions continue with the president of the Fort Pitt chapter of the Daughters of the American Revolution, who own and are administering the nearby Blockhouse, built in 1764 to repel Indian attack, unique as the oldest existing structure of authenticated date in western Pennsylvania. The Daughters have triumphantly repelled an attack of their own, driving back attempts of the civic planners and the state to take over their Blockhouse. A Son of the American Revolution is introduced, ninety-four years old, born the very day James A. Garfield was elected twentieth president of the United States. Then some of the professionals—architects, landscape architects, engineers, city planners—who designed and worked on the building of the park, its bridges, its highway interchange, its wharves, its landscaping, its fort restorations and museum, its fountain.

One of the professionals, a key figure from the day the park was conceived, is not present. Six weeks earlier he had come back to Pittsburgh from Williamsburg, Virginia, his new home, to observe the test run of the fountain. A week before the dedication he had written, "I was tempted to go, but when my common sense, of which I still have a little, said NO!, I had to obey. I am celebrating my 80th birthday today and begin to realize there are limits to my strength. . . . I have found my greatest satisfaction in the way the people of Pittsburgh have vindicated the Commonwealth's judgment in making this unique site an historic park. It was a glorious sight to see people of every descrip-

Presiding at the dedication of Point State Park and its majestic fountain, Theodore L. Hazlett, Jr., told of the thirty years of work that had gone into building an uncluttered city park with a dramatic open view to the west. In the background, across the Allegheny River, stands the city's four-year-old Three Rivers Stadium. (Pittsburgh *Post-Gazette*)

tion swarming into this park to enjoy, for the first time in the history of this city, that sublime landscape of sky, hills and rivers. It has, in a sense, already been dedicated by the people who have accepted it by using it as it was intended. No ceremony or words are necessary to testify to the success of this great investment in human happiness."

The director of the new Fort Pitt Museum is introduced. The names are read of the contractors who had worked on the fountain. The lieutenant governor of Pennsylvania makes a dedication speech, no copy of which, alas, is now available. Members of the Pittsburgh Ballet Theater perform dance selections. The poet Samuel Hazo, director of Pittsburgh's International Poetry Forum, reads a passage from Haniel Long's *Pittsburgh Memoranda*, lines to a comrade killed in World War I:

> Fred, what has happened to you?
> Do you know what God knows, now?
> And is the truth different from what the living
> can catch a glimpse of—
> that one must do one's best by the outward
> world, as neighbor and citizen;
> but that the shortcomings of the real, in which
> all glides to disorder,
> are best healed, considered in ages, by the man
> who holds
> to his own heart and dream: his own heart and
> dream really being,
> from any angle, the reason why the real remains
> imperfect,

never more significant than a child's book of
sketches, random,
a mere hint of what might be in our world.

Some of those present at the dedication ceremonies had worked on the Point State Park project through several decades, and they had come to think of themselves as a band of brothers. That day, they say, they felt two overriding emotions.

First, their thoughts kept returning to the men who had not lived to see their work completed. Theodore Hazlett had mentioned them: "Recent memories of friends no longer here crowd in upon us to the extent that we are overwhelmed." These friends had been the occasioners, the prime movers, of the Pittsburgh Renaissance, and in large measure they were responsible for Point State Park as its crowning achievement. Five names were mentioned most often in the addresses and in conversation after the ceremonies.

• Richard King Mellon, banker, of Scotch-Irish ancestry, a Presbyterian, a Republican, a shy man but one of great power, influence, and capacity for persuasion.

• David Leo Lawrence, Scotch-Irish Roman Catholic, a Democrat, a machine politician, mayor of Pittsburgh during thirteen crucial years, later governor of Pennsylvania. (His son, daughter, and grandson were introduced from the speakers' platform during the dedication.)

• Wallace Richards, a one-time newspaperman,

formerly an official of the New Deal administration in Washington, who was brought to Pittsburgh to serve as executive secretary of the Pittsburgh Regional Planning Association, became General Mellon's "civic adviser," and drove himself so hard that it was thought he died for the dream he had for Pittsburgh.

• Park H. Martin, who had been chief engineer of the county's public works department and who in 1944 became the first executive director of the Allegheny Conference on Community Development, the mainspring of the Pittsburgh Renaissance.

• Arthur B. Van Buskirk, a lawyer, vice-president of T. Mellon and Sons, and chairman, until the year before his death in 1972, of the Allegheny Conference's Point Park Committee.

"In the mid-twentieth century," Theodore Hazlett had said in his opening remarks, "the eyes of the country were upon this city as it sought to rid itself of smoke, floods, and physical ugliness." City planners came to Pittsburgh in the years 1946 to 1960, even from foreign countries, to study what these men and their colleagues were doing. Writers came from the nation's newspapers and from architectural and engineering journals. Some two dozen national magazines published major articles. They all reported the story of the improbable partnership between Richard Mellon and David Lawrence, the one providing private funds, prestige, civic and business leadership, and a cadre of planners of proved technical and

professional ability; the other bringing political clout, the confidence and support of organized labor, and the enabling legislation. *Fortune* magazine had written in February 1947: "Pittsburgh is the test of industrialism everywhere to renew itself, to rebuild upon the gritty ruins of the past a society more equitable, more spacious, more in the human scale." *Engineering News Record* summed up the consensus twelve years later, in November 1959: "More than any other U.S. city, Pittsburgh has demonstrated how a community on the downgrade can arrest its slide, reverse the trend, and build anew. Pittsburgh is a shining example of what engineering, planning, political leadership and business support can do to initiate and carry out a program of reconstruction and development."

The other emotion commonly felt by those who had worked on the development of Point Park was a sense of relief, and sometimes of wonderment, that the park had survived all the hazards and threats of thirty years' construction and had actually been built very much as originally planned. The basic concept had been set forth in the early years to build and maintain a simple, unified park of monumental sweep, uncluttered by buildings, memorials, and statues, with the open space that is so rare in modern cities. The hills and rivers, little changed by man since the eighteenth century, would provide a majestic memorial far more impressive than any man-made monument. The dramatic view to the west, down the Ohio River, the nation's first highway to the heartland of America, should be open and unimpeded.

The concept and the design were explained in continuous publicity in newspapers and magazines, in displays and reprints, on radio and television, and in scores of illustrated talks given before organizations of all kinds throughout western Pennsylvania. But as the park progressed, and especially as it neared completion, it became apparent that people with strong views had forgotten that the design had received enormous publicity, nor did they seem to be aware that the plans had been laboriously passed through a score of city, county, state, and federal bodies, from City Council to the U.S. Corps of Engineers, whose approvals were required by law. Not everyone, it was discovered, liked the sweep of uncluttered open space. Open space was where something should be put. Suggestions proliferated. Put up a one-hundred-foot-high statue of Joe Magarac, the legendary steelworker. Raise a carillon bell tower to ring out the glory of the past. Erect an enormous Calvary cross, a Scot's Cross of St. Andrew, a stainless steel trilon, a memorial to President Lincoln, a public auditorium, a hall honoring all the nation's war dead. Reconstruct Fort Pitt, reconstruct Fort Duquesne. Cancel the fountain. Save Manchester Bridge and Point Bridge and convert them to platforms housing shops, a restaurant, an art gallery, a public library, a 350-room motel, and an industrial museum.

Those responsible for the design and construction of the park marveled that here indeed, on August 30, 1974, were uncluttered open space and a clear view to the west. One of the planners says today, "I was so overcome with the beauty of it all that I stood gazing at the fountain, my eyes wet with tears. I still can't believe that it happened."

The introductions (thirty-one in all), the speeches, and the tributes end. The moment has come to start the fountain. Several of those present are a little apprehensive, for they remember the ceremony on May 18, 1950, when, with the governor and other dignitaries present, the first building was to be demolished. The 1800-pound headache ball had swung in a magnificent arc, buried itself in the side of a brick building, and stayed there.

The master of ceremonies introduces Mrs. Arthur Van Buskirk, widow of the dominant figure in the building of the park. She presses a button. Three 250-horsepower pumps drive a column of water into the air, gradually higher, higher, to reach 150 feet. Three other pumps create a design of peacock tails in the three-quarter acre granite-rimmed basin at the base. There are cheers and applause. The ceremonies are closed, the crowd disperses. Point State Park has been dedicated.

2

The Significance of the Point
In American History

During the demolition ceremony at Point State Park on May 18, 1950, a resident historian declared, in a moment of enthusiasm, "No spot on American soil surpasses in historical importance this very ground on which we stand." Boston and Philadelphia would certainly dispute that, and probably Williamsburg, New York, Gettysburg, and St. Augustine. A case can be made, none the less, for the historian's claim. Great and dramatic events did take place at Pittsburgh's Point in the second half of the eighteenth century. The history of the United States, in fact, and of other parts of the world, was changed by events that occurred at or near the Forks of the Ohio in the years 1749–1758.

We can see why and how if we examine the map on page 10. Imagine that you have traced with your finger the route up the St. Lawrence River from Quebec to Montreal, which are the most important French cities in 1749. You have continued up the river to Kingston . . . across Lake Ontario . . . up the thirty-four miles of the Niagara River . . . and westward along the south shore of Lake Erie. Now you are at Presque Isle (Erie). Go twelve miles south, overland to French Creek . . . south on the creek to the Allegheny River . . . and farther south to the Point, the triangle of ground where the Allegheny meets the Monongahela to form the Ohio River. A courier can make the journey from Montreal to the Forks of the Ohio in as little as two weeks.

Now go the 987 miles down the Ohio to the Mississippi River, through the Indiana and Illinois country where in 1749 some five thousand French are living in four principal villages: Vincennes, Kaskaskia, Cahokia, and Prairie du Rocher. Then go on down the Mississippi to France's New Orleans in Louisiana. We have covered almost three thousand miles of navigable rivers and lakes from the Gulf of St.

The French could travel to the Forks of the Ohio by an almost uninterrupted river highway; the British and Americans had to struggle over seven ridges of the "Endless Mountains." (Adapted from a map drawn by Samuel H. Bryant for Lowell Innes's *Pittsburgh Glass, 1797– 1891,* copyright © 1976 by Lowell Innes, and reproduced by permission of Houghton Mifflin Company)

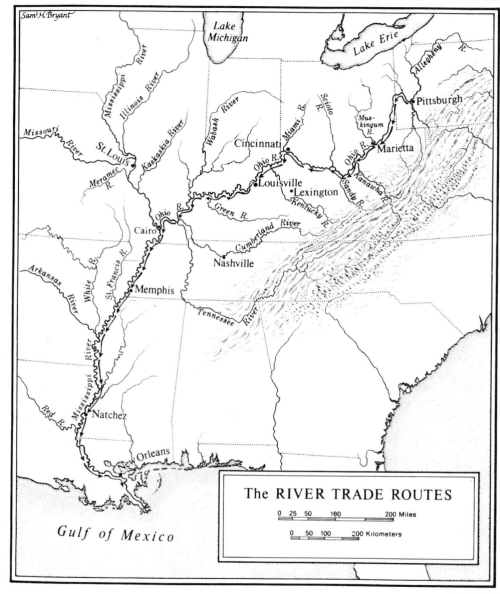

The RIVER TRADE ROUTES

0 25 50 100   200 Miles

0   50 100   200 Kilometers

Lawrence to the Gulf of Mexico, interrupted by only four relatively short portages.

The tracing fingers of the kings and statesmen in London and Paris also made that journey, and they kept returning to the Forks of the Ohio. In their quest for land, trade, and strategic advantage over old enemies, they recognized that this was the key to control of that vast expanse of North America west of the Appalachian Mountains. The French saw that it was the place the British would logically choose if Britain meant to block their passage on the river highway between Canada and Louisiana. "What has been observed," the commander-in-chief of New France wrote to his superiors in Paris, "shows the absolute necessity of the free and certain communication from Canada to the Mississippi. This chain, once broken, would leave an opening of which the English would doubtless take advantage. . . . Many of their writings are full of this project."

The commander-in-chief was quite right; the British and Americans had every intention of taking advantage of any opening. An incursion by the French into the upper Ohio Valley would block an advance into the rich western country, and the British meant to oppose it. They had two advantages: They outnumbered the French ten to one, and their nearest ports and capital cities, Philadelphia, Baltimore, and Williamsburg, were several hundred miles closer to the Forks of the Ohio than were Montreal and Quebec. On the other hand, they

had no water routes to the west, and their way was impeded by seven mountain ridges. Nevertheless, British-American hunters, trappers, and traders, and their land company agents and surveyors, were already crisscrossing the Ohio Valley as far west as the Wabash River.

When the French decided to claim this land and drive out the British, they chose the Forks of the Ohio as the place to make the challenge, though they had neither trading posts nor settlements in that area. In 1749, Captain Céloron de Blainville led some two hundred and fifty French, Canadians, and Indians in an "expédition de reconnaissance" into the Ohio Valley. As he progressed down the rivers, Céloron chose sites for forts, warned the British traders to leave, and buried lead plates inscribed with a proclamation that this land, and all the land drained by its rivers and streams, belonged to the king of France. When he returned to Montreal, Céloron reported that the Indians were unfriendly, that they depended on the British for favorable exchange of goods, and that France, if it did not move rapidly and in strength, would lose the Ohio Valley. By the end of 1753 the French had built a fort at Presque Isle, another on the portage at French Creek, and a third at the confluence of French Creek and the Allegheny, and they were assembling 2,000 troops to garrison a fort they intended to build at the Forks of the Ohio.

The struggle for control of the Ohio Valley lasted for forty-five years, first between the

French and the British (1750–1758), then between the British and the Indians (1763–1764), then between the British and the Americans (1776–1783), and finally between the Americans and the Indians (1783–1795). The early struggle spread to Europe to become the bloodiest war of the eighteenth century; allies turned into enemies and enemies into allies as the fighting continued. Some of the most significant and stirring events of those years took place at the Forks, on the wedge of ground called the Point. Nine episodes may be singled out for their drama and their importance in our national history.

1. November 23, 1753

George Washington, twenty-one years old, an adjutant in the Virginia militia, was in deep thought as he prowled about the terrain at the confluence of the rivers. He had arrived at the Forks of the Ohio that morning and had gone at once to the uninhabited, windswept Point. He wrote in his journal:

I spent some time in viewing the rivers, and the land in the Fork; which I think extremely well situated for a fort, as it has the absolute command of both rivers. The land at the Point is 20 or 25 feet above the common surface of the water; and a considerable bottom of flat, well-timbered land all around it, very convenient for building. The rivers are each a quarter of a mile, or more, across, and run here very near at right angles; Aligany bearing N.E. and Monongahela S.E. The former of these two is a very rapid and swift running water; the other deep and still, without any perceptible fall.

Major Washington then paddled about two miles below the Point to inspect an Indian mound (McKees Rocks) on the south bank of the Ohio, which the Virginia land company had considered as the site for a fort.

I think it greatly inferior, either for defence or advantages; especially the latter: for a fort at the Forks would be equally well situated on the Ohio, and have the entire command of the Monongahela; which runs up to our settlements and is extremely well designed for water carriage, as it is of a deep still nature. Besides a fort at the Fork might be built at a much less expense than at the other place.

Major Washington stayed eight days at the Forks on a journey he was making north to the French forts. As an emissary of the governor of Virginia, he was to order the French to leave the Ohio Valley. As a secondary mission he chose to recommend a site for the land company's fort at or near the Forks. The French declined to leave. Four months later a small force of Virginians began to build a fort (and in a sense founded Pittsburgh) at the Point.

2. April 17, 1754

A French fleet of 300 canoes and 60 bateaux appeared on the lower Allegheny in the early afternoon and landed on the south shore a mile or so above the Point. Men unloaded the boats with practised precision and marched off, 500 strong, to take up positions across the base of the triangle at the Point. They trained two of their eighteen cannon on the small fort there, completed only that morning by the Virginians. It was no more than a squared-log storehouse with a stockade around it, but it bore an impressive name, that of Britain's royal heir, Prince George.

Captain Contrecoeur, the French commander, sent an officer, two drummers, and an Indian to Fort Prince George under a red flag of truce. He gave the defenders—thirty-three soldiers, eight artisans, and a few Indians—one hour to surrender. If they accepted his terms, they would be permitted to leave the next day with their arms, tools, and other belongings. If they resisted, they and their fort would be destroyed.

The Virginians surrendered. Their commander, an ensign, had dinner in Contrecoeur's tent that night. The two men talked amicably through an interpreter of the claims of Britain and France for the Ohio Valley. Contrecoeur expressed astonishment that the British should have presumed to trespass on land universally recognized as the property of the king of France.

The French dismantled Fort Prince George and used its timbers in building their own fort at the apex of the Point—an earth and timber structure with bastions at the four corners, 150 feet square, with a drawbridge over a ditch, the whole named in honor of the Marquis Du-quesne, governor-general of New France. Early in August, Contrecoeur received a letter of congratulation from Montreal. "At the sight of you," the Marquis Duquesne wrote, "the English have withdrawn, looking foolish, and in less than an hour's time you have become master of the battlefield. It is admirable that under your direction nothing has occurred that would resemble an act of hostility."

3. July 7, 1754

On this day of triumph for France, a 700-man army beached its canoes at Fort Duquesne and proceeded to celebrate a splendid victory over the British three days earlier.

They had left Fort Duquesne on June 28 under the command of Captain de Villiers. They paddled up the Monongahela to Redstone (Brownsville) and there began a march over Chestnut Ridge in pursuit of Lieutenant Colonel George Washington and his small army of Virginians and South Carolinians. Washington had advanced part way over the mountain, intending to descend the Monongahela and attack Fort Duquesne, but now he was in full retreat to a stockade he called Fort Necessity, laid in an open area known as the Great Meadows (near present-day Uniontown).

Villiers reached Fort Necessity on the morning of July 3, surrounded it, and at once began a firefight that lasted all day and into the evening. He had 600 well-equipped soldiers, mostly Canadians, and 100 Indians. Washington had fewer than 400 men, of whom 115 were so ill from exhaustion and lack of food that they could not fall in for duty. His Indian allies had left him, some of them to join the French. His losses in the fighting were heavy, and his return fire was ineffective against the enemy concealed in the woods.

Despite his advantages, Villiers that night offered Washington terms of surrender that were relatively generous, though humiliating, and Washington accepted them. He and his men were allowed to march back to Virginia bearing their arms. They were pledged not to return over the mountains for one year. They turned two captains over to the French as hostages to guarantee return of twenty-one French prisoners Washington had taken in a small battle some weeks earlier at Jumonville's Glen.

At Fort Duquesne the rejoicing continued for several days. The French had lost only two Canadians and one Indian at Fort Necessity. The Indians were so impressed by the one-sided victory that they clearly would now become allies of France or would at least remain neutral. In signing the capitulation, moreover, Washington had unwittingly also signed a statement, written in French, that he had "assassinated" the French commander in the April encounter. French statesmen circulated this "confession" among the capitals of Europe to show that Britain, not France, was the aggressor in North America. Now in complete control of the Ohio Valley, they believed that the British, disgusted with

their failure, would give up the attempt to take the country west of the mountains.

They have misjudged the British. The government votes £50,000 to pursue the war in America and mounts a campaign for 1755 to assault French positions in North America at four main points. One of these is Fort Duquesne. Major-General Edward Braddock will march from Virginia to take Fort Duquesne with two regiments of British infantry, intending then to move north and take Fort Niagara.

4. July 9, 1755

Captain Contrecoeur had been receiving almost daily reports from his Indians on the progress of a large British army that was marching on Fort Duquesne. It numbered some twenty-six hundred men, and it was cutting a road northwest over the mountains from Wills Creek (Cumberland, Maryland). "These troops," Contrecoeur wrote to the governor-general in Canada, "remain so constantly on guard, always marching in battle formation, that all the efforts that our detachments put forth against them are useless." Contrecoeur considered resistance out of the question; he was badly outnumbered, his Indians were unwilling to fight, and the British had heavy artillery to demolish his defenses. He debated whether to negotiate a surrender with the honors of war, or to burn the fort and take flight on the rivers.

His long-awaited replacement, Captain Daniel de Beaujeu, who had arrived several days earlier, was determined to attack the British. He planned to do so before they reached Fort Duquesne; in this way he might slow down or stop their advance until French reinforcements arrived, and perhaps might avoid a siege. Contrecoeur, opposing the plan, told him he would have to fight with such men as he could persuade to follow him as volunteers. He finally gave Beaujeu command of the troops, but he held back 400 men to defend the fort.

The Indians said to Beaujeu, "Father, you want to die and sacrifice us. The English are more than four thousand, and we are only eight hundred, yet you wish to attack them. Certainly you must see that you are making no sense. We ask of you until tomorrow to make up our minds."

Early next morning, July 9, Beaujeu put his French and Canadians in Indian dress and began to distribute powder, bullets, and flints. He himself was stripped to the waist, wearing only a gorget on his chest to indicate his rank. A French officer described what happened next: "M. de Beaujeu left his fort with the few troops he had and asked the Indians for the result of their deliberations. They answered that they could not march. M. de Beaujeu . . . said to them, 'I am determined to confront the enemy. What—would you let your father go alone? I am certain to defeat them!' With this, they decided to follow him. The detachment then was composed of 72 regulars, 146 Canadians, and 63 Indians."

The hours passed while Contrecoeur waited.

The sound of cannon was heard from the east. Word of the action filtered back to the fort. The French were too late for the ambush they hoped for; the two forces met in a head-on clash at Turtle Creek, on the Monongahela some nine miles above the Point. Beaujeu was dead, killed in the early exchange of fire. The Canadians and Indians had begun to panic but had been rallied by Captain Dumas, Beaujeu's second-in-command.

By late afternoon the battle was over. The British army had been massacred, and its remnants were in full flight to the south; of an advance force of 1459 men, almost 1,000 had been killed or wounded. Braddock was dying. Colonel Washington had distinguished himself in the battle and had managed to escape with the fugitives fleeing southward. French losses were only 23 killed, 15 of them Indians. Huge quantities of captured military stores were being carried to Fort Duquesne: wagons, horses, cattle, and artillery; Braddock's war chest containing his highly confidential orders and correspondence; and enough presents to supply the Indians for the next year. The Indians were staggering under the loads they carried: scalps, arms collected on the field, and spoils taken from the wagon train. Some were proudly wearing the red coats, sashes, and tricornered laced hats of the slain British officers. The Indians had 30 prisoners, including several of the women who had been traveling with the army.

James Smith, a young American captured by the Indians some weeks earlier, now a prisoner in Fort Duquesne, had seen the detachment march out that morning and saw them return in the evening with "the voice of joy and triumph."

Those that were coming in, and those that had arrived, kept a constant firing of small arms, and also the great guns in the fort, which were accompanied with the most hideous shouts and yells from all quarters; so that it appeared to me as if the infernal regions had broke loose.

About sundown I beheld a small party coming in with about a dozen prisoners, stripped naked, with their hands tied behind their backs, and their faces and part of their bodies blacked—these prisoners they burned on the bank of the Allegheny river, opposite to the fort. I stood on the fort wall until I beheld them begin to burn one of these men: they had him tied to a stake, and kept touching him with firebrands, red-hot irons, etc, and he screaming in a most doleful manner—the Indians in the mean time yelling like infernal spirits.

As this scene appeared too shocking for me to behold, I retired to my lodgings both sore and sorry.

Captain Contrecoeur wrote an account of the battle to his minister in France. The governor-general, he said, "doubtless has informed you, Monseigneur, of the last victory I gained on the 9th of July at Fort Duquesne. . . . If my services seem of sufficient value to you, Monseigneur, to merit some reward, I dare ask you to bestow the Cross of St. Louis on me, and to further the promotion of my two children."

5. September 14, 1758

Now again, as they had three years earlier, the French at Fort Duquesne were watching and waiting the advance of a British army. Brigadier General John Forbes had the largest body of troops ever seen in North America— 2000 British regulars and 4000 American provincials, including two Virginia regiments, one of them under Colonel Washington. Forbes's march toward the Forks of the Ohio differed from Braddock's in two ways. He was (to Washington's outspoken disapproval) cutting a road straight over the Pennsylvania mountains instead of coming northwest from Virginia. And every forty miles or so he was prudently building a strong fort to fall back on in case of a defeat—at Carlisle, at Raystown (Bedford), and at Loyalhanna Creek (Ligonier).

Everything was quiet at Fort Duquesne on the night of September 14. In their camps outside the walls of the fort, the Indians had let their fires go out and lay wrapped in their blankets, asleep. Most of the French inside the fort were in their beds or bunks. Incredibly, no one was aware that an enemy force of 400 men was lying on the hills a few hundred yards to the east, with 350 others a mile or so behind them.

These troops were led by Major James Grant, a British career officer chiefly distinguished for his contempt for American provincial officers and men. General Forbes was at Raystown; Colonel Henry Bouquet, his second-in-command, was at the Loyalhanna fort, which was to be the jumping-off place for the attack on Fort Duquesne. Bouquet had planned to send a patrol to the Forks of the Ohio to capture prisoners, but Grant persuaded him to dispatch a larger force and recover some of their own men held captive. Against his better judgment, Bouquet sent him off on September 9 with 750 men: 300 kilted Highlanders, 100 Royal Americans (British regulars recruited in America and paid by the Crown), and 350 Pennsylvania, Virginia, and Maryland militiamen. As a mark of identification in night fighting, Grant had each man wear a white shirt over his tunic.

Now, so close to the French fort, to this "nest of robbers," Grant lay for some hours wondering what to do next. He finally gave in to what Forbes later called "his thirst for fame" and decided to capture Fort Duquesne. He believed the French had only three or four hundred men, and these he proposed to draw from the fort into an ambush. In his later report on the battle he wrote, "In order to put on a good countenance and to convince our men they had no reason to fear, I gave directions to our drums to beat the reveille. The troops were in an advantageous post and I must own I thought we had nothing to fear."

Wakened and warned by this commotion, some 800 French and Indians seized their arms and rushed into action. Instead of plunging into an ambush, they shrewdly went up each river bank in small parties, circled around, and began to shoot down Grant's confused and panic-stricken troops, who were prime targets in their white shirts. They killed 278 men and 22 officers and took 37 prisoners. Shortly before he was captured, Grant was seen sitting on the bank of the Allegheny, his head in his hands. He refused to flee, moaning, "My heart is broke. I shall never outlive this day." Those who escaped fled to the east, protected and saved by a rear guard of 100 Virginians, of whom 50 were killed in this action.

There was a celebration at Fort Duquesne for another brilliant defeat of the British with almost no losses—the fourth in four years. The rejoicing subsided, however, when the French Indians, loaded with booty and fearful of the large army at Fort Ligonier, announced that it was now time for them to return to their villages for the fall hunting.

With the permission of Captain de Ligneris, the French commandant, Grant wrote a letter of explanation to Colonel Bouquet. He blamed everything on Major Andrew Lewis, who had commanded the Virginians, and closed with, "I flatter myself that my being a prisoner will be no detriment to my promotion in case vacancies should happen in the army." Seventeen years later, at the outbreak of the American Revolution, Lieutenant Colonel James Grant will tell Parliament that he would need only 5000 men to make America an obedient colony.

17

6. *November 24–27, 1758*

Captain de Ligneris knew in the autumn of 1758 that this time the French position at the Forks of the Ohio was truly hopeless. He had only 400 men, his supplies were low, and there was no promise of reinforcements. His Indian braves had left him, and their tribes were suing for peace. Even now, an Englishman, a Moravian missionary named Christian Post, was negotiating a peace treaty in the Indian camp across the Allegheny from the fort; the Indians refused to pull down the British flag that marked his presence and turn him over as a spy.

An attack Ligneris had made on Fort Ligonier in October had accomplished nothing, and his scouts reported that "General Frobus," the British commander, was not going into winter quarters, as he had intended. Instead, he had suddenly sprung into action and was sending forward a fast-moving column of 2500 picked men and a light artillery train, led by competent, experienced officers, including Colonel Bouquet and Colonel Washington. Ligneris concluded (correctly) that a French prisoner or deserter had told the British general how weak the French position was.

Ligneris assembled his officers and discussed what they should do. They concurred that resistance was useless and that they should evacuate the fort, saving what they could and destroying the rest. Ligneris gave orders to put the cannon and munitions in bateaux, leaving fifty to sixty barrels of spoiled powder in the magazine; to place explosives in the bake oven; to stack faggots in the cabins and in the buildings in the forts; and to dismantle the plank roofs and lean them against the log walls. He divided eight days' provisions among the units and packed the small amount of goods remaining to be given to the Ohio Indians "to induce them always to take our side and attack the English." The bateaux were to go down the Ohio to the Illinois post, and with them his prisoners of war. Some of his men were to follow on foot down the right bank of the river. He and 192 men would march northward to Machault (Franklin), the nearest French fort.

When all his scouts were in and accounted for, when the bateaux had embarked, and after the Machault contingent had crossed the Allegheny and started north to a point where they would wait for him, Ligneris ordered a troop detail to set fire to the faggots and light the powder trains. By the light of the burning buildings, he and his men stepped into the one remaining bateau and started up the river. At the sound of the explosions he stopped and sent three men overland to assess what damage had been done. They reported that one of the two magazines had exploded; the powder train had burned out on the other. Nevertheless, the enemy would salvage "nothing but the ironwork of the community buildings."

The British force, including Washington's brigade, was encamped twelve miles away on the night of November 24 when they heard the explosions. An Indian scout reported next morning that he had seen a huge cloud of smoke at the Point. The British resumed their ponderous, cautious march, cutting a road for the artillery as they progressed. They reached the Forks at six that evening, to find a destroyed and deserted fortress, some thirty chimneys standing above the charred and roofless buildings.

General Forbes arrived at the Point the next day, carried on a litter suspended from two horses. He was so ill from the bloody flux that he had described himself in a letter as "extremely weak, having been reduced to the last extremity." He ordered "A Day of Publick Thanksgiving to Almighty God for Our Success" on the twenty-sixth, with a divine service at 1 P.M. outside his tent. Washington was one of three colonels taking part in the formal raising of the British flag. Five years earlier, almost to the exact day, he had stood at that spot on his mission to the French outposts. He had spent five years of his life working and fighting for this triumphant moment, but his thanksgiving was marred. Forbes should have used Braddock's road from Virginia, the owner of this land. Instead, he had built a road that led back to the laggard, obstructionist, pacifist, Quaker-dominated city on the Delaware.

A celebration of the great victory was held the next day, after which one hundred men who had fought in the September engagement went to Grant's Hill to search out and bury the bodies of their comrades. Thirty men marched to Turtle Creek and there buried more than four hundred fifty skulls, with the few bones not carried away by the wolves.

Between the flag raising and the sermon, the celebration and the grave details, everyone of importance seems to have been writing letters on November 25–27.

General Forbes had named the fort at Loyalhanna "Pittsbourgh" in honor of William Pitt, secretary of state for war, but now, in a letter dated "Pittsbourgh, 27 November 1758" he improved his gesture.

I do myself the honour of acquainting you that it has pleased God to crown His Majesty's arms with success over all his enemies upon the Ohio. . . . I have used the freedom of giving your name to Fort Duquesne, as I hope it was in some measure the being actuated by your spirits that now makes us masters of the place. Nor could I help using the same freedom in the naming of two other forts that I built (plans of which I send you), the one Fort Ligonier and the other Bedford. I hope the name fathers will take them under their protection, in which case these dreary deserts will soon be the richest and most fertile of any possessed by the British in North America.

Colonel Washington wrote to the governor of Virginia:

Preparative steps should immediately be taken for securing the communication from Virginia, by constructing a post at Redstone Creek, which would greatly facilitate the supplying of our troops on the Ohio.

Colonel Bouquet wrote to Anne Willing in Philadephia, who had declined to marry him unless he left the military service:

The French, seized with a panic at our approach have destroyed themselves—that nest of Pirates which has so long harboured the murderers and destructors of our poor People. . . . I hope to have soon the pleasure to see you, and give you a more particular account of what may deserve your curiosity: chiefly about the beauty of this situation, which appears to me beyond my description.

An unnamed correspondent sent a dispatch to the *Pennsylvania Gazette*:

I have the pleasure to write this letter upon the spot where Fort Duquesne once stood, while the British flag flies over the debris of its bastions in Triumph.

Blessed be God, the long looked for day is arrived, that has now fixed us on the banks of the Ohio . . . in the quiet and peaceable possession of the finest and most fertile country of America, lying in the happiest climate in the universe. This valuable acquisition lays open to all his Majesty's subjects a vein of treasure which, if rightly managed, may prove richer than the mines of Mexico, the trade with the numerous nations of Western Indians. It deprives our enemies of the benefits they expected from their deep laid schemes, and breaks asunder the chain of communication betwixt Canada and Louisiana.

Despite all their bad luck and all their blunders—at Fort Necessity, Braddock's Field and Grant's Hill,

and at Fort William Henry and Fort Ticonderoga in the north—the British win the final victories and the war. They take Louisbourg, Niagara, Kingston, Quebec, and Montreal. They drive the French out of North America. A treaty is signed in Paris in 1763. In Francis Parkman's famous and memorable phrases, they "quarreled for a prize that belonged to neither," and "half a continent changed hands at the scratch of a pen."

At the Forks of the Ohio the British build their largest and costliest fort, covering seventeen and a half acres near the bank of the Monongahela, more than two and a half acres of it within the ramparts. Fort Pitt is constructed of brick, stone, timber and sod; it has five bastions, a drawbridge, eleven underground rooms beneath the ramparts, and a magazine under the ramparts for powder and shot.

The Indians watch the erection of Fort Pitt with dismay and resentment. They had expected, or at least hoped, that the victorious British would once again retire over the mountains and allow the relatively peaceful and mutually advantageous trade relationships of earlier years to return. Instead, the British obviously intend to settle and claim this land as their own. Early in 1763 they announce that by the terms of the peace treaty with France they own all the territory west to the Mississippi. Now, moreover, without the need to woo and win the Indians away from the French, the British are becoming arrogant. They ignore Indian courtesies, stop giving presents, pay less for skins and furs, and raise the prices of arms, lead, powder, rum, kettles, mirrors, and other supplies.

A view of the Point in the eighteenth century. Two vessels are tied up on the shore of the Monongahela waiting for high water to carry passengers and freight down the Ohio. (Carnegie Library, Pittsburgh)

7. May 27–August 10, 1763

The Indian rebellion began in May 1763 and it spread at once throughout the western country, directed by a remarkable leader, Pontiac, a principal chief of the Ottawas. Indian scalping parties ventured as far east as Carlisle; at least two thousand settlers and traders were killed or captured, and the eastern towns were filled with refugees, known as the "back inhabitants." Twelve frontier forts were attacked and eight fell. Some were overrun; others surrendered on the promise of safe conduct to an English settlement; most of the men, women, and children in them were butchered, burned alive, or carried off as prisoners. Trade goods valued at £100,000 were plundered.

The attacks began near Pittsburgh on May 27, when a family and most of its servants were killed on the Youghiogheny near West Newton. Two soldiers were killed at Fort Pitt two days later. Refugees fled to the fort, and by the end of May, in addition to the 125 regulars in the garrison, it held 305 women and children and 205 men. More refugees appeared from time to time, telling frightful stories of what they had seen and suffered. Captain Simon Ecuyer—like Bouquet a Swiss professional soldier in the service of the British—worked for eleven days in what he called "an unbelievable way" to prepare Fort Pitt for a siege. He burned to the ground some two hundred houses and huts between the fort and Grant's Hill and dismantled those in the lower town, using the materials to construct shelters for the refugees within the fort. He shored up the Ohio bastion, the one nearest the Allegheny, which had fallen away in a thirty-four-foot spring flood; he used barrels filled with earth, bales of deerskins belonging to the merchants, and sharp-pointed poles facing outward. He set up a smallpox isolation hospital under the protection of the drawbridge; built a forge and two bake ovens in the fort; placed beaver traps and spiked "crow-feet" in the ditch; and fenced the cattle and horses in an enclosure under one of the walls. He built a fire engine, placed casks of water about the fort, and trained the women and older children to use the fire buckets to extinguish fire arrows. He distributed tomahawks and placed everyone on half rations. Drums beat reveille every day at an early hour, and the men were at their alarm stations well before dawn.

The fort was under intermittent siege throughout June and July by Delawares, Shawnees, Wyandots, and Mingoes. Smoke in the distance told of houses and barns fired. At times, when there were no Indians in sight, parties could venture out under guard to gather hay, wheat, corn, and greens. The first heavy attack came on June 22 and was beaten off. Two days later two chiefs appeared before the fort, ceremoniously laid down their weapons, advanced, and "made a speech." William Trent, trader and militiaman, reported the conversation in a diary he kept throughout the siege. The braves began by saying that all the other English forts, including Ligonier, had fallen (which was not true) and that a great number of warriors were coming to capture Fort Pitt. Out of friendship and regard, the chiefs had persuaded the warriors to delay their attack long enough for everyone in the fort to leave and go safely to the English settlements.

They desired we would set off immediately. The commanding officer [Ecuyer] thanked them, let them know that we had everything we wanted, that we could defend it against all the Indians in the woods, that we had three large armies marching to chastise those Indians that had struck us . . . but not to tell any other natives. They said they would go and speak to their chiefs and come and tell us what they said.

They returned and said they would hold fast of the chain of friendship. Out of our regard to them we gave them two blankets and a handkerchief out of the small pox hospital. I hope it will have the desired effect.

On July 27, at another such parley, Trent wrote: "As soon as they came over, Captain Ecuyer's answer to their speech was delivered them, letting them know that we took this place from the French, that this was our home and [we] would defend [it] to the last, that . . . we had ammunition and provisions for three years. (I wish we had for three months.)" Ecuyer added: "Brothers, I will advise you to go home to your towns and take care of your wives and children. Moreover I tell you that if any of you appear again about this fort I will throw

bombshells, which will burst and blow you to atoms, and fire cannon among you, loaded with a whole bag of bullets. Therefore, take care, for I don't want to hurt you."

The fort was under almost continuous siege from July 28 through August 3. Indian women and children appeared on the far shores, which, Trent explained, meant that the Indians felt they would now take the fort and had brought their families to carry away the spoils. Seven people in the fort were killed in the fighting; Captain Ecuyer was wounded in the leg by an arrow. Fires on the roofs caused by blazing arrows were successfully extinguished. The defenders' most effective weapons were their howitzers among the sixteen cannon and "hand grenadoes" thrown on the attackers crouching behind the banks of the two rivers.

On August 5 three "expresses" managed to get into the fort; they brought the news that Colonel Bouquet was leading 350 Highlanders and 115 Royal Americans to raise the siege. He had left Carlisle on July 18. The Highlanders had been at the taking of Havana the year before and some sixty of them were so sick with malaria that they had to be carried in the wagons. Arriving at Ligonier on August 2 and finding no word from Fort Pitt, Bouquet decided to leave his oxen and most of his cattle and provisions and proceed at a faster pace. When the expresses left Bouquet's camp, he was less than forty miles away and was traveling with 340 packhorses loaded with bags of flour.

He would proceed by way of Bushy Run rather than a safer but longer branch of the Forbes Road. From sounds they heard at Turtle Creek, the expresses concluded that the Indians were gathering to attack the column.

The Indians around Fort Pitt disappeared, and for four days there was an ominous, eerie silence. Trent wrote: "The troops not arriving according to expectations makes us fear they have been attacked on their march." The provisions were almost gone—food, liquor, and tobacco. "I have," Ecuyer wrote, "four hams and no flour."

Indians appeared on the river banks on August 5, shaking bloody scalps and calling triumphantly that they had destroyed the British army.

On the tenth an express brought the information that Bouquet had been under attack at Bushy Run for two days and a night. The action "continued doubtful," he said, "till the enemy by a stratagem [a feigned retreat] was drawn into an ambuscade, when they were entirely routed, leaving a great many of their people dead on the spot."

Bouquet buried his dead—115 men and 8 officers, more than one-fourth of his force—and resumed the march to Fort Pitt. In one of the great dramatic scenes of early American history, the red-coated Royal Americans and the Highlanders in kilts and tartans came into sight in the early afternoon of August 10. They marched to the fort with drums beating and bagpipes skirling. Colonel Bouquet and Captain Ecuyer, two Swiss mercenaries in the wilds of America, embraced each other. The column was surrounded by more than six hundred haggard but jubilant men, women, and children who had been penned up in the fort for ten weeks and now for the first time were freed of the fear of death or captivity.

8. September–November 1764

Pontiac's rebellion was repulsed but it was not crushed. The Indians retreated to their westward stronghold between the Ohio River and Lake Erie, and for a time there was quiet on the frontier. Then in the spring of 1764, when the French traders in the Illinois country began to supply the Indians with lead and powder, the scalping parties moved out again. Farmers returned from their fields to find their cabins burned and their families massacred or carried off. Refugees again fled into the settlements or retired over the mountains. It was necessary now for pack trains to travel in armed convoys.

Henry Bouquet arrived at Pittsburgh on September 18, 1764, at the head of a mile-long column: two regiments of British regulars, a force of Pennsylvania militia (it had lost 700 men by desertion on the march from Carlisle), wheeled artillery pieces, 1300 pack horses laden with supplies, 400 head of cattle, and flocks of sheep. The army pitched its tents and pastured its animals around Fort Pitt. It remained there for twenty-four days.

Defense against the Indians had always meant repelling their attacks and then pursuing them after they had struck. Bouquet had a mission based on a different concept: He was to march on the Indians deep in their own territory, force them to sue for peace, and bring back all the surviving prisoners they had taken in the past decade.

Bouquet waited at Fort Pitt for a corps of 250 Virginia volunteers who were to join him there. He used the time to drill and train his troops. There was much competitive target practice at one hundred yards, with prizes of $3, $2, and $1 for the winners in each brigade. The armorers, coopers, and artificers were put to work repairing arms and making cartridges. Two men convicted of desertion were given 1,000 lashes each. On September 26 all units marched to the north slope of Grant's Hill and formed three sides of a hollow square. William Anderson and Francis Steedwell, deserters, were conducted to that place and "shot to death." It was hoped that the examples thus provided would "make a deep and lasting impression on the minds of the troops."

The Virginia corps arrived, and Bouquet was pleased to find they were trained, hardy woodsmen. Preparations for the march began. Each man was issued a blanket, a canteen, a pair of leggins, two pairs of good shoes, three shirts, and a "tomhawk" to be carried on a leather strap. Each musketeer carried twenty-four rounds. In the absence of sabres, each trooper of the Light Horse was issued a long-handled axe. An order read:

One woman belonging to each corps and two nurses for the general hospital will be pricked [marked down] upon the commanding officer of corps to proceed with the army. No exception will be made to this order. It will be therefore in vain for any other woman to attempt following the troops, nor will any be suffered to remain here. All the women now in camp and those unnecessary in garrison are to be sent down the country. They will be permitted to go with the waggons which are to set out from hence this day.

Two days were spent ferrying animals, supplies, and 1500 men in bateaux to a temporary camp on the Allegheny shore across from the fort. The army marched on October 3, proceeding down the north bank of the Ohio and on to the Muskingum River, cutting a road as it traveled, covering seven or eight miles a day. At the Muskingum, Bouquet made a fortified camp and held a conference with the Indian chiefs. He gave them twelve days in which to collect and return all their white captives, on threat of destroying their villages and food supplies and waging a relentless war. To assure their compliance, he pushed some thirty miles deeper into the heart of the Indian settlements. No other force was to match that advance for thirty years; two American armies that tried it in 1790 and 1791 were massacred.

Bouquet returned to Fort Pitt on November 28. He carried with him 206 rescued captives—

125 women and children under the care of the matrons, 81 men, some of them black—and a pledge from the Shawnees to deliver up more than one hundred other captives at Fort Pitt the following spring. Indian children born to white mothers he left behind. With him he brought fourteen chieftains as hostages to ensure that the tribes would deliver up the additional captives and would send deputies to New York to sign a treaty of peace. In his orderly book Bouquet had written: "As there will be many among them who are very much attached to the savages by having lived with them from their infancy, these if not narrowly watched may be apt to make their escape after they are delivered up. The guards and centinals therefore on this duty must be particularly attentive to prevent such accidents happening."

9. May 10, 1765

On this day a group of Shawnees appeared on the shore of the Allegheny River across from the fort and made camp. They beat their drums, sang peace songs, and came across the river in canoes. With them they had 140 white captives. The chiefs and the British officers met in the council house in the fort. Lawoughgua, the Shawnee spokesman, rose. Addressing the English as "father" for the first time, he spoke of what it meant to his people to restore the captives:

Father, here is your flesh and blood, except . . . a few that was out with some of our hunting parties, and those will be brought here as soon as they return. They have been all tied to us by adoption, and although we now deliver them up to you, we will always look upon them as our relations whenever the great Spirit is pleased that we may visit them. . . . We have taken as much care of these prisoners as if they were our own flesh and blood. They are now become unacquainted with your customs and manners, and therefore, Fathers, we request you will use them tenderly and kindly, which will be a means of inducing them to live contentedly with you. . . . Here is a belt [of peace]. . . . We hope that neither side will slip their hands from it so long as the sun and moon gives light.

There was a decade of peace on the frontier. Colonel Bouquet, hailed as a hero throughout the colonies and in England, was promoted to brigadier general (two grades lower than the rank he would have had in European service) and sent to Pensacola, Florida, to take charge of the Southern Department. There, within a few months, at age forty-seven, he died of a fever. Historians have speculated on what might have happened if Bouquet, the hero of Bushy Run and of the march to the Muskingum, had lived. He would surely have been placed in command of British units in the American Revolution. If so, General Washington would have met with a far more formidable opponent than William Howe, Cornwallis, Burgoyne, or St. Leger. The story of the American War for Independence might have had a quite different ending.

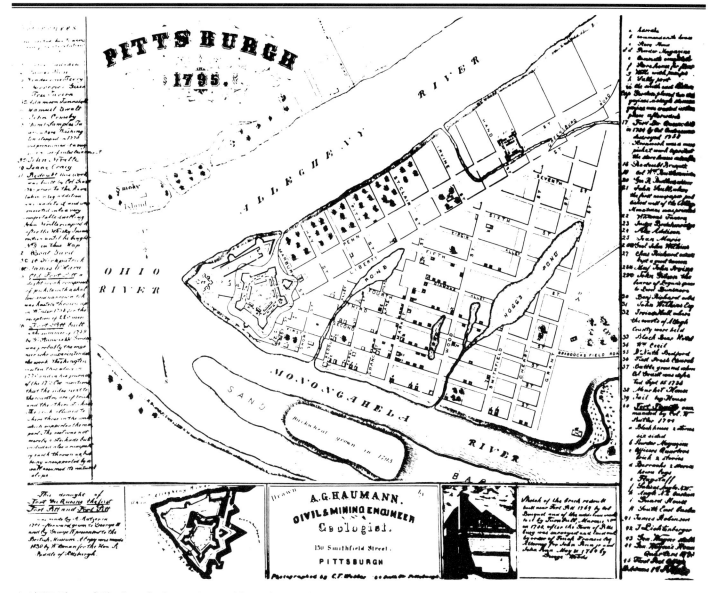

A 1795 Plan of Pittsburgh shows the position of Fort Pitt at the Point, the much smaller Fort Duquesne at the apex, and, extending up the shore of the Allegheny River, the orchard and garden that fed the garrisons. Hogg's Pond came to be known as Massacre Pond after Major James Grant's bloody defeat by the French in the summer of 1758.

There were far-sighted people in 1763 who recognized the danger to Britain of driving the French out of North America and making Canada a British possession. Indeed, there was sentiment during the peace negotiations in 1762 for returning Canada to France in exchange for some of the French "sugar islands" in the West Indies.

The danger to Britain lay in the fact that the American colonies now no longer needed British protection against their traditional enemy, France. By 1765, Americans felt secure enough, in the absence of that enemy, to protest British taxation, trade policies, and the quartering of British troops in American cities and homes. Thomas Hutchinson, governor of Massachusetts, said in 1773, one year before he had to flee for his life from Boston, "I once thought nothing so much to be desired as the accession of Canada. I am now convinced that if it had remained to the French, none of the spirit of opposition to the Mother Country would have yet appeared, and I think the effects of [the acquisition] of Canada worse than all we have to fear from the French and Indians."

Some historians have concluded that if the French had been victorious, or had been permitted to remain in Canada in 1763 their presence would have made an American rebellion against Britain unlikely, even impossible.

Charles M. Stotz, historian, architect, and one of the designers of Point State Park, has carried that idea a step farther. He holds in his *Drums in the Forest* (1958) that if the French had not claimed the Ohio Valley, there would have been no war in North America between France and England. At no time had the British considered invading Canada to drive out the French, or questioned France's right to occupy the lands above the St. Lawrence and the lakes. The war erupted because France challenged Britain at the Forks of the Ohio. If the French had not made that challenge, there would probably have been no war. If there had been no war, France would have remained in Canada. If France had remained in Canada, there would have been no American Revolution in 1776.

If we accept these conclusions, we may agree that the significance of Pittsburgh's Point in eighteenth-century history is this: When the French planted their flag at the Forks of the Ohio by force of arms in 1754, they set in motion a chain of events that culminated in the Seven Years' War in Europe and set the stage for the American War for Independence from Britain.

3

The Point as Part of Pittsburgh, 1800–1914

At the time of the dedication of the Point Park fountain in 1974, Ralph E. Griswold, the landscape architect for the design team for the park, raised an intriguing question. In a casual conversation he asked, "What would Pittsburgh have looked like if the French had defeated the British and stayed in the Ohio Valley? Of course," he said, "it wouldn't have been called 'Pittsburgh' but 'New Paris' or 'The City of Louis XV,' or something like that. It would have been the capital of New France, not Montreal or Quebec, which were icebound as ports in the winter and were at the far end of the communications chain from New Orleans. There is reason to believe that the French intended their capital to be at the Forks of the Ohio.

"Architecturally, they would have laid out a city here according to the concept of the French monarchy of that time. It would have grown into a Beaux Arts city, the style that came out of the monarchy. Imagine a model. With their charac-teristic flair for *le grand plan,* they certainly would have created a monumental park at the Point. One great axis, an avenue or mall, like the Champs Elysées, right up the middle of the triangle, leading from the Point to the top of Grant's Hill, where the spectacular capitol building would overlook the city. A row of public buildings flanking each side of the avenue. Streets running out at right angles toward the rivers, like ribs from a spine. The streets would meet diagonal boulevards running along the rivers, but set back from the shores, like the quays of the River Seine. There would be open public spaces between the boulevards and the rivers, as in Paris. There would be no commercial development of the river fronts.

"Well, the French didn't win, and when the British took charge, they had no such concept of a capital city, and Pittsburgh developed quite differently."

By 1800, Pittsburgh was the leading commu-

29

nity in a county (Allegheny) with more than fifteen thousand inhabitants. It had been surveyed and laid out as a town in 1764 and again in 1784. It had a newspaper, a courthouse, a volunteer fire company, three churches, a lodge of Freemasons, the Pittsburgh Academy, a post office, and regular mail service to the east. It had a shipyard, iron foundries, sawmills, a promising glass industry, and a brisk trade in the manufacture, consumption, and export of Monongahela rye whiskey. There were nearly fifty shops. There were many taverns to feed and house travelers visiting the city on business and settlers headed for the western country, some of whom had to wait for days and weeks for the rivers to rise and become navigable.

The Point continued to be involved in great events until the end of the eighteenth century. George Rogers Clark assembled and outfitted his small army there in 1778, on his way to immortality in one of the epic chapters of the American Revolution. The Whiskey Rebels marched to the Point in 1794 in a historic contest that established the power of the federal government to levy excise taxes in the sovereign states. Three generals—Harmar, St. Clair, and Wayne—came to the Point to lead armies against the Indians in the Old Northwest Territory. But now the Point no longer had an independent history of its own. It was important, not in itself, but as part of a community, incorporated as a city in 1816, already known as the Gateway to the West.

In 1836 Philip H. Nicklin, a traveler from Philadelphia who used the name Peregrine Prolix, published a remarkable account of a visit to Pittsburgh the year before. In *A Pleasant Peregrination through the Prettiest Parts of Pennsylvania*, he described his journey from Bedford Springs to Somerset (thirty-eight miles in 8½ hours) and from Somerset to Pittsburgh (sixty-seven miles in 16 hours). His sensation on first seeing Pittsburgh was one of disappointment, because "the country through which you have come is so beautiful, and the town itself so ugly." The government of the town, he felt, was more intent on filling its purses than in providing for the gratification of the taste, or for the comfort, of its inhabitants. Pittsburghers, he found, were "worthy of every good thing, being enlightened, hospitable and urbane." The town was "full of good things in the eating and drinking way, but it requires much ingenuity to get them down your throat unsophisticated with smoke and coal-dust."

Peregrine Prolix inspected the Point and expressed a prophetic opinion:

The Pittsburghers have committed an error in not rescuing from the service of Mammon, a triangle of thirty or forty acres at the junction of the Allegheny and Monongahela, and devoting it to the purposes of recreation. It is an unparalleled position for a park in which to ride or walk or sit. Bounded on the right by the clear and rapid Allegheny rushing from New York, and on the left by the deep and slow

Pittsburgh in 1817, taken from a sketch drawn by Mrs. E. C. Gibson, wife of James Gibson, member of the Philadelphia Bar, while on her wedding journey. (Carnegie Library, Pittsburgh)

Monongahela flowing majestically from Virginia, having in front the beginning of the great Ohio, bearing on its broad bosom the traffic of an empire, it is a spot worthy of being rescued from the ceaseless din of the steam engine and the lurid flames and dingy smoke of the coal furnace. But alas! the *sacra fames auri* [the holy hunger for gold] is rapidly covering this area with private edifices; and in a few short years it is probable that the antiquary will be unable to discover a vestige of those celebrated military works, with which French and British ambition, in by-gone ages, had crowned this important and interesting point.

Peregrine Prolix had intended to go down the Ohio by steamboat, but the water was so low that he returned to Philadelphia by canal. His packet entered the canal at its western terminus (at the basin near the future Union Station), crossed the Allegheny on a suspended aqueduct, and followed beside the river for some thirty miles, on the way to the portage by railroad over the mountain.

A year later, Jonas R. McClintock, Pittsburgh's first popularly elected mayor, proposed in his inaugural address (March 31, 1836) that a park be built at the Point. His proposal encompassed a continuous wharf, promenade, and park area for the triangle waterfront, with a new Duquesne Way enriched with grass, shrubs and "umbrageous trees." He was to answer politically fourteen years later for an unkept promise; the Pittsburgh *Dispatch* on January 5, 1850, wrote:

LOCAL NEWS

The Point.—That part of the city near the junction of the two rivers, although first seen by travelers ascending the river, is the worst built, the dirtiest, and the least comely portion of the whole city. Although inhabited when much of the most beautiful part of the city was a wilderness, it is now farthest behind hand in improvement; and a traveler who should judge of Pittsburg from the view at the Point, would suppose it to be the most miserable place in the Union. The difficulty there has been that fine property was in the hands of a few people—minor heirs and others—who would not or could not sell or improve it, and those leasing it could not afford to improve handsomely some of these vast estates now coming into market; and we hope to see the day when handsome edifices, which will do credit to the city, will take the place of the miserable sheds and shanties along the river and on Penn and Liberty streets. Then Duquesne Way may become a really handsome promenade—if Commerce should not take possession and displace the "umbrageous trees" which were to have been planted there.

For some decades the remains of Fort Pitt had been, in the words of Zadok Cramer's *Navigator* of 1808, "a considerable obstruction to its being regularly built on." The fort itself had been dismantled and its bricks used for other construction, but not until the ramparts and ditches were leveled after 1830 was there building on the lower fort area itself. Lower Penn Avenue had been a fashionable residential street, but now industrial and commercial development began, replacing houses with shops and small factories. A map of the Point in 1852 showed a public school, a Presbyterian church, two banks, and nine engine shops and iron or brass factories.

In that year, on the evening of December 10, a new force came into Pittsburgh that at once liberated, stimulated, befouled, and defaced the city. A Pennsylvania Railroad passenger train that had left Philadelphia the day before chugged into the Golden Triangle to the cheers of the assembled populace. Two years later several blocks of buildings at the Point were torn down to make way for the Duquesne Freight Depot served by railroad tracks running down Liberty Avenue, one of the city's main thoroughfares.

By 1860 the city had some ten thousand residential dwellings. Pittsburgh was a leading industrial center, primarily in coal, iron, steel, boat building, and glass—half the glass then being manufactured in the United States, some of it of exquisite quality. Pittsburgh supplied much of the armaments for the Northern forces during the Civil War.

Bridges were built across the rivers at the Point—the covered wooden Union Bridge across the Allegheny in 1874, the steel suspension Point Bridge across the Monongahela in 1876. With industrial development, the level of the land at the Point rose some twelve feet. Families began to leave the small houses and large tenements in this, the first ward. Of those who stayed, many were immigrants, a colony of them known as "Point Irish." One such family, that of Charles B. and Catherine Conwell Lawrence, living at the corner of Greentree Alley and Penn Avenue, had a son on June 18, 1889. They named him David Leo. David's father had built the house; the father was in the hauling business, later worked for the county as a warehouseman. Young David, a Roman Catholic, became a Shabbas goy. Beginning at sundown on Friday and ending at sundown on Saturday, he would make the rounds of homes of orthodox Jews and, for a payment of coins laid on the doorstep or the kitchen table, tend the furnace, light the cook stove and the lamps, and perform other work forbidden on the Jewish Sabbath. At fourteen, David became a clerk-stenographer in the law office of a Democratic political power, later entering his insurance firm.

By 1902, two railroad yards covered much of the lower Point. Isaac Craig's eighteenth-century mansion next to Colonel Bouquet's Blockhouse, made of brick taken from Fort Pitt, had to be destroyed. The Blockhouse itself, owned by the Daughters of the American Revolution since 1894, was surrounded by fill and railroad tracks and lay below an elevated freight yard. A turn-of-the-century count of the commercial and industrial buildings showed:

The Kinzer & Jones Foundry
An Ice Company
Murray Pop-Bottle Works
Thomas Cavvey, Second Hand Barrel Storage

THE JOHN J. WRIGHT LIBRARY

The "Gateway to the West" in 1859. (Allegheny Conference)

The three rivers are now carrying an enormous volume of freight, as shown by these flotillas of barges. (Deszo J. Demetsky)

Albert Conwell's Stable
A Galvanizing Shop
Haney's Stables
Logan's Mattress Factory
O'Daherty's & Company Liquor Store
W. W. Lawrence Paint Factory with Stable
  and Warehouse
J. C. Buffman Company, Soft Beverages
Henry Hank's Lumber Yard
McGuiness's Store
French's Felt Foundry
Speer's Box Factory and Planing Mill
S. S. Marvin Company, Stables
Lumber Yard
St. Mary of Mercy School
Worton McKnight's Office Building and Factory
Machine Shop
Rice's Castle (no further identification)

Because of high water in the spring of the year, these buildings had shallow, plank-lined cellars or none at all. The lower Point was obviously no longer important as a business, industrial, residential, or historic area; the major buildings were being constructed on higher ground uptown.

In the meantime, Pittsburgh had achieved, in a manner of speaking, a new kind of fame. Charles Dickens visited it in 1842 and wrote acidly in his *American Notes,* "Pittsburg is like Birmingham in England; at least its towns-people say so. Setting aside the streets, the shops, the houses, waggons, factories, public buildings, and population, perhaps it may be. It certainly has a great quantity of smoke hanging about it." Herbert Spencer, friend of Andrew Carnegie, felt that one week in Pittsburgh was enough to make a man think of suicide. The American biographer James Parton viewed it from Mount Washington and, writing in the *Atlantic Monthly* in 1868, called it "Hell with the lid taken off"—the first of many such comparisons with the infernal regions. Lincoln Steffens said of Pittsburgh, "It looked like hell, literally."

Pittsburgh also became known for its industrial strife, notably for the railroad riots of 1877 and the Homestead steel strike of 1892. Social critics cited Pittsburgh over and over as the outstanding example of American capitalism out of control. Paul U. Kellog, editor of a famous six-volume study of the city, *The Pittsburgh Survey* (1908–1914), called Pittsburgh "the capital of a district representative of untrammeled industrial development, . . . a district which, for richer, for poorer, in sickness and in health, for vigor, waste and optimism, is rampantly American."

Pittsburghers winced under the attacks, and they struggled to rescue and redeem their city. In the twenty-five years from 1888–1912, they mounted programs that produced impressive and lasting capital improvements in the city. Pittsburgh's cultural life was enhanced by construction that began in 1889 at the Point in the narrow strip between the freight yards and the Allegheny River. A group of civic leaders, inspired by the success of Philadelphia's Centennial Exposition of 1876, formed the Pittsburgh Exposition Society to raise $450,000 to build three giant structures: Exposition Hall, Mechanical Hall, and Music Hall. A fire destroyed Music Hall in 1900, but an even more splendid replacement was built at a cost of $600,000. For almost thirty years, the Exposition Society buildings were the hub of Pittsburgh's social and cultural life. There were band concerts, symphony concerts, song recitals, opera, lectures, skating, a wide variety of fairs and expositions, a Ferris wheel, a roller coaster, a merry-go-round, a boardwalk along the Allegheny, and rides in the steamer *Sunshine*. The second floor of Exposition Hall held large dioramas of the Battle of the Monitor and the Merrimac, the Johnstown Flood, the San Francisco Earthquake, and the Sinking of the Titanic. In the early years, a twenty-five-cent ticket was "sufficient for all attractions."

Other turn-of-the-century developments in what has been called Pittsburgh's First Renaissance are described in the author's biography of H. J. Heinz, *The Good Provider* (1973):

Since 1889, three splendid city parks. Two colleges—Carnegie Institute of Technology and the remade, renamed and relocated University of Pittsburgh. Five hospitals, including one for maternity cases and one for children. A zoological garden. The world's second largest conservatory. The $6 million Carnegie Institute, with its museum, library, music hall, foyer (called by one architectural historian "the most splendid ceremonial hall in America"), and its art galleries, where the world-famous International Art Exhibition had been held each fall since 1896. A school for the blind and a school for the deaf and dumb. A water filtration and purification system that in two years (1906–1908) cut typhoid fever cases by more than two-thirds. Skyscrapers twenty to twenty-five stories high. A new railroad station. "The world's most perfect playhouse."

Pittsburgh, moreover, had removed the railroad tracks from Liberty Avenue. It had built a fine paved boulevard from the downtown area to the East End, cut out of the side of a hill. It was buying the bridges across the three rivers and making them toll-free. It was building one of the country's most beautiful sports arenas in the Schenley Farms area. It had just established a Bureau of Smoke and a corps of fast-moving policemen on bicycles. Its public school system was recognized as one of the best in the country. Money had been raised to cut away a monstrous "hump" of earth and relay streets at the eastern end of the Golden Triangle. All these comprised a body of improvements and additions that any city would be proud to have.

The floods continued, however, and the smoke remained. The bees, one observer said, made bituminous honey. Slum areas spread as families moved out of the inner city to settle in the new suburbs. A City Planning Commission was established in 1911 and the Bureau of Smoke Regulation in 1914. They had the power to research, recommend, and issue annual reports, but not much more. In 1910 the courts had ruled that smoke control was illegal in a case

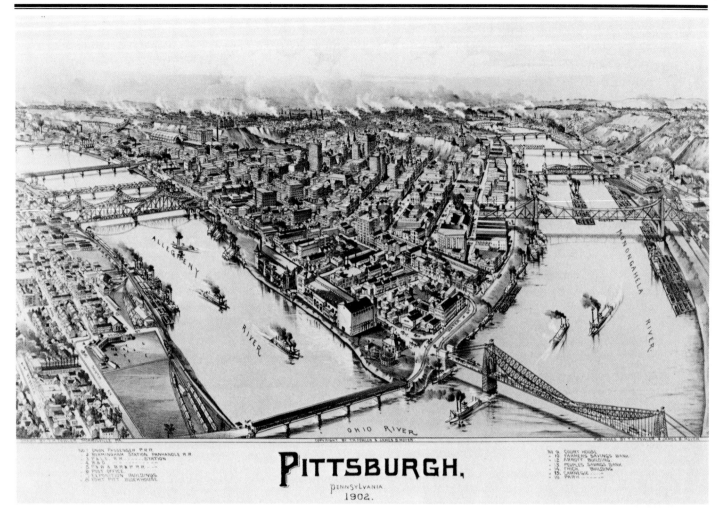

PITTSBURGH,

PENNSYLVANIA
1902.

Twelve Bridges are visible in this 1902 view of the Golden Triangle, including the covered wooden Union Bridge extending from the Point to Allegheny City. The huge Exposition Buildings line the lower shore of the Allegheny. (Historical Society of Western Pennsylvania) involving the Jones & Laughlin Steel Company. "Persons living in Pittsburgh," the decision said, "must submit themselves to the consequences incident to a manufacturing district. If the growth and expansion of manufacturing industries make present resident neighborhoods undesirable, residents must either accept the changed conditions or seek other localities."

As the problems multiplied with growth of population and traffic, city officials and civic leaders turned to planners from other cities (few of which were better off than Pittsburgh) to prescribe remedies. The steps that were taken, the trial-and-error procedures that were followed in the new science or art of city planning, are tied to developments over the next thirty years. They provide food for reflection for those who today believe that everything should have been done sooner, or better, or differently, and especially for those gifted with the American capacity to oversimplify problems that other people should have solved.

The first well-known expert to come to Pittsburgh was Frederick Law Olmsted, son of the designer of New York City's Central Park. Olmsted was a professor of landscape architecture at Harvard, past president of the American Society of Landscape Architects, chairman of the executive committee of the National Conference on City Planning, and designer of an impressive list of public parks and other municipal improvements in many cities. His 1910 report on Pittsburgh, prepared for the Pittsburgh Civic Commission just at the start of the automobile age, was subtitled, "Improvements Necessary to Meet the City's Present and Future Needs." It devoted twelve eloquent pages to the waterfront and the lower Point. "In its water front Pittsburgh has a great public asset which now lies undeveloped both from the point of view of transportation and that of recreation and civic beauty. . . . Pittsburgh, like most American river towns, where she has not actually turned her water front over bodily to the railroads, has left it in a most inefficient primitive condition."

He called for the city to develop its downtown mud banks with public wharves and floating quays in the European manner, and to build "a wide marginal thoroughfare for the relief of traffic congestion," with a border of landscaped park area, promenades, and broad embankment gardens "for recreation and as an element of civic comeliness and self-respect." He declared that such a mixed use could be carried out attractively, and he reproduced pictures of scores of famous European waterfronts to prove that it was so.

One of the deplorable consequences of the short-sighted and wasteful commercialism of the later nineteenth century lay in its disregard of what might have been the esthetic by-products of economic improvement; in the false impression spread abroad that economical and useful things were normally ugly; and in the vicious idea which followed, that beauty and the higher pleasures of civilized life were to be sought only in things otherwise useless. Thus the pursuit of beauty was confounded with extravagance.

Pittsburgh, he thought, still had "opportunity for redeeming the sordid aspect of its business center" by following the European example. "The outlook over the [Monongahela] river with its varied activities to the hills immediately beyond, would be notable in any part of the world. Furthermore, the rivers and the hills are the two big fundamental natural elements characteristic of the Pittsburgh District. Thus, any provision close to the heart of the city, whereby the people can have the enjoyment of these mighty landscapes, is of peculiar importance." Two things were needed for enjoyment of this spacious and impressive landscape. The hillsides, the "steep slopes" across the rivers, "should be treated with respect as a vital part of the great landscape of the city. It should be protected from defacement and its earthy portions should be reclothed with the beauty of foliage." And "a locally agreeable place" should be provided from which the scene could be enjoyed.

The agreeable place he chose was at the lower Point. The unfortunate freight yards, the Exposition buildings, and the two bridges he accepted as necessary and inevitable, but the area at the apex should be rescued and landscaped.

Here is the spot where the Ohio River has its birth: here was built the fort which broke the peace of Europe and around which turned the frontier struggles of the war that gave America to the English-speaking race. It is here that all the most inspiring associations of the city are chiefly concentrated. Poetically, this spot, at the meeting of the rivers, stands for Pittsburgh. . . .

The Point is left pocketed beyond the freight yards and is visited only by the throngs who use the old Point bridge. It seems to be rather forgotten and disregarded by most Pittsburghers. But its historical and topographical significance can never be altered, and it is to be hoped that the City will rise to its opportunity and nobly form the Point into a great monument.

The Olmsted report was much discussed and left its mark on men's minds, but its recommendations were tabled for a later generation to act upon.

In 1914 the Municipal Art Commission presented and endorsed a study by the architect E. H. Bennett of Chicago for improving the Point. A year or so later the commission lamented, "The importance of the project for securing a comprehensive and proper plan for the Point district failed to be generally appreciated to the extent of securing enthusiastic cooperation, and the Commission found itself meeting with failure and discouragement in its efforts along these lines."

A typical street of the lower Point early in this century shows run-down residential dwellings, with one of the three Exposition Buildings in the background. (Carnegie Library, Pittsburgh)

4

The Seeds of the Renaissance

Near the close of the First World War, in October 1918, Pittsburgh turned again to municipal rehabilitation. Fifteen leading businessmen met in the boardroom of the Mellon National Bank and voted to form a Citizens' Committee on a City Plan for Pittsburgh, the main purpose of which was "to prepare and secure adoption of a comprehensive city plan." As executive secretary they named the man who had persuaded them to act, Frederick Bigger, 37, a graduate architect (University of Pennsylvania, 1903), a native Pittsburgher who had practiced in Seattle and Philadelphia and had returned to Pittsburgh in 1913 to work on the Municipal Art Commission's fruitless study for improving the Point.

The committee changed its name to Municipal Planning Association, opened an office, hired a staff of three assistants, retained George Ketchum's firm to handle publicity and raise money, and printed a newsletter called *Progress*.

The association expended $250,000 between 1920 and 1923 on six studies of the city's playgrounds, transit, parks, rails, waterways, and streets. Major improvements were completed or begun in Pittsburgh in the 1920s—among them the Liberty Tubes and Bridge, the Armstrong Tunnels, the Boulevard of the Allies, and the Gulf, Koppers, and Grant buildings—but there was no apparent progress toward anything that could charitably be called a comprehensive city plan. Some critics charged that on the basis of results achieved, the association's planning money was wasted. Others saw it as a necessary preliminary step to educate the public and to mobilize its support, without which public officials are always reluctant to act, even in the worthiest causes.

Another program to rescue the Point was launched in 1930. Senator David Aiken Reed introduced a resolution in Congress to erect a national memorial at the Point to honor George

Rogers Clark and his company of heroes, conquerors of the Old Northwest Territory. The memorial, for reasons that are not clear, was to be an illuminated lighthouse at the apex of the Point, occupying the small tongue of land projecting beyond the junction of the two bridges. Concurrently, a group of Pittsburghers attempted to enlarge the memorial by eliminating the freight yards and rebuilding all the lower Point. Their plan, based on a design drawn up by A. Marshall Bell, onetime director of public safety, and Edward B. Lee, architect, contained in addition to the lighthouse a national memorial park with freshwater aquarium, botanical gardens, and a pioneer museum; space for a town hall or commercial museum for the products of the world; a site for historic monuments and a park; a recreational park or site for future memorial buildings; a water park and boat landing; and parking space along both shores for 4,000 cars.

Senator Reed's lighthouse and the Bell-Lee complex of memorial buildings and parks died aborning. Vincennes, Indiana, with a stronger claim on General Clark than Pittsburgh's, raised $900,000 with which to buy the twenty-two-acre site of old Fort Sackville, and Congress appropriated $2 million for a George Rogers Clark memorial on the site in the form of a massive Doric temple. It was dedicated by President Franklin Roosevelt in 1936.

In the depths of the Great Depression, in the spring of 1933, the Municipal Planning Association closed its office and furloughed its staff. The Dow Industrial Average was 41, United States Steel was selling at $22 (down from $262 in 1929), mills were closed for lack of orders or were working at a small fraction of their capacity, and the association had no money for rent, payroll, planning, or building.

In May 1936, a few weeks after the worst flood in the city's history, the Planning Association was revived, with Frederick Bigger as technical consultant and Howard Heinz (head of the company his father had founded) as president. The following year Bigger persuaded Wallace Richards, thirty-three, serving as a planner and manager of the government's huge housing development at Greenbelt, Maryland, to become the association's executive director. In 1938 the association changed its name to the Pittsburgh Regional Planning Association.

In April 1937 Frank C. Harper, a sixth-generation Pittsburgher, former newspaper editor and columnist, now executive director of the Pittsburgh Chamber of Commerce, delivered a lecture and offered a resolution at a meeting of the Historical Society of Western Pennsylvania. He proposed to launch a movement to build a national shrine, a memorial park named for George Washington, at the Point. His resolution was adopted and pushed by the society's president, John S. Fisher, former governor of Pennsylvania. On September 28, 1937, Harper, Fisher, and other representatives from the society appeared before the City Planning Commission and requested "cooperation in a plan to set aside that part of Pittsburgh known as 'the Point' for a National Park site." City Council thereupon passed a resolution creating a Point Park Commission. Mayor Cornelius D. Scully named the members, with Harper as chairman. Allegheny County and the state announced their support.

The Historical Society and the Point Park Commission held a black-tie "Community Dinner" at the William Penn Hotel on Saturday evening, March 26, 1938, "to promote the Point Park Project and meet officials of the National Park Service." The proposal was to create a thirty-six-acre park and in it to erect a flood wall, re-create Fort Duquesne and Fort Pitt, build a museum and an exposition hall, and set aside parking space for 7,000 automobiles. There were eight speeches at the dinner, plus an invocation and a benediction.

The following month the chairman of the City Planning Commission, Frederick Bigger, issued a ten-page document of major importance in the history of what had come to be known as "the problem of the Point." Bigger addressed it to the City Planning Commission and called it "Analysis and Recommendations re Proposals for Triangle Improvement." He reported on an extraordinary suggestion that the two bridges at the Point be moved back from the apex of the Point. The Manchester Bridge, he said, might be moved up the Allegheny at a cost of $1,250,000; but the Point Bridge (over the Monongahela),

being an inverted cantilever structure, could not be moved. In any case, placing the two bridges farther up the Triangle was impractical because of construction costs, loss of tax revenues from requisitioned properties, difficult problems of planning, and delay in building a Point Park while the bridges were being relocated. On Point Park he said:

There is not time to develop even a sketch plan to reveal the possibility of treatment of the Point Park flanked by the ramped bridge approaches, which is the relationship involved by the plan recommended. . . . However, it is already clear that a raising of the elevation of the ground of the Park, either as an entirety or in several terraces would make it entirely possible for anyone in the Park to have an absolutely clear and unobstructed view of the Allegheny River for a distance of at least 600 feet . . . and of the Monongahela River for a distance of at least 800 feet.

Moreover, the treatment of the western apex of the Triangle Park could be that of massed plantings, including trees to block out in part the view of the rather ugly bridges; or that apex could be developed with an attractive and not too large museum building, housing historical exhibits, of such height as to partially block out the rising ramps close to the bridges, and with its roof make an attractive terrace and observation point.

It is still further suggested that there are two ways of emphasizing the historical status of the Point without erecting a replica of a huge fort. One way would be to have, as a unit of the landscape design, a model on the ground of the entire original Point

The father of city planning in Pittsburgh, Frederick Bigger, is shown in February 1961, two years before his death. He is talking with Robert B. Pease, who, younger by more than a generation, became executive director of two organizations important to the Pittsburgh Renaissance. (Pittsburgh *Press*)

with fort, moat, and abutting rivers. The other way would be to have a still smaller model of the same thing within the museum building; and to have it mechanically adjusted to show little scale figures of soldiers, citizens, and Indians.

On July 1, the City Planning Commission approved Chairman Bigger's recommendation on Point Park, calling for:

the immediate development of sketch plans under the guidance of or with consultation by competent designers and landscape architects, to be submitted

to Federal Authorities showing a desirable adjustment of the Triangle plans to an historic memorial park at the Point; and define how said park area might be designed to benefit the entire community and be worthy of its historical significance.

Representatives of the City Planning Commission, the Point Park Commission, and the Pittsburgh Regional Planning Association met in Washington on December 9, 1938, with officials of the National Park Service "in order to officially clarify the relationship and the point of view of the National Park Service to a proposed historic park at the Point." The representatives returned to Pittsburgh with a new and sobered awareness of the problems involved in dealing with federal authorities:

1. The Park Service would delegate an archeologist to come to Pittsburgh to make a survey and determine elevations and limits of Fort Pitt. (No problem.)

2. The Park Service could not enter into official negotiations with the City of Pittsburgh about a Point Park until all the area to be included in the site of the historic shrine had been acquired by the city and deeded to the Park Service. (Problem: the city could not possibly finance the acquisition of all the property within the site.)

3. The Congress of the United States might then, after conveyance of the area to the Park Service, make a special appropriation to the Park Service for development of the area. (Problem: *Might* make an appropriation?)

4. The Park Service, in the event this congressional action was taken, would reproduce the topographic conditions as to elevations of land existing at the time to be memorialized. (Problem: Reproduction of topographic conditions existing in the 1760s would result in a lowering of the elevation to or near pool level of the Allegheny and Monongahela rivers.)

5. The Park Service would reproduce wholly or in part the forts or buildings existing at the time to be commemorated. (Problem: Reproduction of all or part of Fort Pitt with a clearing of all land occupied by the fort would result in, first, a park within the walls and battlements of a primitive fortification; and, second, serious interference with traffic facilities to the Point and Manchester bridges.)

6. The Park Service would protect the area from river inundation or other encroachment with flood walls and fences. (Problem: Construction of flood walls around Point Park would greatly reduce the size of the Point and, as lowered to the elevation of 1763, would create a well or pit having no outlook to the rivers and no point of observation except the top of Mount Washington across the Monongahela.)*

The representatives thereupon decided "to explore the possible sources of funds for the park, including congressional action, Public Works Administration, Works Progress Admin-

istration, National Park Service, State, County, City, and private contributions." Up to this hour, the only consideration had been to build a national memorial park. Now for the first time thoughts turned to the possibility of building a state park.

In 1939 the Regional Planning Association raised $50,000 to retain Robert Moses, commissioner of parks and parkways of New York City, to "investigate the arterial problems of Pittsburgh, with particular reference to improvement of conditions in the Triangle." A large staff worked three months and produced for Moses a neat, gray volume containing twenty-six pages, twenty-three handsome maps and photographs, and nine recommendations. His total program would cost an estimated $38 million. "It was fortunate," he said, "that there was a wealth of existing information and that almost every phase of the problem had been conscientiously explored before. . . . The trouble is that in major municipal improvements we are generally more distinguished for plans than we are for action, and that often we get so tangled up in conflicting programs, each with substantial merit and each with its strong adherents, that accomplishment is forgotten in the fog of controversy."

Moses set forth certain philosophical principles with which he approached his assignment:

At the risk of being charged with lack of historical perspective and enthusiasm, we must say that the relics and historical association [of the Point] should

*John P. Robin points out that National Park Service views and methods had not then been "urbanized," as they were to be a decade or so later.

be regarded as comparatively unimportant in the solution of present and future city planning problems. Construction of the Point and Manchester bridges at the site of old Fort Pitt has determined that traffic rather than history must be the decisive factor in the reconstruction of the apex of the Pittsburgh Triangle and in the establishment of Point Park.

It is useless to bemoan the bad planning which brought these bridges together at this point, or to adopt the fantastic suggestion that they be torn down and reconstructed elsewhere. They are there to stay. . . . The suggestion that these bridges be removed is apparently based on the assumption that this would facilitate federal reconstruction of the entire tip of the Triangle as an incident in the restoration of historical Fort Pitt. It is hard to believe that anyone would take this idea seriously, even though the National Park Service has shown a polite interest in it. The game of dressing up modern public improvements as historical monuments is played out. This was a quaint and ingenious device calculated to solve local problems at federal expense. The fact is that the era of easy money and federal largesse of this kind is over and that the planners of the future Pittsburgh may as well be realistic about it.

As to traffic congestion in the Golden Triangle, Moses felt it was necessary to emphasize an important fact that had been overlooked or minimized by those who had previously studied Pittsburgh:

This fact is that no American municipality which has its roots in the period of rapid, unregulated growth, and which is still active and growing, can completely solve its peak load traffic problem. The peak exists only in the early morning and late afternoon for less than an hour on each occasion. This constitutes no reason for enduring intolerable conditions. These conditions can be modified and the discomforts can be greatly mitigated, but they cannot be entirely eliminated except at exorbitant cost and on a basis which would appear fantastically extravagant at all but the peak periods.

Moses deplored the preempting of an immense amount of space in the Triangle by railroad facilities, active and obsolete. All visitors, he said, were struck by the waste and blight represented by the dead and abandoned Wabash railroad bridge and station in the very center of the Triangle. The Pennsylvania Railroad, while an active and going concern, occupied a grossly disproportionate amount of land in the Triangle and was a major cause of traffic difficulties, uneven and haphazard development, and civic ugliness. The railroad properties which were dead or dying obviously should be removed and converted to active public use.

One of Moses' nine proposals concerned a waterfront highway running from the Manchester Bridge at the Point along the Allegheny to Eleventh Street. Its design should be different from the one being built along the Monongahela (Fort Pitt Boulevard); it would include a river wall topped by a landscaped esplanade and would not be a combined elevated and depressed roadway system "set back from the river and without protection from floods, such as is being completed on Water Street."

The Water Street plan seems to us to have various defects, and we believe that it should not be applied to Duquesne Way. The depressed roadway on Water Street will be flooded several times each year, and at such times parking will be impossible and the lower level will be a mud bank. We question whether the parking plan will accommodate any large number of cars without great confusion. . . . We do not believe that this is the best treatment of a potentially attractive river edge.

He recommended creation of a municipal authority that would charge tolls for use of the bridges leading into the Triangle. He suggested that a license tag might be sold at a low annual rate to all automobile owners in lieu of a toll charge, perhaps ten dollars a year for passenger cars and fifteen dollars for trucks. Vehicles not having the tag would be charged a toll of five cents. "Motorists," he said, "must be practical about these matters."

On Point Park, Moses recommended:

The traffic at the apex of the Triangle should be unsnarled by a complete reconstruction of the Point so as to eliminate obtrusive, unnecessary and obsolete structures, including the disgraceful old Exposition buildings. . . . Establish a landscape area to be known as Point Park featuring a shaft or monument of Pennsylvania black granite, steel, glass and aluminum, and keeping the Blockhouse in its present location but raised to the new elevation of the proposed park.

Moses closed with a tribute to the city:

Pittsburgh is a fascinating city—busy, alert, self-reliant, the symbol of a uniquely American industry. It has been so engrossed in business that it has only recently got around to a consideration of the incidental problems which business creates—problems of comfort, convenience and beauty. If a tithe of the energy which drives the city is directed toward these problems, the results will be quick and certain.

A by-product of the Moses plan was a furious controversy among various planners and institutions over who had been the first to recommend what Moses recommended. Park H. Martin, county planning engineer, declared that the County Planning Commission had been urging those same projects for some time and had formally recommended seven of Moses' nine points in its 1936 improvement program. The present writer, after interviewing Wallace Richards, wrote two articles reviewing the Moses plan in the Pittsburgh *Bulletin-Index* magazine (November 23, 1939, and July 11, 1940). The articles referred to "bickering, back-stabbing, and behind-the-scenes fighting such as confronts no other U. S. city"; suggested that "perhaps this lack of harmony exists because the problem is so difficult it often seems hopeless"; and offered a characterization of Frederick Bigger that has since been widely quoted: "Nationally famed as a topflight city planner, slight, dyspeptic Frederick Bigger has personally laid practically all of the groundwork for Pittsburgh's long-range planning. . . . He

Pittsburgh Might Have Looked Like This

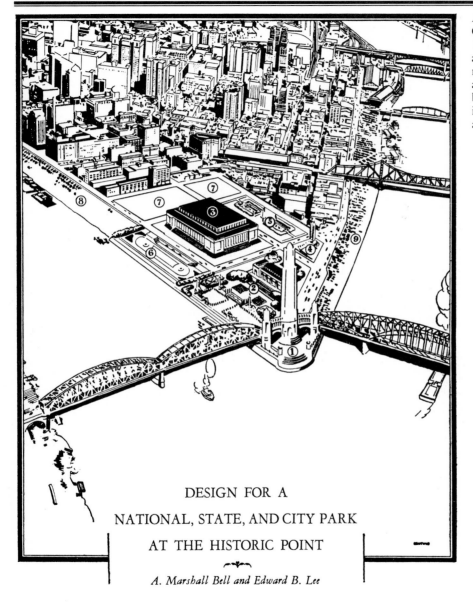

DESIGN FOR A

NATIONAL, STATE, AND CITY PARK

AT THE HISTORIC POINT

A. Marshall Bell and Edward B. Lee

A towering illuminated monument to George Rogers Clark (1) was proposed in 1930. Shown also are a pioneer museum and park (2); a town hall or commercial museum (3); a historic monument site and park (4); site for future memorial buildings (5); water park and boat landing (6); parking space for 4,000 cars (7, 8 and 9).

The Art Commission of Pittsburgh proposed this small park at the apex of the Point in the 1930s. (Pittsburgh *Press*)

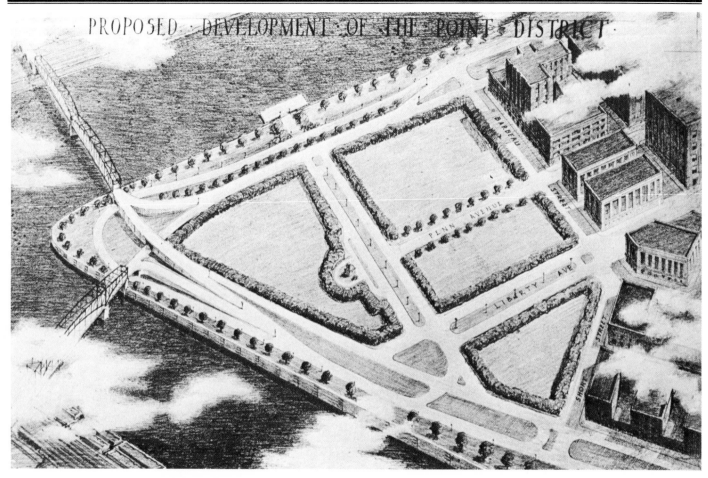

PROPOSED · DEVELOPMENT · OF · THE · POINT · DISTRICT ·

An early proposal covered pretty much the same thirty-six acres that were eventually chosen for Point State Park. (Pittsburgh *Press*)

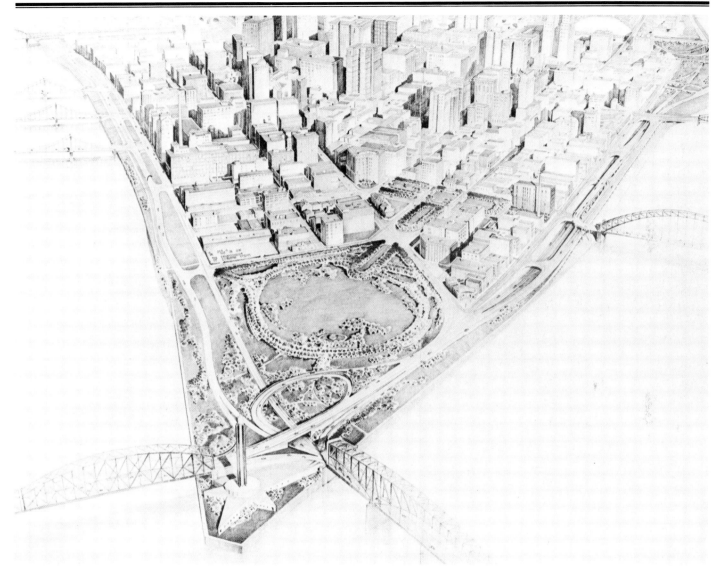

Robert Moses proposed this design in 1939: a landscaped interchange with a shaft of Pennsylvania black granite, steel, glass, and aluminum. The two bridges at the Point, he said, could not and should not be removed. (Carnegie Library, Pittsburgh)

The plans had been drawn and approved, but in 1961 an architect from Baltimore proposed to replace the fountain with this stainless steel trilon. Such viewing towers make some sense in a city built on a flat terrain, but Pittsburgh already had a high view from a nearby mountain top. (Blakeslee-Lane, Inc.)

has been ahead of his time for so long that he is slightly bitter over waiting for the world to catch up with him. He has been privately critical of the much-touted Moses Report as a mere rewrite of what he has been saying for twenty years or more." And of the report itself: "Since many conflicting interests are fighting over as many conflicting plans for Pittsburgh, a chief virtue of the Moses Report lies in what it does *not* recommend. The investigators have offered variations on familiar themes, but admittedly have found almost nothing that had not already been considered, and readily recognize that much has already been started or is definitely planned. But in recommending certain projects, in tying together its program into one organic, dramatic entity, it tends to eliminate other strongly-supported proposals. . . . Actually, the idea of the Moses Report was to coalesce all previous study and spur action."

Action, indeed, was spurred, by whatever cause. The fast-moving events of succeeding months indicated that Pittsburghers now really recognized and intended to do something to remedy their problems.
• The Regional Planning Association formed a new committee to study and promote a "Pitt Parkway" to run east from the Monongahela shore at the Triangle toward the new "Dream Highway" (Pennsylvania Turnpike) then being constructed. Chairman: Richard King Mellon, forty, banker.

• The Regional Planning Association formed a new committee to study and promote capital improvements in the Golden Triangle. Chairman: Edgar Jonas Kaufmann, department store magnate.
• The Chamber of Commerce formed a Golden Triangle Division to "crystallize citizen effort behind a movement to stop depreciation of real estate values within the Golden Triangle by making it a better place in which to work and transact business." Chairman: Richard King Mellon. (Mr. Mellon was publicly criticized for holding an organizational meeting in the Duquesne Club to which only a narrow cross-section of interested persons and institutions had been invited. It was a mistake he did not forget and did not repeat.)
• All planning groups agreed to give priority to two of the Moses proposals: the Duquesne waterfront boulevard along the Allegheny, and a crosstown boulevard, free of crossings at grade, to run from river to river at the wide base of the Triangle.
• Mayor Cornelius D. Scully appointed a new six-man Point Park Commission in October 1940 to reopen negotiations with the National Park Service for a park that would "take the form of a National Historic Site." Chairman: City Councilman Frederick W. Weir.
• The Point Park Commission employed a registered surveyor and obtained a WPA grant to begin excavation work necessary for the reports required by the National Park Service for a

National Park Site. Digging began on January 21, 1941. Wesley L. Bliss, a professional archeologist, was retained the following year.

• City Council in July 1941 passed a strong antismoke ordinance that was planned to bring all users of fuel under the program by October 1, 1943. The ordinance was based on regulations imposed successfully in St. Louis (whose officials confessed to a visiting Pittsburgh research team that they had learned all they knew about smoke control from Pittsburgh's Mellon Institute for Industrial Research).

The seeds of the city's community renewal program were beginning to sprout and flower when the United States entered World War II. The program halted in December 1941, pushed aside for a more urgent community effort.

5

"The Prodigious City"

There is a tendency among those who write about Pittsburgh-before-1946 to paint things considerably blacker than they actually were. This is generally done to make a better story. In order to draw a sharper contrast between the happy present and the miserable past, the writer will allow a reader to think there was always a pall of smoke over the city, the street lights normally burned at noon, and the inhabitants wore gauze masks over nose and mouth when they ventured outdoors. To illustrate this text, the photographer may tend to underexpose his negative, and the picture editor will naturally select the darkest picture of smog he can find in his files. Long-time residents often voice supporting evidence today of the horror of it all. Arthur Rooney, for example, was quoted in December 1979: "In the old days the lights never went out. We'd leave for school in the morning with clean clothes and get there

covered with soot." But in reality, conditions were not that bad.

Still, they were bad enough—so bad that no exaggeration was needed. And they were never worse than in the autumn of 1945, after four years of war, eight years of depression, and a century of errors, unregulated growth, and inaction and misfires in city planning. Renewal work had stopped in 1942. Pittsburgh was a chewed-up, run-down, decaying community. Urban blight had made deep and telling inroads. In the 330 acres of the downtown business section, the Golden Triangle, assessed property values had fallen to an all-time low and were dropping at a rate of $10 million a year. The air was often bad, sometimes very bad. Several hundred communities were dumping their sewage into the rivers above Pittsburgh. Housing was inadequate. The city had not met its United Fund drive goal for more than ten years. No major expressway had been built, none was in design, and peak-hour traffic in and out of the city was often a nightmare—always when it was raining. Pittsburgh was headquarters for half the steel produced in the United States, but steel production was moving east and west. Pittsburgh was headquarters for more than one hundred major industrial corporations, but a number of companies were thinking of moving away and some had optioned offices in other cities.* Management found it difficult to persuade engineering, scientific, and accounting people to move to Pittsburgh, or to stay there if they came. In the winter of 1944 the *Wall Street Journal* surveyed the prospects of 137 cities in postwar America, putting them in four classifications. Class D cities were those that had bleak futures and little promise for growth. Pittsburgh was in Class D.

The Point itself had never been in so low a condition. The river banks in places were littered with debris. Fifteen acres of freight yards and terminal and a half mile of elevated tracks were still there, largely unused. The abandoned marble Wabash Station, a 1904 vestige of the Goulds' unfortunate dream of power and profit, was being used as a govern-

ment warehouse for commodities. Exposition Hall had held its last show in 1918 and was now a pound for towed-away automobiles. There were vacant lots. There were a few rooming houses, some of which had been speakeasies in the Prohibition years and some of which were now places where, in the words of one observer, male patrons made short visits. There were some shops, a run-down twelve-story hotel, a good Professional Building, a residence converted to a women's club, an exclusive men's club that had been taken over as a lodge for the Elks. It was, in sum, a blighted area.

The Point and the Triangle itself had lost their last contact with the rivers. The Monongahela wharf, a wide cobblestone slope running down from Water Street, had once given the city an open shore and a view over the river to the high ridge on the south. The wharf had been a meeting place, a Saturday garden market, a mooring place for boats and barges, and finally, inevitably, a parking place for cars. This last stretch of open space along the Monongahela had disappeared with the building of the Fort Pitt waterfront highway in 1938–1939.

Remarkably, despite all the abuse and misuse, despite the scars and ravages, the features of the city were so strong that Pittsburgh was still a place of striking beauty. Storm Jameson, one of Britain's finest modern novelists, lived and worked in the city after the war, and she wrote in the New York *Times* in 1949, "Pittsburgh is fascinating and tremendous, and if they would

*The Aluminum Company of America was one; according to Frank L. Magee, general production manager, 1943–1946, Arthur Vining Davis had bought a square block on Park Avenue in New York City and intended to move Alcoa out of Pittsburgh when the war ended.

clean it up it would be one of the most beautiful cities in the world."

A Belfast-born architect, artist, educator, and environologist has puzzled out an answer to this paradox in a remarkable study of Pittsburgh's "design image" and "design objectives." Patrick Horsbrugh, born in 1920 of Scottish lineage, left a school of architecture in London for seven years of military service, five of it as a wartime pilot in the R.A.F. He practised architecture, industrial planning, and urban design in postwar Britain and in special projects in Canada and the Middle East. In 1960 he joined the architectural faculty at the University of Nebraska, moving five years later to the School of Architecture at the University of Texas. Since 1967 he has been on the faculty of the Department of Architecture at the University of Notre Dame, where he initiated and directs the graduate program in Environic Studies. In 1963, serving as a consultant to Pittsburgh's Department of City Planning, he produced a three-hundred-page work called *Pittsburgh Perceived: A Critical Review of Form, Features and Feasibilities of the Prodigious City.* (Mr. Horsbrugh has made slight emendations in his original text for its use in this work.) He wrote:

Pittsburgh is unique in its topographical advantages, for it has no equal among the inland cities of these United States. . . . Pittsburgh is a city of exceptional beauty. Better, still, it is un-selfconscious about that beauty. . . . Pittsburgh's beauty is one of natural inheritance, which successive generations have done everything to ignore, to defy, and even to defile—yet somehow it survives and is available as ever for anyone who will pause to perceive.

Pittsburgh's beauty has been forced to yield here and there, but in some remarkable way its resilience from human desecration has intensified this extraordinary condition of beauty.

He wrote of the city's three great natural advantages. All, he felt, were unappreciated, but they were strong enough to withstand man-made injuries.

First, the physical and emotional effect of water: "A location whose landscape permits water to be glimpsed between hills or looked down upon from a variety of positions, giving different combinations of reflections and juxtapositions, possesses a continuing source of enchantment season by season. There is no scene of human contrivance not improved by association with water. . . .

"Consider, now, the elements of Pittsburgh in this romantic mood of visual stimulation. The indifferent industrial facades along the riverbanks become mysterious and evocative. The stinking atmosphere of Herrs Island demands to be explored. The rotting rubbish screes along the waterfront of the Strip, mercifully concealed by the self-sown willows, now so desolate and deserted, ensure uninterrupted solitude within sight and sound of busyness. The wasted water fouled, the deserted railway yard, eye-high with delectable weeds and grasses, wonderland of butterflies in their season, are now as undisturbed as fields a hundred miles remote. The soaring steel mills represent a spectacle that is striking enough by land, but dramatic in the extreme when seen both in fact and in reflection.

"Water is so alive by both day and night that its presence sets the quality of the place, and its existence must be recognized by all who plan and build. Not a single street in Pittsburgh, nor building for that matter, is effectively designed to recognize the proximity or significance of water. . . .

"The Golden Triangle is not only the focal point of the urban and economic form of Pittsburgh, it is also the visual hub from which the principal views radiate and upon which the attention persistently returns. . . . The Golden Triangle itself is immeasurably enhanced by the value of the waters, even though its structures are now isolated from each river by the continuous bridge embankments with their roaring ribbons of traffic. To descend from the city's streets to the water's edge is something of an ordeal. . . .

"In reaction to the damage caused by floods, the Golden Triangle has defended itself from the waters at the aesthetic price of total separation. There is no pavement within the Triangle from which the nearby water can be seen; only from elsewhere can one enjoy the aquatic setting.

"Venetian delights are now denied the inhabitants of the Triangle, Bangkok's splendors must remain unapproached, and Stockholm's water intimacies remain unrivaled, largely because Pittsburgh has replaced its foreshores with highways and their heavy embankments. . . .

"The endless surprise and kinetic qualities of the Pittsburgh scene viewed from the reflective waters should have made this prodigious city the envy of every metropolis in the union." (This was written before the completion of Point State Park.)

Second, changes in elevation afforded by varied topography: "Allegheny County has the idealized basic form for which a designer of cities for the future might well search. It is varied; it undulates without the severities of canyons or escarpments; it is firm enough to allow penetrations (tunnels), incisions (highway cuts), and the concentrated loads of high structures and wide spans. It drains well, although somewhat erratically, and in particular, it supports a wide variety of vegetation in abundance and even in luxuriance.

"By reason of topography, Pittsburghers can enjoy the values of height and the entertainment of self-analysis and examination which height affords. Its features cater to the widespread instinctive desire for both contrasts in form and for supervision.

"Flat cities must strive mightily to create height. . . .

"The powerful economic and engineering reasons for siting cities on regular ground must recognize, also, the urgent necessity for emotional relief through contrast. Here Pittsburgh has such richness of topography that if this is understood and henceforth used to advantage, the city could become a ready reference for totally different standards for the selection of sites for new cities. . . .

"The Pittsburgher may enjoy the scenes from the funiculars, or from Mount Washington's streets, or by climbing West End heights. They may look down upon their city from numberless vantage points. They may enjoy the sights of social vitality, of industry, the splendors of the Golden Triangle. . . . All of these are experiences and information-giving opportunities which the flat-town dweller does not possess."

Third, the variety and richness of the vegetation: "It is unnecessary to deal in the detail of the botanical registry to emphasize the variety of plants, shrubs, and of trees in particular, which flourish in this region. There are many favored parts of the continent where the vegetation is limited in variety, and where it may even be considered by the unenlightened to verge upon monotony, but this cannot be said of western Pennsylvania, nor of the contents of the many Pittsburgh parks and cemeteries which are exceptional in their size no less than in their ecological magnificence.

"More important, however, than all these fine parks, expensively maintained, are the natural, uncared-for trees and shrubs that clothe the steeper hills, often in the face of the most determined discouragements. . . . The most

luxuriant growth of trees and vegetation . . . that has ever graced a great city . . . had come to the salvation of these once-ravaged hills. The result has been to recreate Pittsburgh as the most verdant, possibly the most "rural" metropolis on the continent.

"It is the constant sight of these tree-clad hills that elevates Pittsburgh to a position of pre-eminent beauty among the inland cities of these United States."

Horsbrugh on Pittsburgh's possibilities: "However fascinating its history, however prodigious its feats of industry, however valiant its people, however noble their buidings, the quality and character of the City of Pittsburgh depend upon the remarkable, even the triumphant combination of water, of topography formed by that water, and of the vegetation sustained by that water, all that is collectively known as the *landscape.* It is in the appreciation of the landscape that a people, and therefore a city, aspires to and achieves greatness. Herein lies Pittsburgh's singular opportunity to demonstrate not only its prowess as a titan of industry, but its cultivation as civilized society by maintaining the conditions of contrast, so urgently required by every city of size throughout the country, by a determined program of landscape consciousness, conservation, and control."

Pittsburgh had still another unappreciated advantage in 1945—one that Patrick Horsbrugh did not cover. It was a negative advantage, but

"The most luxuriant growth of trees and vegetation . . . that has ever graced a great city . . . has come to the salvation of these once-ravaged hills. . . . Pittsburgh [is] the most verdant, possibly the most rural metropolis on the continent."—Patrick Horsbrugh, architect, in *Pittsburgh Perceived*, 1963. (Allegheny Conference)

one that made things magnificently possible. It was the condition of the fifty-nine acres at the Point. The condition, in the view of the city planner, was almost perfect.

There was virtually no residential population that would have to be placated, uprooted, and relocated. Of the commercial buildings, most were substandard. There were no architectural treasures to preserve—or to rouse protest if they were razed. There would be relatively few property owners to negotiate with, one of whom, the Pennsylvania Railroad, owned more than a third of the area.

The Point, moreover, was blessed by the fortunate failures of those who had sought to develop it in decades past. They had failed in their efforts to build monuments and memorials that it would have been sacrilegious to remove. There was no lighthouse at the Point, no shaft of black granite, no statue of George Rogers Clark, no Doric temple, no freshwater aquarium, pioneer museum, commercial museum, or town hall. The Point, for better or worse, could be a blank tablet on which this generation would be free to attempt to design and build the most beautiful of city parks.

6

The League of Yes-and-No People

A persistent legend has grown up around the beginnings of the Pittsburgh Renaissance. Journalists on assignment to describe what was happening in Pittsburgh told over and over a story of Richard King Mellon's return from the war in 1945. As it appeared in *Time* magazine on October 3, 1949:

Home again as a brigadier general [colonel] in the Army Reserve,* Mellon took off his uniform. . . . On the night he and Mrs. Mellon returned to Pittsburgh the city was engulfed in black smog so thick that from the William Penn Hotel they could not see the lights of the Mellon National Bank half a block away.

*Mellon had been a student pilot in World War I. He reentered service on April 2, 1942, as a major, handled Emergency Relief in Washington, became director of Selective Service for Pennsylvania in July 1943, and in March 1945 became assistant chief of staff of the International Division of the War Department. He was discharged as a colonel. He became a reserve brigadier general in June 1948 and retired as a lieutenant general in 1961.

"I had almost forgotten how bad it is," said Constance Mellon. "Now I understand why a lot of people leave it and why a lot of people will never come back to it."

"We *must* come back to it," he said.

"Well, you have a lot of ideas about it. Will they ever get done?"

"They *must* get done."

Having discovered that there was a problem and having decided that there should be a Renaissance in Pittsburgh, Mellon "took up his ideas with his colleagues around the Duquesne Club: such men as Pickleman H. J. ('Jack') Heinz, Edgar Kaufmann of Kaufmann Department Store, U. S. Steel's Ben Fairless, Alcoa's Roy Hunt. . . . All of them were conscious of the city's needs."

As *Reader's Digest* told the story, "The start came in 1945 when General Richard K. Mellon . . . returned to the 'Smoky City' from overseas. On his first day home his wife,

A rare picture of Richard King Mellon, young and smiling, taken before World War II, when he was acquiring the knowledge and motivation that caused him to undertake a renewal program for his city. (Carnegie Library, Pittsburgh)

Constance, laid down the law: 'You've got to do something about Pittsburgh—or we'll move away.' " 'I couldn't afford to lose such a wonderful wife,' says Mellon. 'I decided to do something.' "

The story is a pretty one, but it ignores some pertinent facts. Richard Mellon, stationed in Harrisburg and Washington throughout the war, had been back in Pittsburgh a number of times in the years 1942–1945, and he and Constance Mellon were not unaware of the city's smoke problem. He had had a great deal of firsthand experience in the city's renewal programs before the war. He was one of five individual supporters who in 1939 brought Robert Moses to make a plan for improving Pittsburgh. He had been a member of the Regional Planning Association since 1938 and the active chairman of one of its most important committees; on the death of Howard Heinz in 1941 he became, at the urging of Arthur E. Braun and Wallace Richards, the association's president. He and his colleagues had already drawn up plans for postwar Pittsburgh; in 1943 he had formed the key organization that was to be named the Allegheny Conference on Community Development.

There are varying accounts of who first conceived the idea of creating the Allegheny Conference, but there is general agreement that it was one or the other of three principal figures— or perhaps all three at once. They were Dr. Robert E. Doherty, soon to retire as president of Carnegie Tech; Dr. Edward R. Weidlein, president and director of the Mellon Institute for Industrial Research; and Wallace Richards, executive director of the Pittsburgh Regional Planning Association, called Richard Mellon's "civic advisor," sometimes his "public conscience."

According to James McClain, planning officer of the Planning Association, later planning director of the Allegheny Conference, "In the early 1940s a person from the state government came to the city to urge some post-war planning efforts. He talked with Wallace Richards and Park Martin. This is when Wallace got the idea to start the ACCD." According to J. Steele Gow, for many years executive head of the Falk Foundation, Arthur Braun (an elderly banker and publisher who was treasurer of Pittsburgh Regional Planning and had great behind-the-scenes influence in Pittsburgh) asked Gow to accept a visit from Richards. "Mr. Richards came out and spent two hours or more with me that first afternoon, telling me his ideas about Pittsburgh, how he had always thought of Pittsburgh as a vibrant place, with great potential, and that when he got here he found that it was an old city that was living pretty much on its past. . . . He said he would like to have some of the leaders of Pittsburgh get together and consider how a hopefully successful attack could be made on some of these problems that seemed to be deterring Pittsburgh from the progress which was its right and which he thought it had in it to accomplish. I listened with great attention because what he was saying to me almost directly paralleled what Bob Doherty . . . had said to me just a couple of weeks earlier. Bob had also come to Pittsburgh just recently from Yale's School of Engineering, where he was dean, and he was greatly disappointed by Pittsburgh's resting on its

laurels instead of looking to the future and planning ahead. . . . He had talked to me just about the way Wallace Richards talked that afternoon.

"So when Richards left I called Mr. Braun and told him . . . that I thought the first step was to bring these two men together and have them cross-fertilize the other's thinking. That was done, and Bob Doherty and Wallace Richards held several talks before anything else was done. When they found themselves thinking sufficiently alike or knew where their contrasts and differences were, it was decided that a group should be organized and raise some money to get a program to revitalize Pittsburgh under way."

A commonly accepted story is that Richards won support for his ideas in the winter of 1942–1943 at a breakfast meeting in Washington, D.C. Three people were present: Wallace Richards, Dr. Weidlein, and Richard Mellon. Weidlein recalled the event some years later, "We talked about the future of Pittsburgh in the postwar years and came to the conclusion that unless something was done Pittsburgh would become a dying city. Our discussion led us to the thought of creating an organization which could do a job of research and study and evolve a community plan for improvements."

Weidlein gave a slightly different version when interviewed in September 1972: "Mr. Mellon and I were down in Washington. I was associated with the War Industries Board and he with the Army. We would have many talks about what we were going to do to Pittsburgh and we often felt that we were either going to do something with it or give it back to the Indians. So that was the beginning. . . .

"So Mr. Mellon said, 'When you go back to Pittsburgh, you get ahold of Wallace Richards and he will arrange a luncheon and you and Dr. Doherty see if you can't get together all of the various divisions in one organization to see if we can't be a united front to attack all the problems related to the redevelopment of the city.' "

Park Martin once asked Wallace Richards point-blank who had conceived the idea of the Conference, and "Richards did not claim the idea nor disclaim it, but rather attributed it to Dr. Robert E. Doherty. . . . Richards said that Dr. Doherty and Dr. Edward Weidlein, in the early part of 1943, met for breakfast in the Carlton Hotel in Washington, at which time Doherty presented his concern for the region and the idea of a super planning group that would be concerned with what was called the Allegheny Region, to Richard K. Mellon and his brother-in-law, Alan M. Scaife. As a result of this meeting Mr. Mellon evidenced his interest and support of the idea. Dr. Doherty and Dr. Weidlein were to return to Pittsburgh and invite a selected group of business and political leaders to a luncheon to consider the formation of such an organization."

Among these mildly conflicting stories and conjectures about who was at the breakfast table at the famous breakfast in Washington, one thing is certain: Wallace Richards's intentions ran considerably deeper than the call by Doherty and Weidlein for research, study, and a community plan. There were already competent research organizations in Pittsburgh, and there were six master plans covered with dust on the shelves. The need was for a nonpartisan, nonprofit, privately financed, action-oriented civic organization that would have the resources not only to develop a postwar plan, but also the influence to obtain support for it from other civic organizations and the power to convert it to steel, stone, and mortar. The leadership, Richards felt, should come primarily from the city's top industrialists—those he called "the yes and no people."

The Washington conversations were carried back to Pittsburgh and discussed. A second informal meeting was held there in the early spring of 1943, when Mellon sat down with Richards, Weidlein, and Alan Magee Scaife, his brother-in-law, head of the Scaife Company (industrial steel tanks), now an army major. A formal organization luncheon meeting, titled "Citizens Conference on the Post-War Situation for Allegheny County," was then held at the William Penn Hotel on May 24. Dr. Doherty officiated; many of the others present were the heads of the city's leading corporations. Doherty spoke of the need for "resuscitation of a devitalized and deteriorating metropolitan area." He and Dr. Weidlein, he said, and a few others with whom they had talked, felt that "a citizens committee or conference, such as this group, might sponsor that general coordination of study and planning that appears so essential." Dr. Weidlein recalled, "We just talked aimlessly at the first meeting in May"; but the group did vote to constitute itself as the Citizens Sponsoring Committee on Post War Planning for the Metropolitan Area of Allegheny County.

According to Steele Gow, "Doherty picked some twenty-five or thirty leading people in Pittsburgh and invited them to a luncheon to hear a presentation of these ideas, and he asked them to pledge initially $25,000 to explore the possibilities for a year or so and see what could be done. The audience sat on its hands, it didn't applaud the idea, it made no comment, raised no questions, and gave no money. The meeting fell completely flat.

"Doherty . . . said he was not going to let it go at that. He was going to call that group together with some others very soon, but was going to go around to see some of them personally in advance and try to make them realize how important this subject was so that they could help to sell the others. So he paid visits to some key individuals we helped him select and . . . within a very few weeks that second meeting was held and I think the $25,000 was raised without much trouble.*

At this second meeting, held on June 29, 1943, the CSCPWPMAAC renamed itself the Allegheny Conference on Post War Community Planning. (One senses that a public relations man was struggling for a usable, pronounceable title.) It named Dr. Doherty as temporary chairman, Dr. Weidlein as vice-chairman, and Wallace Richards as secretary. It limited its membership to directors, to be known as sponsors, with twenty-five of these to serve on an executive committee. This, the basic study and planning body, appointed nine groups to draw up postwar plans in as many fields.

And the Conference made a momentous policy decision. In the normal pattern of civic service, a top industrialist represented his company at an organizational meeting but thereafter was seen no more; he sent a deputy, sometimes a vice-president employed for such service, to represent him at the subsequent working sessions and to serve on committees. Now an unwritten, self-imposed, strict rule was made known: Members should participate in the work of the Conference and its committees as individual citizens, not as corporate officers.

*Dr. David H. Kurtzman said in 1971, "As a matter of fact, the one thing that contributed more to the Renaissance than anything else was a story in the Chicago *Tribune* which said that Pittsburgh is passé, it's gone. For years that story was quoted. It wrote Pittsburgh off as a major city. . . . This . . . put Pittsburgh in a position where everybody wanted to get on the bandwagon."

The member, not a surrogate, not a second-string executive, was expected to be present at meetings and to work personally on his committees. The Conference did not want a mere luncheon club of deputies; it wanted a decision at the time of the meeting from a man who was empowered to say yes or no—not from an absent member to whom the question would be referred by his stand-in. Robert B. Pease, who joined the Urban Redevelopment Authority as a young Carnegie Tech graduate in 1953 and fifteen years later became executive director of the Allegheny Conference, recalls a saying: "If the chairman of Alcoa wanted to send the president of Alcoa to represent him at a Conference meeting, he would not dare to do it." It was said that no one ever asked to become a member of the executive committee—he was invited; and that no one ever turned down an invitation to join.

For the next two years the Pittsburgh program lay in abeyance. Conference leaders knew, however, that they had started a movement that was a counteraction to those who were thinking of leaving Pittsburgh, taking their companies with them. If Mr. Mellon and his Conference colleagues really meant to stay, there might be hope for rescuing the city.*

*George I. Bloom, active for decades in Pennsylvania politics, has told me that there was a time when Richard Mellon himself was thinking of leaving Pittsburgh and establishing his residence in New York City. Mr. Bloom recalls distinctly a meeting in which Governor Edward Martin worked hard to persuade him to stay in Pittsburgh.

Early in July 1945, Wallace Richards made a telephone call to Ralph E. Griswold, head of a firm of landscape architects based in Pittsburgh. He said that the state, intending to build its own office building in the Point area in Pittsburgh, had asked the Planning Association to recommend a site. Would Griswold be interested in working on a location for the building?

Griswold replied that he would be interested.

Richards said, "I'd like you to work with another architect, Charles M. Stotz."

Griswold said he would be happy to work with Charlie Stotz. Then he added, "You know, I'm already consultant on a study of the whole Point in connection with the proposed national historical park, for the Point Park Commission, and for the City Planning Commission. Would it be possible for us to coordinate the two studies?"

Richards said, "Well, I have no authority to go beyond the location of the office building, but it sounds like a sensible idea. I'll call Dick Mellon right away."

He called back within an hour and said, "Go ahead, broaden your study. I'll call Charlie Stotz and tell him."

"It was that chance remark and that decision," Griswold says today, "that started people thinking about the Point as a whole. I was dealing with Willard N. Buente, chief engineer of the City Planning Department, and he was so provoked with me for agreeing to work with the Regional Planning Association that he immediately dropped the city's work on a park at the Point. Fred Bigger had quarreled with Richards and had left the Planning Association to spend full time on the City Planning Commission, and he too was not pleased with me for taking an assignment from Richards.

"I had been working for City Planning only a few weeks, but I could see there was a complete stalemate there. The city people were determined to have a national park at the Point. It was an unalterable rule of the National Park Service that the restoration of a historic structure *must* be a total restoration and one placed on its original site. So the Park Service people said, 'We'll have nothing to do with it unless you give us the whole Point and let us rebuild Fort Pitt on it.' That would have run to Stanwix Street, almost to the edge of Horne's store, with no room left for a real park and no provision for the traffic at the Point. There we were. It would never work. The city would never buy all that land and turn it over to the Park Service."

Griswold and Stotz prowled the Point area and retired to home or office to set down their findings and their ideas. They made their exploratory studies in a manner common to architects, laying large sheets of transparent tracing paper (known in the profession as "bum-wad") one atop the other, the design progressing as each was finished. They had worked well together on a number of other projects, including the restoration of Old Economy in Ambridge; but in two weeks of hard

work on Point Park they produced nothing that satisfied them. The location of a site for the state office building depended on the design of the park, and in designing the park they were caught in a three-way deadlock of the traffic planners, whose sole or main concern was the flow of vehicular traffic over the two Point bridges; the historians, who wanted at least one reconstructed fort; and those who thought of the Point mainly in terms of public buildings set down in a park. Their own designs, and the designs of all who had preceded them, contained what was really nothing more than a landscaped interchange.

Ralph Esty Griswold, born in Warren, Ohio, in 1894, graduated from Cornell in landscape design. He had served as a lieutenant in camouflage in the AEF in World War I, continued his professional studies after the war in Paris and Rome, and started out as a landscape architect in Cleveland in 1923, moving to Pittsburgh in 1927. His commissions over the next twenty years included landscape design for country clubs, municipalities, and colleges throughout the country, industrial parks, the Warm Springs Foundation in Georgia, and the Richard Beatty Mellon estate at Ligonier. He was a Fellow of Landscape Architecture at the American Academy at Rome. In years to come he would design the American Military Cemetery at Anzio, Italy, and the restoration of the Agora (marketplace) in Athens. He was best known in Pittsburgh in 1945 as superintendent of Pittsburgh's Bureau of Parks (1934–1945) and as landscape architect for the initial stage of Chatham Village, a medium-density housing development in Pittsburgh which Professor Patrick Horsbrugh calls "an outstanding example of community planning that is renowned the world over among sociologists, architects, and physical planners, not less than among real-estate economists and philanthropists."

Charles Morse Stotz, born in Pittsburgh in 1898, a Cornell graduate in architecture, the son of architect Edward Stotz, had begun to practice with his father and his brother Edward, Jr., an engineer, in 1923 in the city's oldest architectural firm. After years of designing industrial research centers, churches, college buildings, and some one hundred fifty private residences, he developed an architectural avocation in the study of eighteenth-century military architecture and in the restoration of historic buildings, in which highly specialized fields he became a national authority. Among his many projects were the restoration of Old Economy Village in Ambridge, Pa., Drake's oil well at Titusville, Pa., the Bradford House in Washington, Pa., and in the 1960s, Ligonier Square, Compass Inn, and the Fort Ligonier reconstruction. In 1932 he organized the Western Pennsylvania Architectural Survey, which covered twenty-seven counties and recorded twenty-five hundred buildings; and in 1936 he wrote *The Early Architecture of Western Pennsylvania*, a classic in its field. He had served as president of the

Pittsburgh chapter of the American Institute of Architects and had worked in civic planning in various capacities since 1936. As president of the Pittsburgh Art Commission for twenty-five years, he was involved in plans proposed for developing a park or memorial at the Point.

"We made one study after the other," Griswold says, "and it was just like marking time. We always came up against the fact that we had those two bridge ends looming thirty feet up in the air. There simply was no park area to design—only a tiny peak of land and water-front beyond the bridges. How were people to get down to that? Who would want to, and why? Everyone had agreed that the bridges had to stay there—Olmsted, Moses, Bigger, the Regional Planning Association, the City Planning Commission.

"One day Charlie threw down his pencil in disgust and burst out, 'We'll never get anywhere with those damn bridges where they are!'

"We looked at each other," Griswold says, "and talked about it for a while. Then we went to see Wally Richards. By this time it was understood that we were making a proposed preliminary design for a state park at the Point. We asked, 'Would it be possible to present a design with the bridges moved back from the Point?' We explained what that would mean, what it would do. Richards listened and said he would talk to Mr. Mellon.

"Richards called us a few days later. He told us to make *two* studies for the Regional Plan-

Three key men in the design and building of Point State Park: from left to right, Ralph E. Griswold, landscape architect who served as the prime design contractor; Arthur B. Van Buskirk, chairman of the Allegheny Conference's Point Park Committee; and Charles M. Stotz, the architect primarily responsible for moving the old bridges at the Point. (Pittsburgh *Press*)

ning Association—one with the bridges in place where they were and with the 'landscaped interchange'; the other with two new bridges moved back to where we thought best, with the design of a real Point Park."

Since bridges and traffic flow were now involved in the study, two other professionals were added to make a four-man design team: George S. Richardson, of the engineering firm of Gordon, Richardson, and Associates, and Donald M. McNeil, a traffic engineer from the Pittsburgh Bureau of Traffic Planning.

George Richardson, born in Colorado, held degrees in civil engineering from the University of Colorado. After experience with the Pennsylvania Department of Highways, Bethlehem Steel, American Bridge Company, and the Allegheny County Works Department, he entered private business in 1937, specializing in bridge and highway design and construction. He designed the George Westinghouse Bridge (1931) with its record 470-foot concrete center span, and the Homestead High Level Bridge, among many others. In 1967 he and his firm would plan the erection of the 630-foot-high Gateway Arch at St. Louis for the Pittsburgh–Des Moines Steel Company. Of him Charles Stotz says, "He was a giant in his profession."

Don McNeil, a registered professional engineer, joined Pittsburgh's Bureau of Traffic Planning on graduating from the University of Pittsburgh. He became a traffic engineer in

1932, one of the first in the country to hold that title and position. He was one of the organizers of the Institute of Traffic Engineers in 1930, serving as its national president in 1953–1954. He would leave his miserably paid position as head of the city bureau in 1952 to found a successful and profitable private consulting engineering firm, specializing in traffic engineering and transportation and parking problems.

Richardson said at once that the Manchester Bridge on the Allegheny River was old and destined for early replacement, and that the Point Bridge across the Monongahela was cantilevered and could not be moved. "If you cut the ends, it will fall into the river," he said. He then expressed the "preliminary opinion" that new bridges of proper design in the most advantageous positions would not only be more efficient and aesthetically pleasing, but would be less expensive than remodeling or retaining the old bridges with addition of the necessary approaches.

Charles Stotz recalls the next episode. "My memory is clear that we were instructed by Richards that the Point Bridge could be removed, but that the Manchester Bridge must be retained. The struggle to make a workable scheme by leaving either bridge in place was a stumbling block of large proportions. By this time Richardson was asked to join us. I do not remember his attitude about this but believe he agreed both must go. However, we did not receive an OK to eliminate the Manchester

Bridge. I was on vacation with the family at Van Buren Bay near Dunkirk and after worrying about it and making a phone call to Pittsburgh I came back to town for a meeting. I was personally adamant that no scheme could be satisfactory unless we were free to deal with the bridges, their replacements, and traffic interchanges as required for an adequate park solution. We had a meeting in the Regional Planning office that lasted until midnight. Wally Richards finally conceded not to insist further in the matter and agreed to recommend that both new bridges should be moved upstream some distance needed to accomplish a workable traffic interchange."

The four men presented their *Point Park Development Study* to Wallace Richards at his office on October 1, 1945. It was written as from the Regional Planning Association to the state. A document of some importance in the history of Pittsburgh and southwestern Pennsylvania, its introduction reads:

The redevelopment of the Point Park area still remains unresolved in spite of the fact that it has had more plans offered for its solution than any other planning problem in the Pittsburgh region.

A glance at the list of Point Park plans will show the persistent interest in this complex problem over a period of years.

Why this problem remains unresolved can best be explained by an analysis of these plans. None of them has successfully combined the three major plan factors, the rivers, the fort sites, and the highways, to the satisfaction of the aesthetic, historic, and traffic viewpoints.

The plans with good traffic solutions have poor park designs, ignoring the riverfronts and fort sites. Yet no plan which ignores these important factors can be permanently acceptable. If such a plan were carried out it would be successfully challenged sooner or later. From then on there would be a demand for a change, a situation which should be avoided if at all possible.

In the hope that such a situation may be avoided, the Regional Planning Association has sponsored the preparation of collaborative studies by planners representing several viewpoints, including bridge construction, traffic planning, park design, and historical architecture. These technicians have worked with the Regional Planning Association staff in preparing this report and the following plans, which are offered to any agency interested in the redevelopment of the Point Park area.

The planners presented two alternative proposals, accompanying each with maps, drawings, traffic diagrams, aerial perspectives, and cost estimates. The advantages and disadvantages of each were set forth in some detail.

The first proposal, Type A Study, demolished the Point and Manchester bridges and relocated their replacements nearer the base of the Triangle.

If the highways and bridges had not already usurped the waterfronts and Point, every planner would agree that the ideal plan would be based on a Park Development of the Monongahela and Allegheny waterfronts culminating in a monumental terrace commanding a sweeping view of the Ohio River. That is the basic geographical, historical, and aesthetic significance of this site. There is none other like it in the world. It means Pittsburgh to everyone.

ANY OTHER CONCEPTION OF THIS PROBLEM IS A COMPROMISE AND WILL FOREVER APPEAR AS SUCH.

Up until now, most of the study has been given to what kind of compromise would be most acceptable or least objectionable. Little effort has been made to try and find a solution of this problem which avoids the necessity of one-way compromise.

Type "A" study offers a solution which reclaims the actual Point area with its riverfronts, panoramic view of the Ohio, and a major part of the historic fort sites for PARK DEVELOPMENT. In this sense it is truly a POINT PARK PLAN incorporating all the significant natural and historical features.

This type of plan requires some compromises on the part of traffic and the reclamation of the Fort Pitt site and it envolves a heavy penalty in cost. But this cost penalty is attributable to the original mistake of placing the Manchester and Point Bridges in their present locations.

In considering cost, the decision which will eventually have to be made is, "Can we afford not to remove the bridges from the Point?" If they are not removed in connection with the redevelopment of the Point area, the resulting compromise will be subject to change in the future, which will make the ultimate cost far greater.

Four of the eleven advantages listed for the Type A Study were: (1) the Monongahela and Allegheny waterfronts and the Ohio River view are an integral part of the park area; (2) the

Blockhouse of Fort Pitt is retained in its exact original location and given a prominent place in the park plan; (3) it concentrates the traffic separation between the park and the business district where it is least conspicuous and interferes least with park functions; (4) the park area would be permanently free of traffic confusion. The disadvantages were higher cost; reconstruction of some of the work completed on the Water Street and Duquesne Way boulevards; more difficult bridge approaches; and the need to acquire more property.

The second proposal, the Type B Study, left both bridges in place. Among its meager advantages, other than lower cost, was, "It satisfies those who are primarily interested in the traffic problem and indifferent to the Point Park Development." The disadvantages were expressed eloquently: "(1) the highways and bridges usurp both waterfronts and the Point, forcing an interior park development with no relationship to the geographic, historic, or aesthetic character of the site—it is a downtown park but in no sense a Point Park; (2) it is an unsatisfactory answer to the visitor who wants to see the historic Point he has heard so much about—all he can be shown of the Point is a colossal traffic intersection, with an apology; (3) it is primarily a traffic solution with a park attached."

Wallace Richards obtained the approval of the executive committee of the Planning Association for showing this double-barreled "preliminary proposal" to the state. Early in October he departed for Harrisburg with Park H. Martin, executive director of the Allegheny Conference. Their appointment was with Governor Edward Martin. Says Ralph Griswold, "I think they were a little scared." The thought is not unlikely, considering that Richards had been asked to pick a site for an office building and was presenting a radical and costly proposal for a state park.

Governor Martin, a lawyer from Waynesburg, Pa., had managed two successful careers concurrently in his sixty-six years. As a soldier he had been in the Philippines during the Spanish-American War, then served in the Mexican border campaign and in France in World War I. He had been relieved of division command in 1942 as over-age in grade, retiring as a major general. In politics he had risen through state Republican offices to become governor in 1943. He was the author of a history of the 28th (Pennsylvania) Division, which he had trained in World War I, and he had received honorary degrees from thirteen Pennsylvania colleges. He would be elected to the U.S. Senate in 1947.

Wallace Richards and Park Martin spread out their proposals before the governor. They prefaced their presentation with an explanation of what they had done and the statement that they would ask him to consider two different proposals for a park at the Point in Pittsburgh.

There was a pause, and for a moment the fate of Point Park hung in the balance. Indeed, since the park was later to become the springboard for and the symbol of the whole renewal program, it is probable that the success of the Pittsburgh Renaissance, at least in degree, was at stake at that trembling moment.

By all the rules of precedents and the nature of Republican governors, Edward Martin's response should have been automatic. He should have asked, "Which proposal costs the least?" On the other hand, the state's coffers were overflowing with funds accumulated during four years of war, when capital projects were few and a long time apart. Money, moreover, was cheap; it could be borrowed for 2½ to 3 percent.

The governor broke the silence with the questions: "Which one is the better proposal? Which do you prefer?"

He was told. He then said, "Put the other one away. I don't want to see it."

Says George Richardson, "Park and Wally didn't need an airplane that evening to fly back to Pittsburgh."*

*One may assume that Richard Mellon had telephoned the governor before Richards and Martin made their trip, and that he advised him on the merits of the two proposals. It is known that Mellon had discussed the park proposals with Governor Martin. As Arthur Braun told it, "Mr. Mellon and Governor Martin were good friends and spent much of their free time discussing matters of mutual interest. One evening Governor Martin told Mr. Mellon of plans being considered to develop the Independence Hall area in Philadelphia in accord with its historic interest. Mr. Mellon

Governor Martin lost no time making the headline announcement that his administration would finance major improvements in Pittsburgh, including the clearing of thirty-six acres at the lower Point, removal of the two unsightly bridges, construction of two new bridges upstream, and creation of a state park at the Point. The news broke on October 25, 1945. There was to be a mayoralty election in Pittsburgh on November 6, and some people saw this timely revelation of Republican largesse as a move to help the Republican candidate defeat the Democratic candidate.

The Democrat was David Leo Lawrence, the undisputed boss of the party in Pennsylvania, a machine politician not known for civic-mindedness, now for the first time seeking election to public office. Lawrence had a hard decision to make. "The announcement," he said flatly, "was to embarrass me and make me lose the election." His colleagues told him that if he approved Martin's program, he would be accused of sacrificing party interests, selling out to big business, and "sleeping with the Mellons." Some advisors said he should charge that the publicized improvements were nothing but a

Republican trick, a campaign promise that would never be kept.

Lawrence was not surprised by the Martin–Allegheny Conference program; he had, in fact, already considered it with some care. This had come about because of action taken by John J. Kane, chairman of the Board of Allegheny County Commissioners, another Democratic machine politician, a former labor leader, now directing Lawrence's campaign. Kane had conceived the extraordinary notion that the Republican businessmen were serious about their municipal rehabilitation program and that furthermore it might be a good thing for Pittsburgh. Park Martin affirmed in November 1971 that Kane, during the mayoralty campaign in the summer of 1945, sent an agent to his office to get a copy of the Conference recommendations, with word that he intended to show it to Lawrence.

Lawrence held a strategy meeting. Present was his former secretary and political advisor, John P. Robin, just back from army service. Robin agreed with Kane's estimate of the situation. The Republicans, he added, were counting on Lawrence to attack the program. Instead, Lawrence should hail the governor's announcement as good news, the best thing that could happen to Pittsburgh. This was exactly what the Democrats had been hoping and planning for, and they were delighted that the administration in Harrisburg had finally

agreed that this was a worthy purpose, and further mentioned that Pittsburgh had a highly important area that should be developed as part of the State's project. This was the Point, at the confluence of the Monongahela and Allegheny rivers. . . . Governor Martin agreed to Mr. Mellon's suggestion. That is when the Point Park was established."

come around to their way of thinking. As the new mayor of Pittsburgh, Dave Lawrence would welcome and cooperate fully with the governor's program.

Lawrence shortly thereafter announced a platform of seven planks, one of which was that he would support the program of the Allegheny Conference for improvement of the City of Pittsburgh and the County of Allegheny. Lawrence was elected on November 6, by the slim margin of 14,000 votes.

7

"Our Mission as Keepers of the Gate"

Governor Edward Martin's announcement of October 25, 1945, authorized the creation of a state park based on the concepts of the Regional Planning Association's *Point Park Development Study*, but the study was only a preliminary exercise and needed a great deal more work. Wallace Richards set November 14 as the date for presenting the completed plan to the Allegheny Conference, then to the public, then to the state. Griswold, Stotz, Richardson and McNeil resumed their search for a finished design that would preserve the waterfronts of the Point, celebrate its historic significance, and provide an uninterrupted traffic flow for trucks, cars, and eight streetcar lines.

Richard Mellon, as chairman of the Regional Planning Association, presided at the November 14 session, a dinner meeting held at the Duquesne Club. To a large and broad assemblage of business, civic, and political leaders, members of the association, and assorted plan-

ners, engineers, and architects, he declared that "Pittsburgh needs something to increase the enjoyment of living here and induce business to come here." Since its founding in 1918, he said, the Planning Association had spent $1,090,000 on plans later turned over to public agencies. Governor Martin, he added, had committed $4,000,000 for the park, including the purchase of land. "The money is ready. We cannot afford to let Pittsburgh down this time." Now the Point Park project was within the immediate grasp of the city, and he urged concerted action by every interested agency to make it a reality. The governor and the secretary of the Department of Forests and Waters had asked the Allegheny Conference to represent the state in coordinating and guiding the project, and the Conference had accepted the charge.

He introduced Wallace Richards, who gave the history of the *Point Park Development Study*. Richards emphasized strongly that the study

The time is November 14, 1945. Ten men are inspecting the model of the park proposed that day for the Point. They are, from left to right, H. J. Heinz II, County Commissioner John J. Kane, Edgar J. Kaufmann, Councilman Fred W. Weir, Mayor-elect David L. Lawrence, Mayor Cornelius D. Scully, Robert E. Doherty, Arthur E. Braun, Councilman Thomas E. Kilgallen, and Park H. Martin. (Carnegie Library, Pittsburgh)

was "tentative and wholly preliminary and in no sense final." It would be made available to public and private agencies "as a starting point, in the hope that it will be an incentive to action and of possible value in the preparation of the official plan adopted for Point Park." Richards introduced the four collaborators, the authors of the study. Using slides and a large model, Griswold, Stotz, Richardson, and McNeil spoke in turn on their part of the work: landscape design, architecture of buildings, highways and bridges, and traffic. The park design they presented is of peculiar interest in view of the design that emerged several years later. An unidentified Pittsburgh *Press* reporter described the $6 million "long-cherished dream" in a story with headlines larger than any since the end of the war on September 2, 1945: "The park suggested by the planning group would be basically simple, taking full advantage of the beauties of the site, yet with plenty to remind visitors of the world-changing events that transpired there.

"Its focal point, as one entered it from the Boulevard of the Allies or Penn Avenue, would be a round building designed as a memorial to Fort Pitt.

"In the center of the building, below floor level, would be a large scale model of the British fort. Daytime illumination of the model would come through glass carved with heroic figures of pioneers, Indians, frontier soldiers, pack trains, wagons, boats, and the like.

"Two semi-circular outer corridors would be lined with dioramas showing, with life-like realism, the history of the Point.

"The visitor would walk out of this building onto a terrace formed by two restored bastions of old Fort Pitt. Straight ahead of him, down a ramp, would be the historic Blockhouse, untouched. Beyond that, in the center of an open space, would be a restoration of Fort Duquesne, with which the French hoped to hold middle America.

"Planning Association officials explained that they had abandoned the idea of restoring all of Fort Pitt because it would extend too far uptown, interfere with roadways, and could be shown better, anyway, in a model.

"A restaurant with an outdoor dining terrace would stand among the trees to the right of the Fort Pitt Memorial. It would have a glass front, enabling diners to sit on different levels inside and look out over the park.

"Beyond the restaurant, on the Allegheny River, would be a basin for small pleasure craft, with a boathouse where boats might be rented.

"Down both sides of the triangular park would run wide walks, flanked by willow trees and benches.

"Where these walks met, and visible from the entire park, would be a fountain symbolic of the meeting of the rivers. Three huge jets of water would symbolize the three rivers. . . .

"No roadways would run through the park. . . .

"Toward the city, beyond the elevated struc-

Point Development Study made in November 1945 by Griswold, Stotz, George Richardson, and Don McNeil. The Regional Planning Association presented it to the state; Governor Edward Martin approved it and asked the Allegheny Conference to form a committee to supervise the design and construction.

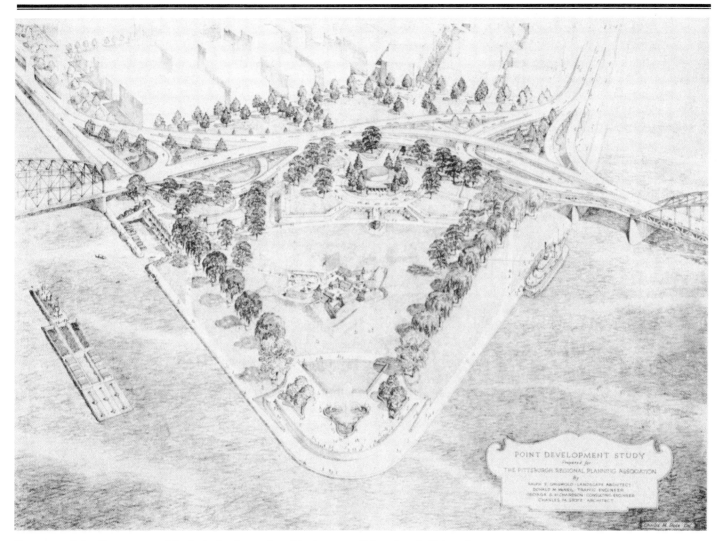

POINT DEVELOPMENT STUDY
Prepared for
THE PITTSBURGH REGIONAL PLANNING ASSOCIATION
By
RALPH E. GRISWOLD · LANDSCAPE ARCHITECT
DONALD M. McNEIL · TRAFFIC ENGINEER
GEORGE S. RICHARDSON · CONSULTING ENGINEER
CHARLES M. STOTZ · ARCHITECT

Features of the first proposal included a fountain with three small jets (symbolizing the three rivers), a rebuilt Fort Duquesne, a round Fort Pitt Memorial Hall, a restaurant (in the trees at upper left), and a marina for small boats.

tures connecting the [new] bridges, would be several squares of land that would be acquired as park property, and landscaped. They might be used later for suitable buildings.

"As a final touch—after traffic conditions have been improved by the contemplated new arteries—the Boulevard of the Allies would be lined with trees as far as Grant Street, and Liberty Avenue as far as Stanwix, to provide suitable avenues leading to the park."

The Boulevard of the Allies and Penn Avenue would be continued to join at the doorway of the round Fort Pitt Memorial Building, "so that its shining walls may be seen from many parts of the downtown area." The restaurant would hold 234 persons inside and 112 on the terrace. It was intended to be "a truly distinguished dining place and the equal of its kind in Pittsburgh or any other city." Just to the right of Penn Avenue as one entered the park area there would be a refreshment and lunch concession built into the structure of the ramp . . . in an inconspicuous location and yet one readily accessible to the public."

To close the meeting, Richard Mellon formally turned over the plans, pictures, and model to Robert Doherty, chairman of the Allegheny Conference. Dr. Doherty announced that a Point Park Committee would be appointed and charged with pushing the project through to actual construction. He closed the meeting with the words, "The Conference will proceed at once to carry out its assignment."

At this point the work of the four consultants was completed. They submitted their accounts and returned to their normal professional practice.

The park development was now like a giant puzzle with interdependent parts, in which nothing could be done in one area until the pieces had been put into place in another. The builders had to wait for the properties to be acquired, had to wait for the properties to be demolished, had to wait for the designs to be approved and the contracts let. Such waiting was to be expected in a major building project as this one, where many interests were involved and a score of agencies had to be consulted, but no one in the heady days of 1945 and 1946 dreamed they would need twenty-nine years to complete the work they had undertaken.

The Point Park Committee, as appointed, had twenty-eight members. According to Arthur B. Van Buskirk, Wallace Richards "came to my office on December 5, 1945, and asked me if I would take the chairmanship of a citizens' committee to advise the state in the development of the state park. This was most historic ground. It had been agreed between Governor Martin and R. K. Mellon and others that this development would be the state's major postwar contribution to western Pennsylvania's future. I said yes, and I moved into the heart of the Point State Park development from the moment of its inception."

The first meeting of the committee was held

in the county commissioners' conference room on December 27, 1945. Griswold and Stotz were members and were present, as were Mayor Lawrence, Robert Doherty, Park Martin as executive director of the Allegheny Conference, and Wallace Richards as secretary of the committee. Chairman Van Buskirk presided. At his suggestion, the members appointed a steering committee to work with other renewal activities, such as the proposed Penn-Lincoln Parkway East and West. They established four study committees on historical significance, highways and traffic, river commerce and recreation, and architecture and design. The minute of the meeting reads:

It was made clear that the Point Park Committee as a whole and the sub-committees in general are not in any sense administrative committees; they serve only in an advisory and coordinating capacity. The Committee makes recommendations through the Allegheny Conference to the appropriate public officials of the city, county and state.

Mayor-elect Lawrence spoke briefly on the whole-hearted interest of the city government in Point Park and offered all assistance possible. He stressed the importance of the project and urged speed in getting initial plans under way.

The choice of Van Buskirk as committee chairman was a happy one. Born in Pottstown, Pa., in 1896, he had been educated at Yale and in law at the University of Pennsylvania. He served two years in World War I as a lieutenant of field artillery and was for two years law clerk to Pennsylvania Chief Justice Robert von Moschizker; he then became an associate, later a partner, in the Pittsburgh law firm of Reed, Smith, Shaw, & McClay. In World War II he served two years in Washington as deputy administrator of the U.S. Lend Lease program. In 1945 he left a vice-presidency of Mellon Securities Corporation to become a vice-president and governor of T. Mellon and Sons. Leland Hazard, his friend and fellow lawyer, said of him, "In those days . . . it was Arthur Van Buskirk who was the spokesman for R. K. [Mellon] on the Allegheny Conference and in the mayor's office. There were others of great vision on the eighteen-man executive committee of the Conference . . . but Van was the man. He came to the monthly meetings at the Duquesne Club with a bounce in his step, a ring in his voice and a sparkle in his eyes— total charisma."

At its second meeting, on January 17, 1946, Chairman Van Buskirk presiding, the Point Park Committee approved a six-point, formal statement of objectives, of which points five and six were, "To make clear that the work of the Committee is a civic activity based on the premise that public officials, charged with the final responsibility for the development of a Point Park, will welcome study of the problem by citizens leading to crystallization of public sentiment concerning the kind of park to be built," and "To recognize the unique opportunity afforded Pittsburgh to secure, at long last, a nationally significant park and to leave no effort unexpended to build it."

Developments came thick and fast in 1946, the miracle year of the renewal of Pittsburgh and the Point.

January 21. Mayor Lawrence submitted to City Council the Point Park Committee's recommendation that a minimum of 36.2 acres be acquired for the Park.

January 27. Richard Mellon and his sister, Sarah Mellon Scaife, announced the gift to the city of 13 ½ acres of family-owned land at Fifth and Penn Avenues in the Point Breeze area, to be developed as a public recreation center. The gift included $100,000 in cash.

March 22. A fire destroyed the Wabash Terminal and railroad trestle and damaged eleven warehouses, all owned by the Pittsburgh and West Virginia Railroad. These stood on twelve acres just outside the eastern edge of Point Park as planned, blocking the possible commercial development of acreage adjoining the park. Wallace Richards called Ralph Griswold early next morning in a state of high excitement to convey the good news. "You won't believe what has happened!" he began. "The Wabash Station has burned down! They will be blaming us for it for sure!"

April 11. Mayor Lawrence set October 1, 1946, as the date on which the smoke control ordinance would be enforced for industry, commercial buildings, and the railroads. The ordinance, passed in 1941, called for the regulations to take effect only when the war had ended. Opponents of smoke control pointed out that the war had not ended, since no peace treaties had been signed with Germany and Japan. Lawrence and several members of City Council declared solemnly that World War II was over, peace was at hand, and smoke control should begin on October 1.

April 18. The Point Park Committee recommended to Governor Martin that the Pennsylvania Department of Highways be authorized to begin studies for the Point Park traffic interchange and the new Point and Manchester bridges. The governor so acted.

May 21. The voters of Allegheny County approved a $34 million bond issue for public improvements, including highways, bridges, and a Greater Pittsburgh Airport.

June 3. The Point Park Committee appointed a Point Redevelopment Study Committee to recommend ways and means of redeveloping the blighted property adjacent to Point Park for appropriate commercial use. Charles J. Graham, president of the Pittsburgh and West Virginia Railroad, was appointed chairman.

July 1. Graham's committee proposed that an area east of the park be developed as a modern business district. Such a development was necessary to supply a setting for Point Park itself, since the park would be spoiled if it was separated from the city by a blighted and decayed area. The committee recommended that the land be acquired by use of the urban redevelopment law passed by the Pennsylvania legislature a year earlier and that it then be developed (unlike Point Park) by private enterprise and capital. Accordingly, the Allegheny Conference recommended to the mayor and City Council that they create a Pittsburgh Redevelopment Authority as an essential instrument in rebuilding the city.

July 8. The authority had not been created and the redevelopment law had not been tested in the courts, but Van Buskirk, Richards, Park Martin, and Charles Graham boarded the *Pittsburgher* bound for New York City. "We saw that the first thing we had to do," said Van Buskirk simply, "was to find a developer. This meant somebody with vast sums of money." Their first choice was Metropolitan Life Insurance Company. They called and presented their proposal to Frederick H. Ecker, president. He was not interested.

On the sidewalk at One Madison Avenue, Graham suggested that they call on the Equitable Life Assurance Society. He said he knew the president, Thomas I. Parkinson. "He and I are members of the Pennsylvania Society, and I am sure he would see us." Richards said, "Why not? What have we got to lose?"

Van Buskirk approved the idea, but he had to leave to keep another appointment. Graham, Richards, and Martin took a cab to 393 Seventh Avenue and were admitted to Parkinson's office. They proposed that Equitable put up several high-class apartment buildings on a plot across from Horne's Department Store. Parkinson listened for a while and then asked two questions. What was Pittsburgh doing to control its smoke? What was being done to control Pittsburgh's floods? The answers satisfied him, and he agreed to open negotiations.

July 15. The state bought the first piece of property for Point Park.

July 18. The county broke ground in Moon Township, sixteen miles west of the Point, for the new $30 million Greater Pittsburgh Airport then second only in size in the United States to New York's Idlewild.

July 25. The state broke ground for the first leg of the Penn-Lincoln Parkway, the first non-toll limited access freeway in Pennsylvania, which was to run 9.2 miles eastward from the south shore of the Point to meet State Highways 22 and 30.

August 19. The city and Horne's Department Store began to widen Stanwix Street (named for Brigadier General John Stanwix, builder and first commander of Fort Pitt). The street, with Commonwealth Place, marked the eastern boundary of the Point redevelopment area.

Fall 1946. The executive committee of the Allegheny Conference authorized the preparation of a state legislative program for Pittsburgh. Working with the Regional Planning Association, the Pennsylvania Economy League, and the Lawrence administration, and guided by Theodore Hazlett, its counsel, the Conference settled on ten bills known as "the Pittsburgh Package." Two bills were introduced in City Council as administrative measures; eight bills were introduced jointly in the Pennsylvania house and senate. The eight bills passed with bipartisan support. They produced enabling legislation to control smoke, create a public parking authority, establish a city Department of Parks and Recreation, broaden the tax base, and build express highways and county-wide waste-disposal facilities.

November 7. The Point Park Committee announced at its fourth meeting that twelve of the thirty-two parcels of property in the Point area had been acquired. The state awarded the first contract for design of the new Point bridge and interchange. It went to George Richardson, consulting engineer.

November 18. City Council and Mayor Lawrence established the Redevelopment Authority of Pittsburgh. Lawrence asked Van Buskirk to serve as chairman, but Van Buskirk replied that it would be better if Mr. Lawrence himself took the position; Wallace Richards joined him in asking Lawrence to serve. Lawrence said that the suggestion was "ridiculous." How could a mayor appoint himself chairman of a city authority? Van Buskirk and Richards persisted and agreed to make their request in an open letter. They were joined by the president of the Chamber of Commerce. Several inspired newspaper editorials urged Lawrence to take the post.

December 2. Lawrence solved a difficult prob-lem by appointing three Republicans and two Democrats to the Redevelopment Authority, with himself as chairman and Van Buskirk as vice-chairman. It was, he said, "the first time I ever appointed a committee that made me a member of the minority party." (Lawrence's appointment of himself as chairman, it was discovered several years later, was illegal; he had no legal right to appoint himself. The question was never seriously raised, however, and the authority was protected by having had in every instance a majority decision without the mayor's vote.)

The ten-member Study Committee on the Historical Significance of the Point Park Project met three times early in 1946. John William Oliver, chairman, rose at the Point Park Committee meeting on April 18, 1946, to read his report. Oliver, trained at the University of Wisconsin, had been head of the history department at the University of Pittsburgh since 1923. Unmarried, a resident of the University Club, he was devoted to the work of his profession, and in this report he was both lyrical and eloquent. His committee approved the Planning Association's design for the park, "a thirty-six acre pool of quiet in the midst of the city, built on sacred ground." He closed with a ringing paragraph that in succeeding years was frequently quoted in the literature of and about the Pittsburgh Renaissance:

Some day at the meeting of the waters there will be erected a fitting monument to symbolize the role this spot has played in the past and will play in the future. Might it not bear some such inscription as this?

"Through this river-gate poured the tide of conquest, of trade, and of ideas which made America. We have kept well these gates. We have fostered and passed on that freedom which came to this continent, not as a perfected democracy, but as the right to continue the struggle for a just balance of changing political, economic, and social forces. Out of this we have helped to form an order of society, not perfect, but with the method to perfect itself. We have learned and become strong through that struggle, and have built not only great material assets, but have bred up human values. Our mission under God, as keepers of the gate, has been to know the right and to give right the might to conquer. The dross of materialism has been translated into the pure gold of the spirit. We have found our joy and duty."

Chairman Edgar Jonas Kaufmann reported at the same meeting for his Study Committee on Architecture and Design. Kaufmann was active until his death in 1955 in various phases of the work of the Allegheny Conference, as chairman of its important Coordinating Committee, on its Point Park Committee, and on the Redevelopment Authority. Van Buskirk called him "a great leader." Leland Hazard called him "the inspired merchant" and "a Renaissance man." William Froelich, who was secretary of Kaufmann's Point Park Coordinating Committee, remarks on the many hours Kaufmann spent on Conference matters:

[He was] a remarkable individual who in meetings would keep prodding and asking questions. If he didn't know, he would ask. He wasn't proud in that respect. He was quite willing to make himself look foolish by asking questions of the engineers, but some of the questions he put to them surfaced certain things that really were problems, ones that had not been anticipated.

He treated everyone the same way, whether it was a young professional like me or someone with whom he was on a peer level. Everyone recognized his selflessness in pushing Point Park, when a number of people were advising him that it would serve Horne's Department Store to the disadvantage of Kaufmann's, uptown from the park.

Theodore Hazlett said, "There had been a real rivalry between the upper Triangle interests and the lower Triangle group, sometimes very bitter. I was encouraged when I saw Edgar Kaufmann support these developments against what were called his own short-term interests. I thought, 'This program is going to work.' "

Kaufmann had been asked to produce a theme for the park, and on April 18 he too was poetic and eloquent. The park should be a symbol of personal freedom and world responsibility. "It is here where man and nature can work together to produce something unique. Such a chance comes very seldom to any community, and Pittsburgh should consider this one with great seriousness. . . . As a state park . . . it should represent a focal point in the progress of human civilization so far as western culture and industry have been able to further it." For this reason, he said, "I believe it is especially important that the Point Park should not be considered and executed primarily as a memorial to the past.

"No mere museum of relics will achieve this; that can be done only by a project dedicated to the two greatest ideas of our time: the freedom gained for individual men and women by intelligent use of machines, and the responsibility of world cooperation and peace.

"Only the most foresighted park planner and an architect worthy of the name genius could thus continue the traditions which make the Point a shrine."

8

"Cantilever Development in Automobile-Scale of Point Park, Pittsburgh"

Edgar Kaufmann was quite serious about his call for "an architect worthy of the name genius," perhaps because he questioned whether anyone in Pittsburgh was advanced enough to do justice to so great a project. Whatever the reason, he offered to retain Frank Lloyd Wright, an indubitable genius, to draw up a design for Point Park. He had earlier commissioned Wright to design Fallingwater, a private residence in the mountains south of Pittsburgh that is recognized as a national landmark of architecture. He had paid for a number of other Wright designs for Pittsburgh, including a parking garage next to Carnegie Museum where the Scaife Gallery now stands, but none was built. Now he proposed to bring Wright to Pittsburgh to meet with the executive committee of the Allegheny Conference.

The meeting took place on a Saturday afternoon in the early summer of 1945. Over a luncheon table in the Duquesne Club, Wright confessed that he had been unjust in his famous advice of a decade or so earlier on what should be done about Pittsburgh: "Abandon it." He agreed, for a fee of $10,000, to draw up a plan for the Point. Kaufmann agreed to pay that amount as a grant to the Conference.

Several weeks later Wright wrote Park Martin and asked for the $10,000. Martin's engineering background was such that he felt a certain uneasiness at paying for services that had not been produced, and he called Kaufmann's office for advice. Kaufmann was in New York, but Miss Clinton, his secretary, said she was to telephone him later in the day and would ask him what to do. She called Martin a few hours later to report: Mr. Kaufmann had laughed about the request and said, "Tell Park to send him the money. He's probably hard up." Martin sent the money.

The following spring, Martin said, "I became concerned about what Wright might propose for the Point, knowing that he was a controversial figure and might suggest something that would cause dissension in the community." He suggested that Kaufmann should send someone to Wright's studio to review the plan. Kaufmann agreed. He asked Martin, Wallace Richards, and George Richardson to make the trip.

They flew to Phoenix and drove to Wright's school and studio, Taliesin West. Wright, then in his seventy-seventh year, had been working nine months on the project, using eleven of his apprentice architects to assist him. Richardson says, "We spent the whole day with him. He started by taking us through the studio he had there for meeting with clients. He had quite a remarkable set of plans for the Point, and a very impractical solution. I was asked to go there strictly in connection with how this would fit into the plans for the highway improvements. It didn't fit at all."

Wright displayed a drawing of what he proposed to build and gave the three visitors a mimeographed presentation piece titled "For the Allegheny Conference—Cantilever Development in Automobile-Scale of Point Park, Pittsburgh." It showed a huge, slope-sided, tiered, circular main building at the Point, one-fifth of a mile in diameter and 175 feet high. This had thirteen levels, each indicated by a helical ascending "Grand Auto Ramp" on the outside, four-and-a half miles long, geared to two-way slow and fast traffic. The building had

a tower on top—in Wright's words, "a glass shaft 500 feet high—a light-shaft memorial to Fort Duquesne—equipped for light concerts and broadcast music." Two cantilevered double-decked "tunnel bridges" extended across the rivers, each in a single span, each built "by means of prestressed steel or cold-drawn mesh cast in high-pressure-concrete with vertical and horizontal glass-enclosures: a characteristic employment of steel in tension in appropriate Architectural Forms."

Wright described the main buildings: "Many commercialized exploits (known as 'concessions') are spread out along the interior of the grand, slow or fast, rising or descending auto-ramps. Others are easy of access in the Winter-garden. Intermediate parking extends from the ramps, three at each level. The Sky-park above is provided with ample parking space and promenades. . . .

"Spacious under-sky but glass-covered play-field, 20,000 seats for summer or winter use. Parking on same or adjacent levels for 3000 cars with access to other parking levels below.

"Note: This under-sky sports-arena seating easily 20,000 for football or baseball by day or night is easily converted to skating rink, hockey field or circus.

"For Grand Opera, unusually good acoustics, probably no loud speakers necessary, and generous seating for from 10,000 to 20,000 people. Everywhere beautiful in proportion it is easy of access. . . .

"Convention Hall, minimum 12,500 seats, parking accordingly. . . .

"Three great rooms for cinema (approximately 1,500 each). . . .

"Upon the inside of the continuous four-and-one-half miles of Grand Ramp direct where access is had from the ramps are several hundred commercial concessions such as hamburg stands, candy, soft drinks, to flowers, books, curios, infinite gadgetry and personal services. Conveniently placed garages and other immediate services as they may appear convenient, etc., etc., are provided all as a source of revenue. The Grand Ramp within would resemble a county fair.

"A vast Winter Garden—tropical plants (a modern arboretum covering the flora of the world.)

"Sky Park, nine or more acres, planted to indigenous trees, shrubs and flowers.

"On and below the main street level, an outdoor concert garden seating approximately 15,000 to 20,000 people.

"On and below this same street level opposite there is a novel zoo wherein extraordinary animal life would be sheltered in characteristic fashion natural to the animal. . . .

"Elevator service is provided at points directly convenient in handling the various popular concentrations. Ventilation and drainage of the vast roof areas is adequately managed by use of the three great pylons supporting the roofs of the audience halls and sports-arena. . . .

"Helicopters may land on the SkyPark. Dirigibles, large and small baloons [sic] may be moored there in the Park to provide excitement. Parachute jumping could also be a feature of this Place."

A building extended westward from the main building to the Point, connecting with "a great glass covered pavilion containing restaurant above, seating 1000 people at tables, 500 at counter. This restaurant surrounds a novel, extensive under-water aquarium for sea monsters seen from below. A great overhead insectorium or aviary. . . . Appropriate greenery and fountain-effects thrown up from the rivers are features throughout. A special enclosed play-park and pool for small children. . . . "

Two "flexible suspended docks" extended from the Point at pool level "for embarking and debarking from river traffic—freight or excursion boats, racing shells, etc., etc." Beyond these a circular swimming pool reached partway across the Allegheny, supporting a free-form tower of indeterminate function, though it seemed to be involved with the fountain.

Wright described other facilities included in the complex of buildings: "Federal, State, County, and City occupational-endeavors of all sorts find homes here. All civic enterprises of a cultural nature for the citizens of Pittsburgh are amply provided for by this scheme in vast varied shelter for use in Winter or Summer.

"As component supporting parts of the great

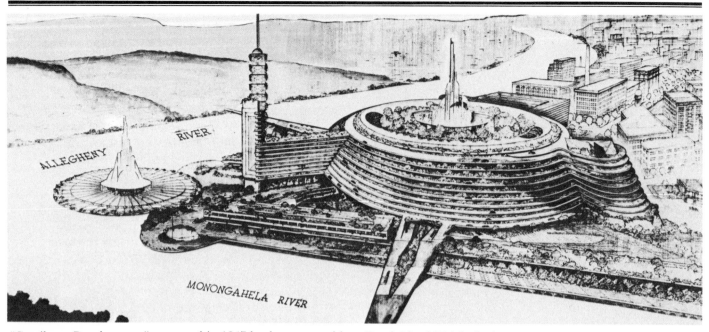

"Cantilever Development" proposed in 1947 by the great architect Frank Lloyd Wright had thirteen levels 175 feet high and four and one-half miles of circular "Grand Auto Ramp" lined with shops—among other remarkable features. (Allegheny Conference)

over-all structure, exhibition galleries, planetarium, forums, great halls for symphony or chamber music, grand opera and conventions of every description, are provided for. . . . A great arena for games utilizes the central roof area of the grand ramp. A large area of green park is by this means thrown up against the sky in comparatively clean air with a wide prospect.

"Adequate office buildings for the State: 150,000 sq. ft.

" Adequate office building for the Federal: 150,000 sq. ft.

"Adequate office building for the Welfare of Pittsburgh: 150,000 sq. ft. Beautifully situated adequate offices for civic, culture clubs and the various charitable activities of Pittsburgh citizens.

"Six ideal smaller chambers to be rented for chamber music, lectures or free for civic gatherings and forums.

"Total accomodation for persons seated in audience or in cars on ramps: 123,000."

Wright explained the philosophy of his "over-all building scheme": It "provides newly spacious means of entertainment for the citizen seated in his motor car Winter or Summer. A pleasurable use of that modern implement is here designed instead of allowing it to remain the troublesome burden it has now become to the City.

"The economy of steel in tension (the spider spinning) cast concrete in compression and enclosures all of glass (all special Pittsburgh products) here gives new scope and appropriate character becoming to the new age which both glass and steel should long ago have created out of the industrial revolution as the threshold of a new era: the Chemical Revolution.

"Throughout this design the Industrial-revolution is raised to the threshold of the imminent Chemical-revolution as not only adequate in scale but natural entertainment for the urban multitudes. The forms employed are essentially economic and satisfying where the nature of glass and steel—our modern miracles—are concerned. For instance the sweeping ramps and inverted or tension domes. More important, an over-all harmony throughout the entire scheme of construction is presented to the Allegheny Conference.

"At no point in this scheme is steel to be used other than in tension and in such a manner that a fibre stress of 132,000 lbs. is feasible. 12,000 lbs concrete is also practicable. Glass is used mainly without frames and set directly in contact with concrete easily replaced in case of breakage. . . .

"The entire scheme is arranged with adequate trees, shrubs, grass and gardening, all of which taken in connection with the broad expanse of flowing river-surface render the whole architectural mass gentle and humane."

George Richardson recalls the meeting at Taliesin West with a look of remembered bewilderment and amusement on his face. "The bridges were just two big cantilevered arms hanging out of this beehive structure. So far as traffic was concerned, all that you could make out of the plan was that the vehicles would come over the bridges and disappear into the beehive, and I don't know what happened to them after that." Richardson, Richards, and Martin examined the drawing in silence, listened to the lecture, read the presentation, and then discussed the project for some time in generalities. There was a pause. Martin asked Mr. Wright how he proposed to handle the traffic to and from the bridges. Wright shrugged his shoulders and said, "Let the engineers worry about that." Martin braced himself to ask the inevitable question, "Mr. Wright, do you have any idea what this would cost?" Wright replied that he did not care. If the idea was good, the community would have to provide the financing. As Richardson remembers it, the Maestro replied, "I don't know. One hundred million, two hundred million. Who cares about money? You can tell what God thinks about money by the kind of people he gives it to."

On his return to Pittsburgh, Martin advised Kaufmann that Wright's plan was impractical, that it would cost at least $150 million and cover most of the lower Point, and that it should not be made public. He told Kaufmann for the first time that Wright's letter requesting payment of his $10,000 fee had ended with the pleasantry, "How is the old moneybags repos-ing?" On hearing this, Martin said, "Kaufmann chuckled."

Ralph Griswold tells what happened in succeeding months: "Edgar had intended to spring a great surprise on the Point Park Committee with Wright's solution to the whole problem. When he saw the drawings he realized he didn't dare show them, even to the Committee. He rolled them up and put them under his desk. When Wright came to town to talk to Edgar about some other project, he asked, "Whatever happened to those plans I did for the Point?" Poor Edgar was embarrassed—there they were rolled up under his desk. He had to bring them out and show them to Van Buskirk to satisfy Wright. Van took one look at the drawings and almost dropped dead in amazement. He said, 'Edgar, you'd better put them back under your desk.' They weren't displayed until two years later, in 1949, when somebody at Carnegie Tech heard about them and persuaded Edgar to allow them to be exhibited there."

Wright was in Pittsburgh at the time, and he talked of his discarded plans to a *Sun-Telegraph* reporter: "These plans may be away ahead of their time. But some day, they will be discovered again and put to work. I have designed a fairyland—but scientific in bone, fiber and flesh. Conventional architects and engineers haven't the imagination to appreciate it. The trouble with most experts is that they have stopped thinking."

Griswold remembers the Wright conception

and the Carnegie Tech exhibition: "They were perfectly beautiful drawings. Of course, they gave a charge to the students, anything by Frank Lloyd Wright. They were almost a student's concept. If you were a young architectural student and were dreaming about national competitions, this would be just perfect. So they demanded, 'Why in hell hadn't we done this?' There we were, in 1946, with a chance to take a giant stride into the twenty-first century and make Pittsburgh forever immortal, and we blew it!

"I assure you, they were gorgeous drawings, and very imaginative. Of course, they had nothing to do with the problems we were facing. It was a Tower of Babylon, and Queen Hatshepsut and a Ziggurat all in one pile. Everything we hoped to do, everything that decentralized the city, traffic-wise, was ignored. He put the whole basket of chips into one great terraced building, with theaters and theaters and theaters, and meeting rooms and meeting rooms. You came in through this thing to get anywhere in town.

"We all told the Martin-Wright story for its humor, but really, it was outrageous, when you consider that we had worked so closely on costs in our planning. We all wanted a number of things we knew we couldn't have, because there wasn't money for them. The highway engineers knew there should be three tunnels at Squirrel Hill instead of two, and they knew there should be an interchange at the south end of the Liberty Tubes, with no crossings at grade, but we couldn't afford it. And then Wright presented this thing to us without any conception of what it might cost!"

Twenty-eight years later, on a trip to New York City, John P. Robin met an urban design architect who was working for a very large foundation. Says Robin: "When he learned I was from Pittsburgh, he raised the Wright issue with me—in 1975! Why hadn't Pittsburgh adopted this wonderful Frank Lloyd Wright plan? It was clear that he thought Pittsburghers were too stodgy, too unimaginative, to accept this really great achitectural breakthrough.

"I tried to explain it to him, but I don't think it did any good."

9

The Authority
to Develop

Almost everything now had to mark time until George Richardson and his associates drew up the engineering plans for the Point interchange and the two new bridges. There could be no firm studies for the park nor for historical restorations until his plans had been produced and approved by "all interested public and private agencies," including the Regional Planning Association, the Point Park Committee, the executive committee of the Allegheny Conference, the City Planning Commission, the City Art Commission, the City Department of Public Works, the City Bureau of Traffic Planning, the City Council, the mayor's office, the County Roads Commission, the County Works Department, the county commissioners, the U.S. Corps of Engineers, the Public Works Department of the state, the Department of Forests and Waters, the governor's office, and, finally, for the decisive approval, the State Department of Highways. Before the park itself could be

designed, questions had to be answered. Where would the bridges be placed? What would be the conformation of the interchange? How much space would these take up? How much space would be left for the park? How much open waterfront?

For the next two years—1947 and 1948—there was, to outward appearances, no progress at the Point. The Point Park Committee did not meet in 1947, and it met only twice in 1948. There was no demolition of buildings at the Point, no regrading of land, no construction.

And yet there was essential progress in certain activities where progress was possible. One was in the acquisition of land for the park. Another was in drawing up undramatic but delicate and important agreements with the Corps of Engineers, the utility companies, and departments of the city and the county. Another was in the work of the new Redevelopment Authority in the commercial area that was to adjoin the park.

Realtors hold, probably with some justice, that engineering problems are relatively simple when compared with the human problems of appraising property, negotiating its acquisition at fair market value, and avoiding litigation and condemnation proceedings.

The subcommittee in charge of acquiring land for the park, responsible to the state, was headed by Louis W. Monteverde, owner of the Real Estate Company of Pittsburgh, one of the incorporating members of the Allegheny Conference. The other subcommittee members were Robert McDowell, a partner in the real estate firm of Porter and McDowell, and Donnell Reed, a banker. Representing the state and handling all its legal work in the acquisitions was Thomas W. Corbett, deputy attorney general in the Department of Justice in Harrisburg, on assignment to the Department of Forests and Waters. Corbett speaks with admiration today of Monteverde's skill and diplomacy. By the end of 1949 he had acquired by negotiation thirty-four of the thirty-five parcels in the park area, including the thirteen acres of Pennsylvania Railroad property. The city made a gift of the Exposition Building land to the state. The total acquisition cost to the state was $7,588,500, a figure all parties agree was a reasonable one. There were no hints of scandal or corruption in any of the proceedings—a fact that seems more remarkable thirty-two years later than it did in 1948.

Acquisition of the properties for *commercial* development in the Point's other twenty-three acres, on the other hand, was a far more complex matter than acquiring property for public use, such as a public park. The right of the state to acquire property for public use under the powers of eminent domain was well established in law. But what the city of Pittsburgh now intended to do was to acquire private properties in the redevelopment area through its new Redevelopment Authority, using condemnation proceedings if necessary, and then turn them over, not to a government agency for public use, but to other private parties for private use for profit.

The Pennsylvania Urban Redevelopment Act of May 24, 1945, gave municipal governments the right to do this. The right was hedged about with elaborate safeguards. The Planning Commission had to certify that the area was blighted. A redevelopment plan and a subsequent redevelopment contract had to be submitted to the Planning Commission for review. Both the plan and the contract had to be approved by the governing body, generally the City Council. Only if approvals were obtained for both was the Redevelopment Authority permitted to sign a contract with a developer, either private or public. The developer was required to follow the agreed-upon land use.

This was a revolutionary new concept, and Pittsburgh was the first to use it in a major redevelopment project. One might conjecture that

Three staff members of the Allegheny Conference look inquiringly at Paul J. Ambler, the state's district highway engineer. They are, from left to right, Theodore L. Hazlett, Jr., counsel, John J. Grove, assistant director, and Park H. Martin, executive director. (Pittsburgh *Press*)

the principle of "reverse permissibility" was involved here—that only a Republican state administration supported by a conservative, business-oriented body like the Allegheny Conference could have pushed through such a radical act in Pennsylvania. (It has been suggested that the state legislators did not grasp what extraordinary powers they were giving the cities.) In any case, three men—Arthur Van Buskirk, Wallace Richards, and Mayor Lawrence—recognized that in the Redevelopment Act they had an absolutely new and invaluable instrument for municipal rehabilitation. If it was upheld in the courts, the power of a Redevelopment Authority would solve problems that had always thwarted city planners.

First, it would bring in private redevelopment capital and thus free a project from the delays and uncertain start-and-stop appropriations of a state legislature.

Second, it would provide a way to keep redeveloped properties on the tax rolls. Private property acquired for public uses—for parks, playgrounds, roads, bridges, public office buildings—paid no taxes.

Third, it would overcome the difficulty—often the impossibility—of assembling private properties for redevelopment by other private owners. The properties in a blighted area have many owners and fractionated uses. Acquisition by purchase has to be conducted secretly, and two or three holdout owners or land speculators can delay an entire project, or kill it. But the new law makes it possible to acquire such properties by negotiated purchase, to use condemnation proceedings if necessary, to create a consolidated private ownership through the authority, and thus to replan and develop a whole area.

Proponents of the act relied on some highly sophisticated legal reasoning in defending the constitutionality of a statute for which there were no clearly applicable precedents. They held that eradication and renewal of a privately-owned blighted area was a public need, because it was important to the health, safety, and welfare of the community as a whole. Therefore such eradication and renewal were actually a public use, and thus the act was legal.

Mayor Lawrence appointed John P. Robin as executive director of the newly formed Urban Redevelopment Authority of Pittsburgh. Robin had been the mayor's executive secretary, his political strategist and civic advisor, and his liaison with the planning organizations involved in the first years of the renewal program. A young man of civic dedication combined with wide reading and an articulate sense of humor, he got along well with the professionals of the Allegheny Conference, the Planning Association, and with most of the city-county political figures. Van Buskirk had his own candidate for the post; he considered Robin too closely associated with politicians, and so he questioned the appointment. Lawrence appointed Robin

First executive director of the Urban Redevelopment Authority (1948–1955) was John P. Robin. He had been Mayor Lawrence's advisor, speech writer, and secretary. Returning to Pittsburgh after two decades of work in other cities and countries, he became chairman of the board of URA. (Pittsburgh *Press*)

acting director, and Robin's performance soon won him the full title.

Discussion with Equitable Life continued. President Parkinson announced that his company had no interest in erecting apartment buildings next to the park but might look favorably, if the authority concurred, on putting up three high-rise office buildings. The authority concurred at once. Negotiations ran into a crisis, however, when United States Steel Corporation announced its intention to erect a tall office building at 525 William Penn Place, farther back in the Triangle.

The Pittsburgh negotiators first read of that development in the morning paper when they got off the train in New York on their way to what they considered a decisive meeting with Parkinson. Theodore Hazlett recalls the events of that morning: "Van Buskirk said dejectedly, 'We might as well turn around and go back. There's no point in seeing Parkinson now.' However, we met first with Robert Dowling of the City Investing Company, who was Parkinson's real-estate advisor. We expressed our dismay to him. He looked at our map, on which we had indicated the small plot to be developed by Equitable, and considered the plot beside Mellon Square where the U.S. Steel office building was to go up. He said, 'Instead of limiting your proposal to a few acres, why don't you make it a bigger offer? Propose to Equitable that they be the sole developer of the entire commercial area you intend to acquire.' We looked at each other. One of our group took a grease pencil and drew a line from river to river along Stanwix Street, pretty close to what is now the eastern boundary of Gateway Center, and he put hatch marks on all the land between that line and the park. Parkinson agreed to consider that enlarged proposal."

Formal negotiations with representatives of Equitable Life began in Pittsburgh on March 6, 1947, and continued through the next three years. The authority proposed to sign a redevelopment contract with the city; the city would enter into a cooperation agreement. The authority would acquire and assemble the properties on twenty-three acres adjacent to the park. It would demolish the ninety-three buildings in the six-block area and grade the land. It would do this with money supplied by Equitable and then sell the property to Equitable. As the new owner, Equitable would erect a minimum of three new office buildings, its plan of development to be approved by the appropriate city and civic organizations. The city, under the cooperation agreement, would change the street patterns as required.

While these negotiations continued, a series of small successes occurred. One by one they fitted into the larger design of the redevelopment project.

March 25, 1947. The City Planning Commission certified the entire Point as suitable for redevelopment, thus clearing the way for the contract with a private developer.

May 9. The state legislature amended the insurance act to permit insurance companies to invest in Pennsylvania real estate.

July 3. Acting Director John Robin, having engaged a secretary, opened the Redevelopment Authority office at 519 City-County Building in a room next to the mayor's office. Theodore Hazlett, Jr., counsel to the Allegheny Conference, was appointed counsel to the authority. ("URA," Hazlett later said, "wanted a Republican lawyer. Me."

July 29. The state supreme court, acting on a friendly suit (*Belovsky* v. *Redevelopment Authority*, 357 Pa. 329), upheld the constitutionality of the redevelopment act. (The Belovsky case was a general challenge by a Philadelphia taxpayer to the constitutionality of the urban redevelopment law. The court verdict was a comfort to the group that was planning Pittsburgh's rehabilitation, but the lawyers recognized that it did not provide a sufficiently sure legal foundation for the specific redevelopment plans being negotiated with Equitable. Further test litigation would be necessary.)

November 26. The state supreme court ruled favorably on the constitutionality of the law permitting insurance companies to invest in real estate.

January 29, 1948. Equitable Life bought a tract of land in the redevelopment area, thereby indicating its serious interest in pursuing the Point redevelopment proposal.

March 23. The Redevelopment Authority sold a $150,000 bond issue to civic-minded citizens, in this way enabling it to continue to function for the foreseeable future. This was the first long-term urban redevelopment authority debt ever issued in the United States. Theodore

Hazlett, who set up the bond issue, said in 1979, "If there have ever been bonds offered to the public with less security behind them than these, I am not aware of it."

During these developments, Thomas Parkinson introduced a new condition. He was under considerable pressure from sceptical officers and directors of his company who thought the whole Pittsburgh development might prove to be an unwise investment. To counter this opposition, he stipulated that Equitable must have binding commitments for tenants to rent at least one-half of the office space in its first three office buildings. (Parkinson, a noted constitutional lawyer as well as president of Equitable, was eventually displaced by his opposition, in part because of the company's difficulties in the early years of Gateway Center.) Van Buskirk began to make the rounds of the large Pittsburgh corporations in search of tenants. His request was a novel one: He asked them to sign, as an act of "civic responsibility," twenty-year leases in office skyscrapers that had not yet been built, had not yet been designed, were to be erected in an area subject to floods at the far edge of the established business district, at rents 20 to 100 percent higher than those they had been paying in their older buildings, on land that had not yet been acquired, but would be acquired under a radical new proposition that had not been tested in the courts. He received

commitments from nine companies: Westinghouse Electric, Westinghouse Air Brake, Pittsburgh Plate Glass, National Supply (oil-field equipment), Jones & Laughlin Steel, Peoples Natural Gas (displaced by Mellon Square Park), Union Switch and Signal, Joseph Horne Company (department store), and Mellon National Bank. These, however, signed statements of intention rather than contracts. Negotiations of the actual leases were protracted and sometimes abrasive.

The law firm of Reed, Smith, Shaw & McClay had been engaged to represent Equitable in Pittsburgh, and Ralph H. Demmler for four years headed the group from that office working on the redevelopment project. "The difficulties encountered in negotiating the long-term leases," Demmler says today, "could hardly have been avoided. Both sides were committing substantial corporate resources to an arrangement with multiple questions. How do you determine needed protection for both landlord and tenant in an agreement to lease space for twenty years in a building that is not even on the drawing board? What kind of space? What kind of air conditioning? What kind of renewal options? Who would bear tax increases and increased labor costs? What about 'cushion space'? What one tenant did not think of, another did. The whole undertaking was complicated by the authority's promise to buy the Jones & Laughlin office building on Ross Street (now the Civic Building), which was a commitment made in order to induce J & L to lease space in Gateway Center.

"Equitable's New York counsel was inclined to be uncompromising, and he was confronted by equally adamant prospective tenants who, after all, were under no compulsion to rent space in the undesigned buildings. At one point the prospective tenants complained to Mr. Parkinson about the hard-nosed attitude of the Equitable vice-president who was in charge of the negotiations. Thereupon a different Equitable officer was put in charge. There were times when it looked as if the deal would plunge off the tracks, but Mayor Lawrence, Arthur Van Buskirk and Edgar Kaufmann were called upon from time to time to break impasses."

Equitable (and, indeed, the Pittsburgh interests) wanted full legal assurance that the redevelopment contract was valid. Demmler persuaded Albert Schenck, a distant relative and one of the owners of the Demmler and Schenck Building on lower Penn Avenue, to bring a test case before the supreme court of Pennsylvania. Schenck sued the city, the authority, and Equitable, contesting the redevelopment law and particularly the redevelopment contract. The case was argued on January 5, 1950, and on January 10 the court sustained the contract (*Schenck* v. *Pittsburgh et al.*, 364 Pa. 25).

In the meantime, the Redevelopment Authority had been making some stipulations of its own. As Mayor Lawrence told the story for Stefan Lorant's *Pittsburgh: The Story of an American City:*

We were having breakfast in Van Buskirk's rooms in the Ambassador Hotel on Park Avenue [when] Arthur said: "What about charging tolls to these companies? Do you realize we're giving them value and the prestige and the power of the act of assembly that gives the Authority the right of eminent domain?" For a few minutes I did not grasp what he was talking about; until then, I and probably the others as well had figured that we were going to operate these authorities on funds from the government. But it did not take us long to realize the importance of Van Buskirk's suggestion. We held on to it and it turned out to be a boon to the rebuilding of the city. It financed a large part of our overhead.

Hazlett recalls that the Redevelopment Authority asked Equitable for a "toll charge" of $100,000 a year, and that Parkinson responded with, "Would you take $50,000?" Van Buskirk said, "Agreed," and as a result Equitable paid a charge of one million dollars over the next twenty years. The nine tenants of Gateway Center, on hearing of the charge, warned that Equitable should not add it to their rent. (They ended up paying half of it.) The money was used to pay staff and administrative costs.

On November 16, 1949, the Redevelopment Authority formally approved the proposal for Gateway Center as presented by Equitable Life. Other approvals followed routinely. The City Planning Commission signed it on November 25. City Council received it from the authority on November 28, began public hearings on January 3, 1950, and approved it on January 10.

St. Valentine's Day, February 14, 1950, is still remembered as the Day of the Great Signing. As one participant puts it, "We had to bring all the trains into the station at one time." The ceremonies took place in the chambers of City Council following hectic nights and weekends of work. Mayor Lawrence, chairman of the Redevelopment Authority, was there. City Council was there en masse, representatives of Equitable Life, heads of the nine companies that had agreed to rent office space in Gateway Center, and one or more lawyers for each. The redevelopment contract was signed, the cooperation agreement was signed, the various leases were signed, and the authority bought old buildings vacated by Jones & Laughlin and Peoples Gas, all this to the sound of popping flash bulbs and with reporters milling around. After the ceremony, Mayor Lawrence had a lunch for all interested parties and their lawyers. Some of them were exhausted, and some remember to this day that on an occasion that called loudly for a drink, Mr. Lawrence served nothing stronger than coffee.

On March 23, 1950, the authority adopted a resolution starting condemnation proceedings against certain properties in Gateway Center. On April 6 it acquired seven major properties in the area, thus beginning the land-acquisition process the state had completed in the park area exactly five months earlier.

Litigation did not end with the signing of legal documents and the beginning of condemnation proceedings. In April 1950 some twenty owners filed suits in federal court in Pittsburgh and in the Court of Common Pleas to invalidate the redevelopment contract on the grounds that the condemned area was not blighted and that it was a violation of the state and U.S. constitutions to seize private property solely for the purpose of turning it over to another private entity. Both courts decided in favor of the contract, holding that a public purpose was being served, and the property owners appealed the federal court decision to the Supreme Court of the United States. In the meantime, in what Ralph Demmler calls "a leap of faith," Equitable continued to design the buildings, to pay the authority for acquired properties, and to clear the land as it was acquired. Theodore Hazlett said, "We took photographs and made engineering drawings of every building that was demolished, as a precaution. We figured we would need them if the courts ruled against us and we had to replace the buildings." Ralph Demmler says, "I made an agreement with one of Equitable's New York counsel that if the Supreme Court invalidated the redevelopment contract, we would join each other in permanent exile in Antarctica."

The final stamp of legality was placed on the contract in October 1950, when the Supreme Court of the United States dismissed the property owners' appeal.

Walter Giesey, Mayor Lawrence's secretary

for several years, said, "The fact that the Redevelopment Authority condemned and acquired land at Gateway Center and had half of it cleared before the case was ever heard by the [U.S.] supreme court took both a lot of guts on the part of the authority members and some pretty damn sound judgment on the part of its legal counsel [Theodore Hazlett]. The Pennsylvania redevelopment law had not [cleared its last constitutional hurdle] until Gateway Center was halfway cleared. I don't know what would have happened. . . . How were they ever to put those buildings back up? It could not be done. Well, those were the risks they took."

In the meantime, other and different negotiations had been concluded and agreements signed with a number of public bodies. The U.S. Corps of Engineers established the harbor line along both river banks, beyond which nothing was normally permitted to extend. In a favorable concession, the corps allowed construction beyond the line if it was below a certain height and would not constrict or impede river flow at flood stage. Thus the park area was considerably enlarged and its shape improved.* The corps also established a flood level for the park area, above which—when the new dams were built upriver—it was felt the water would never rise. Park designs were drawn accordingly.

Railroad and street railway rights-of-way were eliminated. The city vacated existing streets in the park and redevelopment areas and relocated Barbeau Street. An existing cable running across the bed of the Monongahela to the South Side was protected and preserved, and water mains suspended from the Manchester Bridge were relocated. The U.S. Weather Bureau was persuaded (with difficulty) to relinquish its station in a small building at the apex of the Point and to place it elsewhere. The way was now clear to start to tear down the old and build anew—to begin what Arthur Van Buskirk called "the action stage."

*The harbor line on the Allegheny runs along the stepped stone seats, some fifty feet back from the present river's edge. Those who call for a flood wall at the Point should realize that the wall would almost certainly have to be built some distance inland from the present shoreline, thus reducing the size of the park and, of course, ruining the park's concept of open space and unhindered access to the rivers. Newport, Kentucky, is an example of a town cut off from the river by a flood wall.

10

"The Action Stage": Demolition and Design

The first visible evidence of renewal at the Point appeared on Thursday afternoon, May 18, 1950, almost five years after the trip to Harrisburg by Wallace Richards and Park Martin that started the Point projects. It happened as the first event of something called Welcome Week, staged by the Pittsburgh Chamber of Commerce. Following parades led by the University of Pittsburgh ROTC band and the Carnegie-Tech Kiltie band, a crowd gathered at the Point near a two-story warehouse on Exchange Way at the rear of 110 Penn Avenue. This unsuspecting and unoffending brick structure, twenty by thirty feet in size, 103 years old and looking every day of it, had been singled out as the first sacrificial offering to the new god, Urban Renewal.

Hundreds of happy school children were there, led by their teachers, freed from classrooms to watch their elders perform some strange ceremony. Governor James H. Duff was there and made a speech. Mayor David Lawrence was there and made a speech. Arthur Van Buskirk was there and made a speech in which he declared, "We hope we have only scratched the surface and that we will be able to make this community a shining example for the rest of the cities in America." Professor John Oliver, chairman of the Historical Advisory Committee, made a speech in which he declared, "Let us not look on this as an act of demolition or destruction. Rather, let it be the first step in the restoration of one of the greatest of national shrines."

Governor Duff raised and swept his arm. A tall crane swung in an arc and hurled a demolition ball against the building. The ball was held for some time by the shuddering victim, but was eventually freed to renew the attack. A bulldozer moved in to level the rubble.

There was a triumphal dinner that evening at the Schenley Hotel, sponsored by the Allegheny

Demolition at the Point began on May 18, 1950, with the blows of a one-ton "headache ball."
Five years had passed since the first work was undertaken on the park; twenty-four more
were to pass before it was completed. (Allegheny Conference)

Conference and given as a testimonial to Thomas Parkinson, president of Equitable Life, builders-to-be of Gateway Center, and Governor Duff, "whose leadership is making Point Park a reality." Edgar Kaufmann presided and Arthur Van Buskirk was toastmaster.

Over the next sixteen months some forty other buildings were demolished in the park area, the rubble cleared, and the land leveled for short-term lease as parking lots. The elevated structures of the Pennsylvania Railroad went down, and the last of the three exposition buildings. No blasting at all was permitted during the demolition, for fear it would shake and damage the Blockhouse. This special care created some problems when it came time to remove the large concrete railroad bumpers; the heaviest headache ball simply bounced off them. A "rock jack" was finally brought in from California. Holes were drilled in the bumpers and the cylindrical jack inserted; projections were forced out on the sides under hydraulic pressure, and the concrete split. About three hundred thousand cubic yards of rubble were bulldozed into a hill some thirty feet high, covered with top soil, and planted with grass. This was ultimately used for highway fill on the site. Throughout the demolition, police cordons were set up, for traffic flow was maintained to the end.

Most of the stones from the railroad retaining wall, huge sandstone blocks, were salvaged, for they had become a unique commodity and could not be matched. They were eventually used in the slope wall along the Monongahela River and in similar construction along the Allegheny. All the blockstones ("Ligonier blocks") from the alleys and from between the streetcar rails were also salvaged. They were piled up for future use and covered with soil that was allowed to grow up with weeds. Thus camouflaged, they were not carted off by the citizenry. Many were used in park construction, but thousands, alas, were placed in fill. (They sold for about fifteen cents each on the open market.) Workers also collected bricks from those parts of the original foundation of Fort Pitt that were to be disturbed by construction of the interchange highway. They were buried in a pit and covered over for safekeeping, the location being measured off from a pin in a street. When the street was torn up and vacated, the bricks were "lost" for a year or more. When recovered, they were laid on a part of the fort foundation along the southeastern scarp near the Music bastion, in the "archeological display" excavation.

In the meantime, George Richardson's design of the Point Park interchange between the two projected bridges had been going forward, and it had not been going smoothly. It was a frightfully difficult engineering problem to take heavy traffic into and out of such a congested and limited space and still leave acreage for a park. Some ninety thousand vehicles entered and left the Triangle every twenty-fours by way

Demolition in the other twenty-three acres—the Gateway Center commercial development—began a few months later. The once-grand Wabash Building stood on the site of today's Four Gateway Center. At the extreme left is the old McCann's Building, with its famous food market and its cafeteria (forty-five cents for the big lunch, with no limit on the cups of coffee). (John R. Shrader)

Beyond the ragged doorway of the Wabash Building stand two of the first three Gateway Center buildings. (George L. Bower, Pittsburgh *Post-Gazette*)

of the two bridges at the Point, including 718 streetcars on eight trolley routes. "There simply was not room," Richardson says, "to develop a plan up to the standards you would like to have in a highway interchange. State and federal designers tend to apply rural specifications to urban situations, which is often not a practical thing to do, and certainly was not practical at Pittsburgh's Point.

"We had space for, say, a two-hundred-foot turnoff radius from the bridges. Federal specifications called for, say, an eight-hundred-foot minimum radius. But if we had used ramps with an eight-hundred-foot radius, we would have run right through the center of what is now the State Office Building, and there would have been little park. In fact, any interchange design at the Point conforming completely to the highest standards of highway design would have required using most of the area of the entire Triangle."

Richardson and his associated engineers had originally submitted a report to the State Highway Department on April 30, 1948. It outlined three possible plans for the Point interchange, identified as Schemes A, B, and C, each complete with engineering drawings, layouts, profiles, detailed estimates of cost, and an analysis of traffic data and requirements.

Scheme A proposed a new double-deck Fort Pitt Bridge over the Monongahela River. The upper deck would be used for two-way traffic connecting the Fort Pitt Tunnel to the Point

interchange. The lower deck would serve vehicular and street railway traffic traveling in both directions between Carson Street and the Triangle.

Schemes B and C proposed divided highways on a new Fort Pitt Bridge for outbound and inbound traffic carried at the same level, and an independent structure at a somewhat lower level between these roadways for streetcars. The basic arrangement of the bridge was the same for both Scheme B and Scheme C; the difference occurred in the ramps in the Point interchange. Richardson recommended Scheme C as clearly the best "from the standpoint of meeting general traffic requirements." He had found "certain disadvantages" in Scheme A's double-deck bridge. "It is not feasible with a double-deck bridge to provide any arrangement at the Carson Street intersection which will eliminate some of the conflicting traffic movements for both streetcar and vehicular traffic. Also, with vehicular traffic entering or leaving the Point interchange on two decks, duplicate connections are required. In addition to these disadvantages with respect to traffic, the level of the upper roadway for the double-deck span would be approximately 14 feet higher at the Triangle shore pier than for the vehicular roadways on the single-deck span, a condition unfavorable to obtaining good grades on the connections in the Point interchange."

The state highway department sent Richardson's report to the Allegheny Conference, its

Point Park Committee, and various other interested public and private agencies for study and comment. On October 17–18, 1948, the state highway department held a meeting of six public groups in Pittsburgh to discuss the interchange proposal. Those interested mainly in traffic flow were inclined to favor Scheme C, but Point Park committeemen objected that it usurped too much park area and that its two bands of highway crossing the Point would divide the park into three separate areas. Edward L. Schmidt, chief engineer of the highway department, announced that a decision on Scheme C would be withheld to permit submission and consideration of other schemes.

A number of other schemes were submitted. Three were developed in the offices of the Public Roads Administration, one by the County Planning Commission, and one by the City Planning Commission (it called for relocation of Liberty Avenue).

At the sixth meeting of the Point Park Committee, held on November 5, 1948, Van Buskirk appointed a Subcommittee on Plan. In accepting the chairmanship, Edgar Kaufmann expressed his opposition to building any elevated structure between the park and the redeveloped area. He "emphasized the seriousness of the problem facing the Point Park Committee if the Point Park Interchange is to be constructed as now planned." He suggested that the level of the park should be raised "so that the above-surface structures of the Inter-

change will be a part of the Park rather than a barrier between the Park and the rest of the Triangle."

The Point Park Committee then took steps that produced still another interchange plan. It recommended that its parent body, the Allegheny Conference, join with the Regional Planning Association to retain Gilmore Clarke and Ralph Griswold "to study the effect of the highway interchange, as proposed in Scheme C, on the Park and the possibility of landscaping the Park to minimize the effect." Clarke was a partner in the New York firm of consulting engineers and landscape architects, Clarke, Rapuano, and Holleran, designers of New York's Merritt Parkway. Interviewed at his estate at Newtown, Pa., in July 1975, two months before his sudden and unexpected death, Michael Rapuano told of his part in the project: "I went down to Pittsburgh . . . and after quite a long study I came up with a solution to the traffic problem. The design that I used was to propose a double-deck bridge over the Monongahela and a double-deck bridge over the Allegheny. And if you know design of highways, you will see quickly how some of the interchanges they had going on in the Point area I took care of at the end of these bridges on the other side of the rivers.

"Well, when I got my studies completed, I had only a strip connection in the Park—that is, just as it is now, a strip connection between one bridge and the other. And we retained I don't

Progress report, October 1952: Most of the old buildings in the fifty-nine acres of Point Park and Gateway Center have been leveled; the first three Gateway Center buildings are nearing completion. (Associated Photographers, Inc.)

know how many acres of park, twenty-four acres of park.

"When I got this down to Park Martin they approved it quickly. And he said, 'We've got to take this over to Mr. Mellon.' I think we went over to Mr. Mellon in the afternoon. And we presented it to Mr. Mellon and he approved it quickly. The point I never can forget was that Mr. Mellon got on the telephone and he called the governor [James H. Duff]. He told the governor about this plan the Allegheny Conference had had made, and he wanted very much for the secretary of highways and the secretary of parks and another secretary to come to Pittsburgh the next morning.

"And so be it. The next morning two secretaries arrived and we had a meeting around nine, nine-thirty, and I made my presentation. Mr. Mellon said that . . . as far as he was concerned, he was very much in favor of this, as it did solve the problem. And it did one great thing: It saved the park. And these other two fellows said they would take it under advisement. They thought it was a solution. . . .

"I think Mr. Mellon made one of the prime decisions when he was able to see that there was a solution. No design, no city design, no urban design, is any good unless you have a political activant and a political backing. You can't be a designer as such and make it realistic unless the political climate is correct. No, I'll put it another way. That design could have been submitted to Joe Doakes, and because of politics he could have said, 'Nothing doing.' Mr. Mellon was beyond politics, and he could see that we were saving millions and millions of dollars of valuable property for the public and still keeping that traffic moving. When that man had that vision and had the position to be able to call the governor and say, 'I would like to have two or three of those secretaries come down here tomorrow morning,' and when that cooperation came about between the people interested in the welfare of the city, and the politicians—when those three came together that morning you had urban design at its best. That doesn't happen very often."

Ralph Griswold reported on his work with Clarke and Rapuano at the seventh meeting of the Point Park Committee, March 25, 1949. The minute of the meeting reads:

Mr. Griswold stated that [they] had undertaken the study of the Point Park area and Interchange with two major objectives—(1) to study the visual connections of the Park area with Scheme C and try to minimize the effect of the highway ramps proposed in that scheme and (2) to determine the best approach for pedestrian and automobile access to the Park. In studying these phases, Mr. Griswold said, the question of fill was abandoned [as not feasible] and then attention was turned to trying to eliminate the highway barrier between the City and the Park as proposed in Scheme C. This led to certain improvements in Scheme C and finally to development of Scheme E. Scheme E has the advantage of dividing the area into only two sections, keeping the area at its exact present level, and simplifying the highways crossing the skyline so that they cross at only one level.

Scheme E was hailed in Pittsburph as the best solution so far produced for a complex planning problem. Three staff officers of the Regional Planning Association praised it for grouping the roadways together into a single band, for confining more of the interchange to the sides of the park area, and for offering greater possibilities for park development. Both the city and the county planning commissions formally approved it over the state highway department's Scheme C. Kaufmann's Subcommittee on Plan endorsed it:

Scheme E provides for a more spacious and desirable Park development. The reasons for this conclusion are: (1) that Scheme E will divide the Park into only two parts, while Scheme C would divide it into three; (2) if Scheme C were adopted an elevated ramp would cut across the Park near the proposed redevelopment area; this is believed to be detrimental not only to the Park but also to the proposed redevelopment area; and (3) in Scheme E the elevated roadway across the Park is considered to be better than that in Scheme C from the point of view both of structural and park design.

The Point Park Committee sent Scheme E to Harrisburg on March 25, 1949 with the recommendation that it be adopted for construction. Highway department engineers agreed that the grouping of the roadways in a single band across the park was an attractive feature so far as the park was concerned; but they held that

the improvement had been accomplished by changes that were not acceptable with respect to traffic flow. One objectionable feature they cited was an inner loop in a very sharp descending grade and short radius for all traffic moving from the Fort Pitt Bridge to Fort Duquesne Boulevard or the Fort Duquesne Bridge. The stalemate between park and highway proponents continued. It lasted for some eighteen months. Then a new and opportune development unexpectedly provided a solution.

George Richardson obtained a copy of a report that the U.S. District Court for the Western District of Pennsylvania had ordered the Pittsburgh Railways Company to make. The company, obeying the court order, had employed consultants to conduct a survey "on the advisability of substituting bus service in whole or in part for the street car service presently being undertaken." The consultants' report recommended that the company substitute buses for streetcars on nineteen of its routes, including the eight operating over Point Bridge.

"Elimination of streetcars," Richardson says, "made possible an entirely new concept for arrangement of roadways. With this recommendation before me and the possibility of eliminating streetcar service through the Point interchange, I returned to the drawing board. I used the single-band roadway through the park as proposed in Scheme E, but I developed the idea of double-deck bridges, using the upper deck of

George S. Richardson, civil engineer, a specialist in highway and bridge design, called a giant in his profession, faced an insoluble engineering problem: to place a complex, heavy-traffic interchange with acceptable highway design standards in a space only half as large as it needed to be. He is shown here, on the right, talking with Ralph Griswold. (Pittsburgh *Press*)

the Fort Pitt Bridge and lower deck of the Fort Duquesne Bridge for one-way inbound traffic, and the lower deck of the Fort Pitt Bridge and upper deck of the Fort Duquesne Bridge for one-way outbound traffic. The one-way feature automatically provided grade separation of conflicting traffic movements. This greatly simplified the arrangement of connecting ramps and resulted in a much more compact layout of the whole Point interchange, greatly minimizing the amount of park property required for highway development. The new plan was designated as Scheme X and there followed a number of meetings to review the new plan." Richardson's work diary reads:

April 13, 1949: E. T. Baker, chief design engineer for PDH [Pennsylvania Department of Highways] was at GSR [George S. Richardson] office to review Scheme X.

April 14: ELS [Edward L. Schmidt] at GSR office to review Scheme X.

April 21: ELS, Wally Richards and others at GSR office to review Scheme X.

April 30: Supplemental report submitted by GSR to PDH. This report reviewed all previous plans developed in GSR office and by others and presented the final layout for Scheme X, which was recommended for construction.

May 17: Edgar Kaufmann (with Wally and Leland Hazard) at GSR office to review Scheme X. It was decided to start wheels rolling for approval by PPC [Point Park Committee].

June 2: Meeting with Kaufmann Committee to explain Scheme X. It was enthusiastically received.

June 20: Conference at PDH with all area public agencies present. Scheme X was unanimously approved.

July 1: Meeting with Park Martin, Wally, C. D. Palmer, Fitzgerald and Bauer to insure agreement of Pittsburgh Railways Company to cooperate in abandoning streetcar service on "lines to the west."

July 18: Point Park Committee meeting. Former recommendation for approval of Clark and Rapuano Scheme E was rescinded and Scheme X approved.

For the first time since a park at the Point was conceived, there was complete agreement by all parties on the proposed design for bridges and traffic interchange. The Department of Highways gave George Richardson a contract and one year to design the Point Park interchange.

Richardson laments today that, because of the restrictions of site and limited area, "the layout of Scheme X violates many principles necessary to secure the most efficient flow of traffic through a complex interchange. . . . I believe, however, that Scheme X was the best plan that could have been developed under the circumstances. I doubt, if we were free to do so, that any better plan could be developed now which would meet the requirements and restrictions with which we worked. Actually, the scheme operates quite successfully for traffic volumes as projected at the time the scheme was adopted. I believe present-day traffic volumes are on the order of double those used at the time Scheme X was developed. These volumes do cause considerable congestion during peak-hour movements."

Arthur Van Buskirk had said early in the renewal program, "There has to be something in sight, something people can see." More than any other development in and around the city, Point Park filled that requirement. The Pittsburgh renewal program was now being called nationally the "Pittsburgh Renaissance," and Point Park and Gateway Center, in the jargon of the city planners, were being looked upon as the "Renaissance Face."

11

Leaves from a Journal
of These Days

Like most professional men who must bill their services according to the hours they spend on a project, Ralph Griswold, M.L.D, F.A.S.L.A., A.I.A. (hon.), kept an office diary recording the time, place, and nature of his work on Point Park. This diary is an invaluable record for anyone interested in the park or in the Pittsburgh Renaissance. Beyond that, it gives a fascinating look into subject matter not often covered in our literature: the day-to-day activities of an architect engaged in a complex civic undertaking with other people, organizations, and disciplines; and, specifically, what is involved in converting free, imaginative drawings and proposals into working blueprints on which contracts can be solicited and the actual work performed.

Griswold and Associates, in consultation with Clarke, Rapuano, and Holleran, had produced in 1950–1951 a "Land Use Plan" for the entire Point area, including the location of a state office building. They had done this as consul-

tants for two private citizens' organizations (the Regional Planning Association and the Allegheny Conference) that were acting on a request made on November 5, 1948, by the state. Governor John S. Fine had approved their plan on May 10, 1951, as the basis for design of Point Park.

The secretaries of two departments in Harrisburg had asked Griswold early in 1952 to prepare "interim" and "ultimate" plans for the design and development of the park and to draw up terms of a contract under which he would work (now for the first time) for the state. He talked with Michael Rapuano, and they agreed to carry out the assignment as a joint venture of their two firms. They were asked to make a formal presentation of their completed work to the state by midsummer and the Point Park Committee by autumn. It was apparently the first time Pennsylvania—and perhaps any state—had signed a major renewal contract in which landscape architects were the prime contractors.

Griswold's working journal for the first nine months of 1952 concerns the effort to meet the state and the Point Park Committee deadlines, set for July 16 and September 15:

"*January 8, 1952*. Studied Park Martin's memorandum and worked all day on a reply. It is very difficult to work out a contract for which there is no precedent and which involves so many unknown factors.

"*January 14*. Discussed the proposed contract for services in Park's office from 3:00 to 4:30.

"*January 22*. Bill [Swain] continued on the land-use plan.

"*January 30*. Mike [Rapuano] arrived a little late but we had breakfast together and agreed upon a letter to be sent to Park Martin. He will write the letter from his office today. (Philadelphia ASLA [American Society of Landscape Architects] meeting.)

"*March 25*. Met with Wally [Richards], Van Buskirk, Snyder [William Penn Snyder III], [John] Grove, and Secretary [Samuel S.] Lewis in Van Buskirk's office, then viewed the Point Park from the new T. Mellon and Sons office on the 39th floor of the U.S. Steel Building. Then drove up Mount Washington to see the Point area from there, and then through the demolition area. We had lunch in the Mellon suite at the Duquesne Club. After that I discussed contract terms with Ted Hazlett and John Grove at the Conference office.

"*April 29*. Reviewed revised contract form and checked it by telephone with Mike Rapuano in New York. Called Ted Hazlett and made a few corrections.

"*April 30*. Meeting in Van Buskirk's new office with Secretary Lewis, [William R. B.] Froelich [of the Regional Planning Association], Martin, and Hazlett. We moved on to new concepts of progress on the park and Lewis took our contract back with him to discuss with the attorney general. Instead of waiting until May 1st we must get going on preliminary plans immediately. Wrote Mike what has happened and sent a copy of the contract.

"*May 5*. Picked up a plan from [Paul] Ambler showing area to be maintained by state highway department. Talked to George Richardson about the base line, the harbor line, and the general status of his plans.

"*May 8*. Bill started work on the jurisdictional plan.

"*May 15*. Park Martin called for me at 8:15 and drove me to Harrisburg. We arrived in time for a quick bite of lunch before our meeting with Secretary Schmidt at 2:00 o'clock. Our meeting with him reached a satisfactory conclusion in time to meet Secretary Lewis at 3:00 o'clock. We got on fine with him on park matters, but when we got into the matter of our contract for professional services we got all tangled up on typical bureaucratic red tape and found that a session with [Secretary] Alan Reynolds of Property and

Supplies will be necessary to get things straightened out.

"*June 5*. Picked up Ted Hazlett at his home in Fox Chapel and we drove to Harrisburg, meeting Thomas Corbett and Sam Jackson in the attorney general's office at 2:00 P.M. We spent three hours going over the contract and ironed out all the details. It was agreed that Ted should write the contracts in Pittsburgh and after we have signed them to send them to Corbett in Harrisburg. I arrived home at 10:00 and immediately sent a night letter to Mike to come here Monday to sign.

"*June 6*. [William P.] Braun called and gave me an estimate of $12,000 for the land survey and $6,000 for the river soundings and borings. I told him I thought we could do business on this basis. Met in Park Martin's office with Ambler, Barret, Devlin, Froelich, and Robin to clear up jurisdictional items in the Point area. Mike wired that he could not come Monday so I will go there.

"*June 8*. Entire morning and part of afternoon setting up schedule for office to complete the preliminary contract work in 40 days. Also prepared agenda for tomorrow's meeting with Mike.

"*June 9*. New York: We started work about 9:30 following the agenda I had prepared. By 5:00 P.M. the contracts were signed and on their way to Harrisburg, the joint venture agreement executed, and all business complete.

"*June 10*. Reviewed yesterday's business with John [Renner]. Called Froelich and Rust Engineering and Department of Property and Supplies about demolition contract drawings and specifications. Called Martin about the Historical Advisory Committee. Called Ted Hazlett to report on yesterday's meeting with Mike and mailed him a copy of the joint venture agreement.

"*June 12*. The contract with the Commonwealth came through fully executed today. So far as I know, this is the first contract between the Commonwealth and landscape architects for professional services as principals.

"*June 17*. All day with Mike Rapuano and Sigmund Roos, who arrived at 9:30 A.M. We toured the Point waterfronts, talked with Braun and [James] Fulton about survey specifications, talked to the bank about our joint venture account. Hazlett and Charles Stotz joined us for lunch at the Carlton House. We discussed revisions of the joint venture agreement with Hazlett, historic structures with Stotz. Spent the afternoon reviewing plans and details in the office. Called on Park Martin re. Westinghouse report on fountain.

"*June 19*. Made several calls regarding core borings and ended up by making an appointment to see Mendancy in the county office tomorrow. Talked to Ambler about the cost of removing the bridges and ramp at the Point. Set up a meeting with Dr. Oliver at the Allegheny Conference on Monday. Discussed planting with Margaret [Winters], grading with John and Chuck [Cares], and architectural structures with Bill.

"*June 22.* Wrote outline for report to be sent to Mike for comment. Sent photographs of stone walls with suggestions for treatment of wharves to Mike.

"*June 23.* Meeting with Historical Committee in Park Martin's office resulted in indecisive opinion about use of bastions. Reviewed plantings with Margaret and made an appointment with Dr. [O. E.] Jennings for a conference tomorrow. Sent letters to Mike and Secretary Lewis.

"*June 24.* Charles Stotz came in and discussed the bastion design for an hour. Margaret conferred with Dr. Jennings at the museum for one and a half hours on the plant ecology of the Point area. I wrote the minutes of yesterday's Historical Committee meeting. Talked to Fulton regarding surveying proposal and wrote Roos regarding questions raised on some details. Wrote Stotz re. consulting services on architecture. Wrote Dr. Oliver re. his committee report.

"*June 25.* Reviewed historical and maintenance structure computations with Bill and sent data to Stotz and Rapuano. Roos called in answer to my questions on the surveying contract and I transmitted his message to Fulton, who is writing a revised proposal on this basis. Obtained stone wall plans from Property and Supplies.

"*June 27.* Hazlett called re. surveying contract and I made arrangements to write a letter of transmission and pick up copies of the contract at 1:30 P.M. At 2:00 I met with Park Martin and the Sanitary Authority to discuss the sewer location in relation to the park. They had planned a huge exhaust pipe in the middle of our fountain. They agreed to change it.

"*June 30.* Started Bill and Margaret on interim plan and ultimate planting plan. Talked to Rapuano by telephone on urgent items.

"*July 2.* Called Van Buskirk and Martin and set up meeting for Secretary Lewis at 10:00 A.M. Wednesday, July 16. Saw Barret and picked up a plan for water lines and sewers. Saw Stotz and discussed bastion structure and maintenance headquarters. Organized my material for New York tomorrow. Discussed grading with Bill and John.

"*July 3.* [New York] Felt very rocky after a very poor night on the train, but I managed to pull through the day. Worked all morning with Mike, Moice, and Kirkpatrick and occasional chats with [Ralph] MacDonald. We covered most of our agenda before lunch. Lunched at Marias and resumed work at 2:00 By 3:00 we were finished. I bought some ties and trunks at Abercrombies, then relaxed for a couple of hours at Luxor Baths. Had a pleasant dinner at Marias again, then saw "Top Banana." Feeling better.

"*July 4.* Arrived home 9:00 A.M. Full office force working. Working on various problems, planting, grading, all morning. After lunch Bill and I went down to the Point and took photographs of the wharves to send to New York for the perspective sketches.

"*July 5.* Bill revised his bastion plan, John and Chuck worked on interim grading, Margaret finished the preliminary planting plan. Betty [Phillips] and Donna Jeanne [Henry] worked on the books. It was beautifully clear, cool, sunny, an invigorating day with everyone cheerful.

"*July 6.* Sunday: Four hours writing report.

"*July 7.* Finished my rough draft of the report and mailed it to Mike for comments. Sent photos of wharves, sketches of fountain, and print of planting plan to New York.

"*July 8.* Made appointment to see Park Martin about the fountain on Friday. Received approval of the increased price for the surveying contract and mailed revised contract to Braun and Fulton. Worked on the estimate and set up several items ready for calculation.

"*July 9.* Some progress on estimates. Mac-Donald called and wanted advice on using steel sheet piling for river wall. I am to call him tomorrow.

"*July 10.* Had a bad night with chills and fever and nausea. I managed to pull myself together and get to Park Martin's office for a meeting on Point State Park to discuss the fountain area. Also discussed water acidity of the rivers in relation to the steel piling with Park and [a representative] of the Dravo Corporation, who said it was alright for our wharves. Called MacDonald and reported this data.

"*July 12.* Saturday: Everyone worked all day again. John and Bill on intermediate project, Chuck and Margaret on planting. I worked on the estimate.

"*July 13.* Sunday: Bill worked all day revising the intermediate project plan and helping me on the estimate. We organized all the plans for printing and I have everything set for final typing on the report and estimate tomorrow.

"*July 14.* Took all our plans in to Mathias [Blueprinting Company] for prints. Checked the bastion and walk details in connection with the overpass with [James C.] Fisher in Richardson's office. Colored an intermediate plan showing grass and planting. Chuck colored a planting plan showing the trees to be planted in large sizes compared to regular nursery plants.

"*July 15.* Finished the report, estimate and plans. Met Mike and Ralph MacDonald at the hotel when they arrived at 6:00 P.M. Looked over their plans and sketches, discussed estimate. We had dinner at the Carlton House and then drove out to the office and assembled our plans and data for tomorrow's meeting."

The presentation of plans to state officials, scheduled for July 16, was held in the thirty-ninth floor conference room of T. Mellon and Sons at 525 William Penn Way.

"*July 16.* John and I left the office at 9:00 A.M. with all our plans and data for the meeting. John took the plans up in the freight elevator while I parked the car. I met Mike and Ralph

MacDonald in the lobby and by 9:30 we were in the conference room. No sooner had we arranged our plans than in walked Mr. Lewis, 15 minutes ahead of time. Then came Van Buskirk, Wally Richards, Bill Snyder, Park Martin, Ed Schmidt, Paul Ambler, and R. K. Mellon. My presentation proceeded in an orderly manner in spite of interruptions. Our plan, report and estimate, all were approved and it was recommended that our services be continued.

"*July 17.* Wrote Park Martin and Secretary Lewis confirming the sense of the meeting yesterday. Secretary Lewis called to say he was pleased with our meeting and asked for a copy of my article on Raccoon Creek Park."

Two months remained before the September 15 presentation to the Point Park Committee, which would be open to the press and would serve as the vehicle for formal public announcement of the full plan with widespread publicity. During this time Griswold made three more trips to Harrisburg and one to New York; received and acknowledged complimentary letters on the report from Richard Mellon and Arthur Van Buskirk; worked all day Saturday, his fifty-eighth birthday, in order to meet the September 15 deadline; drew up signs to be erected at the Point during the interim work-in-progress; received plans for the wharf and submitted them to the U.S. Corps of Engineers; wrote specifications for negotiating several contracts; sent test boring plans and specifications to Harrisburg; and held a meeting to discuss drainage, water supply, street vacation, and salvage of curbs, stones, and drain inlets. On August 27 he attended a meeting of the Fort Pitt chapter of the Daughters of the American Revolution, owners of the Blockhouse, held in their attorney's office, and described the plans for the park and the reverent care that would be given to the Blockhouse when it was taken over by the state. Finally,

"*September 15.* I hardly had the office organized when Secretary Lewis called and I arranged to pick him up at 10:15. Then Mike called and I picked him up at 10:00, bringing them both out to the office. Lewis was in a fury over the decision not to move Barbeau Street at this time, which threw the whole discussion off beam. The use of park property for parking also caused great objection. Park Martin joined us for lunch at the Carlton and we got matters calmed down for the afternoon meeting, but I was in a state of nervous exhaustion for the Point Park Committee meeting, which went off well in spite of the uproar.

"Our plans were approved, the question of parking licked for all time. We took Alan Reynolds and Mike to the Schenley for cocktails and then to the Allegheny Conference dinner at the museum. The dinner was a pleasant release and I put Mike on the train exhausted but content.

"*September 16.* The news stories and photographs were good. We bought, clipped, and filed material from all three papers. Resumed work on contract drawings and specs on interim project. Mailed application to Corps of Engineers for permit to do waterfront improvements."

The unsigned story in the Pittsburgh *Press* read:

"Pittsburgh's Point Park has been given the green light.

"State officials and a steering committee of the Allegheny Conference on Community Development pressed the button yesterday in agreeing to begin actual construction in the 36-acre park.

"Grass and trees will be planted this fall in three large areas. . . .

"Architect contract drawings will be completed by the end of this week. Bids for the work will be taken within the next four weeks, Samuel S. Lewis, State Secretary of Forests and Waters, announced.

"Along with the first phase, known as the 'interim development,' architects unrolled a basic plan for the 'ultimate development.'

"This second phase will follow just as soon as the Point interchange of the Penn-Lincoln Parkway and new bridges are completed in the park.

"Aim of the planners is to complete the park by 1958 in time for Pittsburgh's Bi-Centennial celebration, marking 200 years since the city was founded.

"In general, the basic blueprint calls for restoring the rivers, forest and views of sur-rounding hills as nearly as possible to the scene George Washington had in looking out over the Point in pioneer days.

"Arthur B. Van Buskirk, chairman of the Conference's Point State Park Committee, told members of the meeting in the Court House that the planning door is still open.

" 'This doesn't foreclose the dreams you want to dream,' he said. 'There still may be major recommendations for points of historical interest, such as a museum, sculpture, and recreational facilities.'

"An archeologist-historian will be retained to work with the contractor in examining all excavations so that historical material may be saved.

"Stone from existing Pennsylvania Railroad walls will be salvaged for the riverfront walls. Streets will remain in place during this phase but the cobblestone paving blocks eventually will be used in the walks and riverfront construction.

"The park actually won't take final shape until the second phase. This follows, in general, the landscape plan previously announced by the State and Conference committee.

"It calls for an eye-line view of the rivers through the center of the park. At the Point a 100-foot column will spout jets of water from a pool 200 feet in diameter.

"Outlines of Fort Pitt and Fort Duquesne will be traced in paving stone along their original boundaries where possible, throughout the park.

"The proposed riverfront will be a bee-hive

of water sports. A river wall of steel sheet piling, containing mooring rings, and wharf, with sloping walls, will encircle the Point between the new bridges.

"Open lawns will extend from Barbeau Street to the fountain, except for a break at the highway interchange."

Other design elements of the Park were revealed in the twenty-two-page Griswold-Rapuano report:

The Blockhouse (Bouquet's Redoubt) was to remain unaltered at its present grade and location.

All planting in the eighteen-acre area west of the highway interchange would be consistent with the policy of restoring the natural conditions that existed before the year 1800. There were two groups of existing trees in this area that were not consistent with the proposed character: thirteen ginkgo trees around the Blockhouse, and twenty-three London plane trees around the existing bridge ramps. Neither of these tree varieties existed in the original forest at the Point; therefore, it was planned to move these to the new planting on the opposite side of the interchange.

All newly graded areas were to be covered with four inches of topsoil and seeded with temporary grass. Permanent planting of grass would be on six inches of topsoil.

For immediate effect, many large trees with good heads would be planted.

Automobiles would not be permitted in the finished park except for the service and maintenance of park functions.

All the maintenance facilities were to be grouped together in one structure in the proposed Monongahela bastion, which was to stand under part of the interchange highway.

The fountain jet and its pool at the very tip of the Point, as well as the transformer and pump room under the fountain plaza, would be designed on the assumption that they would be under flood level occasionally. This low profile was felt to be justified by "the tremendous design advantage gained by looking down on the fountain pool from a higher level vista clear to the Ohio River."

January 15, 1953, clear and sunny, was a beautiful day for a groundbreaking ceremony. Secretary Lewis and Secretary Reynolds, Mayor Lawrence, and representatives from many agencies were present. There were no speeches. A power shovel began to clear an area for the first construction contract. The secretaries shoveled soil for the photographers and posed in the cab of the power shovel. Work began in earnest when the crowd dispersed, and a group of dignitaries retired to the Duquesne Club for luncheon and discussion.

Wallace Richards was not present to see the first results of his work. He had suffered a severe stroke a few hours earlier and was in the hospital under intensive care.

12

The Conference and
the Committee

By this time the nation's press had become interested in the "Pittsburgh Renaissance," and writers were flocking to the city to report on what was happening there. The *Saturday Evening Post* had done it first with a major article by George Sessions Perry on August 3, 1946: "There is good reason to believe that Pittsburgh is in the beginning of one of the most dramatic periods of municipal renaissance that any great American city is likely to undergo in the next decade." *Fortune* came next in February 1947 with its much-quoted pronouncement that Pittsburgh was the test of industrialism everywhere to renew itself. Other major stories followed: *Business Week* on October 11, 1947, and again on March 12, 1949. *Life* on December 1, 1947. *Colliers* on April 9, 1949. *National Geographic* in July, 1949. *Newsweek* on September 26, 1949. *Time* on October 3, 1949 (Richard Mellon on the cover). *Holiday* in October 1949. *Architectural Forum* in November 1949. *Town and Country* in

August 1950. *Atlantic Monthly* in May 1951. *Milwaukee Journal* on September 9, 1951: "Where city planners meet, the talk is that Pittsburgh is doing more than any other city to assure its future." *Fortune* again in June 1952. *Wall Street Journal* on February 24, 1953. *Business Week* on April 11, 1953. *Colliers* again on May 30, 1953: "You'd Never Know Pittsburgh." *Readers Digest* in May 1955: "The New City Called Pittsburgh." *Business Week* again on April 2, 1955. *Life* again on May 14, 1956: "Mellon's Miracle."

Every writer began with how miserable life had been in Pittsburgh before 1946 and expressed astonishment at the improvements that were being wrought. After all, in the words of Jeanne R. Lowe, "Pittsburgh was the city that stood out to many as the symbol of hope for urban reconstruction. . . . It was introducing a new style of doing things for American cities. . . . What it accomplished in the early days was herculean in the light not only of its own heritage but also that of urban America generally. . . . It provided other troubled American cities with at least a starting point for a new civic tradition. It furnished cities with a pattern of action."

The writers all told the story of the alliance between David Lawrence, Democratic machine politician, etc., and Richard Mellon, patrician banker, etc. They described smoke control, flood control, the Urban Redevelopment Authority, Point State Park, and Gateway Center. And they examined the operations of that remarkable organization, the Allegheny Conference, which was making it all possible. They were as interested in revealing how and why the Conference operated as they were in describing its successes. Such civic organizations were not uncommon in the middle third of the century, but they saw that this one was unique in one important respect: It was succeeding. The Conference, indeed, had become nationally, even internationally, famous by the mid-1950s.

Most writers dwelt on the quality of leadership provided by the Conference, concluding that this was the one essential lesson to be learned from the Pittsburgh experience. Pittsburgher Adolph W. Schmidt, elected president of the Conference in 1956, later American ambassador to Canada, was quoted:

First, there must be a focus of power of such strength and authority that the top leadership of the community is willing to rally around and give it continuing support. This does not need to be a single individual or group but can be a combination of several recognized sources as long as they act as an effective unit. Such sources of power are available in every community.

Second, this concentration of citizen power and leadership must make its peace with the elected public officials of the political subdivisions through which public action alone can come. Their understanding, cooperation, and support must be obtained, regardless of political affiliation.

Pittsburgh benefited by a happy concatenation of four strong forces in 1945–1960: continuing and productive business leadership; continuing and productive political leadership; the supporting skills of congenial, experienced technicians; and the existence of a channeling organization that seemed to have been born for this hour. The leadership, of course, flowed downward from Richard Mellon and David Lawrence.

No one has written and spoken more perceptively about R. K. Mellon than Leland Hazard, who became a member of the Conference's executive committee in 1950 and thereafter "performed the work (perhaps, more accurately, made the speeches) which gave me an individual status independent of the Pittsburgh establishment." In articles, an interview, and an autobiography he described Mellon as a shy man who had no close friends and a very few trusted business and civic advisers ("I was not one of them"); who disliked publicity and whose

Twelve men assembled in the Duquesne Club in April 1953 to pose for a second *Collier's* magazine article on Pittsburgh's "Great Awakening." From left to right they are (seated) Leland D. Hazard, David L. Lawrence, Clifford F. Hood, Sidney A. Swensrud, James M. Bovard, and William Penn Snyder III; (standing) Park H. Martin, H. J. Heinz II, I. W. Wilson, Adolph W. Schmidt, Robert C. Downie, and Arthur B. Van Buskirk. (Associated Photographers, Inc.)

"whole nature would have rebelled against open, personal leadership"; who believed that a man should live and work in the community in which he made his money. "He was a builder, a brick and mortar man; if he became interested in some aspect of education, the first thing he thought about in connection with it was adequate housing and adequate facilities for that activity. . . . The Allegheny Conference was a method of implementing his aspirations for Pittsburgh and his determinations for the betterment of his native city."

He was, Hazard said, no Lorenzo di Medici. "He was not interested in music, he was not interested in painting, he was not interested in sculpture, he was not interested in the performing arts. Those activities, those sensitivities, were just not a part of him. . . . His close associates used to tell me, 'God made R. K. Mellon the way he was'; he had certain interests and non-interests." But "he was a man of good intent and of fine community character. . . . He had a good heart and a clear head and he did not evade either the managerial or the philanthropic responsibilities of vast wealth. . . . Some things he was not particularly enamoured with, like television station WQED, but he didn't oppose them. In some things—a good horse, a steeplechase, a wildlife preserve, a park for Pittsburgh's city center—he was as constant as a star."

James McClain said in 1972, in the second year after Mellon's death, "R. K. said he couldn't do everything; some things had to be left out, and some other men in the picture, like Jack Heinz, who were informed about and liked music would have to pay attention to it. . . . The wonderful thing about Mr. Mellon, who was the personification of free enterprise and to whom the public parking authority idea might appear to be socialistic, was that he listened. He listened to Richards and then asked, 'Is it right?' Richards answered, 'Yes.' Mellon replied, 'Then let's do it.' "

Park Martin attested that Mellon faithfully attended the quarterly and annual meetings of the Allegheny Conference,* for Martin had persuaded him to be publicly identified as supporting the Conference program. He was not, however, a member of the executive committee, and he did not attend committee meetings, including those of the Point Park Committee. He rarely intervened directly and personally in Conference matters. He did indeed explain to Governor Martin that renewing Pittsburgh's Point was as important as renewing Philadelphia's Independence Mall. It was said, too, that when the Pennsylvania Railroad opposed the smoke control bill in 1945, he called Jack Appleton, vice-president of the western division, and suggested that he and the corpo-

*Steele Gow, on the other hand: "Dick Mellon very seldom came to any Conference meetings. I don't remember seeing him more than once or twice. He shied from publicity and he was always afraid newspaper people would single him out and interview him on this or that."

rations in which he had influence would consider shipping their freight on the B. and O. And Park Martin believed that Mellon was "largely responsible" for persuading Pittsburgh corporations to sign the leases in Gateway Center. But his role, in Patrick Cusick's words, like that of Mayor Lawrence, was "more reactive than creative."

Steele Gow declared in 1971: "Dick Mellon got much more credit for the Conference than Dick Mellon ever deserved or I think ever expected or ever hoped to have, and he didn't court it himself at all. All the extravagant language that was used about Dick at the time of his death is an illustration. It just wasn't so that he did everything. He stayed in the background, he was modest, he would help when he was asked, he never advanced programs of his own very far, he talked them over with everybody but if they didn't strike fire he didn't put on pressure for them. So he had the admirable trait of being a really modest person. But the public heaped the praise on him and made him the author and the daddy and the grandfather and the great-grandfather and all else of the Allegheny Conference, which he wasn't." Still, Gow would surely have agreed with Leland Hazard's statement, "Nothing, literally nothing, could have been accomplished by the conference over the opposition of R. K. Mellon." Governor Lawrence said in the 1960s, "He is a sort of bull cow in Pittsburgh; as he moves, many others move with him."

Mellon and Lawrence first came together at "a quiet luncheon" at the Duquesne Club organized by Van Buskirk and Park Martin. This was one of a series in which a few selected "decision-making" city, county, and state officials met Allegheny Conference people, including technical staff members. "I think," Patrick Cusick said in 1972, "Mellon and Lawrence had a great mutual respect for each other." Jack Robin said in a 1975 interview, "They never came together personally. I don't think they met informally in their whole lifetime. There was no social relationship. The connection was always at the professional level rather than at an executive level. Lawrence wasn't going up to join the Rolling Rock hunt. He never had any desire. It was a sort of accretion of common purposes.

"See, what happened was that . . . they found that their civic interests were convergent. Also what really happened was the opening, a sort of channel of communications [between them]. As Mayor Lawrence's secretary, I was part of that channel. I was Lawrence's main person in that channel. And Richards and Van Buskirk were Dick Mellon's. And Richards and I were able to get along immediately. . . . Van Buskirk, after some hesitation, learned to trust both Lawrence and me.

"The people who represented the civic groups in city hall were normally the professionals, such as Wallace Richards and Park Martin. . . . Lawrence had an enormously high respect for Richards and Dave Kurtzman and Park Martin, that became a very personal one in which the whole relationship was one of 'What's best for the city?' Lawrence never regarded these men as being emissaries of another power; he regarded them as people having a special knowledge of a special subject area in which cooperative programs could be developed for the benefit . . . of a situation in Pittsburgh. . . .

"Lawrence was a man of enormous force of character and self-discipline. He never flinched from what he conceived to be his duty, as he knew it. He was a man of relatively open mind. He read very little; he read the newspapers and almost nothing else. He learned by contact with sources, by exposure, by experience. . . . He worked long hours. We were in the office on Saturday, we were in the office on Sunday. . . . It was always a pleasure to work with him because he had a great sense of obligation, of duty, combined with a lively and interesting personality. He was never a stuffed shirt. While he took himself with appropriate dignity and pride, he was a man who did not overwhelm you with his own sense of his own importance. . . .

"He came back very strong in three great trials in his life. First, he had gone quite broke in the depression, his insurance company, wiped out. . . . Then, second, he was attacked and had to defend himself against [a political] vendetta. And then, third, his two boys were killed in the same automobile accident in the early 1940s. And his marriage was not a particularly good marriage. His personal life was not necessarily a very happy one. But he was engrossed in his political and governmental responsibilities. . . .

"He had a capacity to grow and change. . . . From a small-town politician he grew to mayor of Pittsburgh in 1945, governor in 1958, to be a real national leader, and a very important one. . . . Sometimes politicians do things for a political effect, and then having done them, they become part of their ego system, their personality, their beliefs. And if they are honest and decent men, having advocated them for political causes, they become strong advocates for believing in them conscientiously. And this is the case, I think, of what happened to Mayor Lawrence."

The structure, philosophy, and methods of the Allegheny Conference had been under test since 1945, and by 1953 they had been certified as sound. Its operating budget had leveled off at about $90,000 a year. The basic rules were still being maintained. Members of the committees were attending their meetings and were working personally as individuals rather than as corporate representatives; they did not send deputies. They obeyed the commandment of the Conference that its work and programs were nonpartisan and that no person or group would attempt to claim political credit. They obeyed the rule that no person or group, other than those retained to provide professional services under contract, would use the Conference for personal or corporate profit.

The Allegheny Conference had begun as a study group, with a high proportion of academic figures among its sponsors, but Park Martin and Richards consciously brought about a change in emphasis. As Martin told it (writing in the third person):

In the early summer of 1945 at a meeting of the executive committee, reporting on the committee work, Martin raised the question of what the Conference proposed to do with the reports. He pointed out that most of the reports concerned projects which could only be accomplished by elected public officials. He remembers the expression of pain on Dr. Doherty's face when he said in reply, "Do you mean I have to deal with politicians?" Martin answered that to get things done, someone had to, to which Doherty said, "If you want to, all right, but I won't." Martin asked, "Do I have your permission to do so?" Dr. Doherty then said yes.

This was the first time that anyone came to grips with the implications of the program. The Conference now was taking a step to do something about its reports. Instead of being only a research and planning group, the Conference would now embark on a course covering coordination and implementation of its plans. . . .

Not long after this, Dr. J. Steele Gow resigned as a member of the executive committee. While not stated, it was assumed that as director of a tax-free charitable trust, he felt it unwise to be a member of a group working with public officials. . . . Gow's resignation was the beginning of the change in the executive committee from the academic type of mind to the corporate executive type.

The Allegheny Conference and, indeed, the Pittsburgh renewal program were now unabashedly business oriented and business dominated. Conference policies were set by the executive committee, whose twenty-five members were almost without exception presidents or board chairmen of industrial corporations.* Leland Hazard said, "An invitation to join the executive committee was considered a command performance." In the heady years of the Pittsburgh Renaissance, 1945 to perhaps 1958, Pittsburgh businessmen active on Conference committees found, to their pleased astonishment, that they were community heroes. They returned to their normal whipping-boy status as soon as the Renaissance program drew to a close.

---

*Among them Alcoa, Allegheny-Ludlum Steel, Consolidation Coal, Dravo, Duquesne Light, Gulf Oil, Harmon Creek Coal, H. J. Heinz, J & L Steel, Mine Safety Appliances, PPG Industries, Pittsburgh Coke and Chemical, Shenango Furnace, United States Steel, and Westinghouse Electric.

Arnold J. Auerbach, taking a census of the executive committee for a Ph.D. dissertation in 1958, found that twenty-four of the twenty-five members belonged to the Duquesne Club, nineteen to the Rolling Rock Club, and thirteen to the Fox Chapel Club. All were registered Republicans. "However, one of those interviewed stated that he considered himself to be an 'Independent' Republican and another stated that although he is registered as a Republican he voted for Franklin Roosevelt."

With a small, seven-man staff (including the executive director), the Conference continued to draw on the technical and professional skills of existing Pittsburgh agencies in developing programs; thus those agencies were brought within the project rather than supplanted. The Conference and its program, Park Martin said, "became the keystone around which the other agencies hovered. . . . There existed some jealousy among some staff members of some of the civic agencies, for apparently they felt that the Conference, because of its broad purpose, would encroach on some of their own activity. . . . For a few years the relations between the Conference and the Chamber of Commerce were strained, since the Chamber regarded the Conference as trespassing on their field. As the Conference became increasingly successful in its work, as it gained public support and support of the newspapers, and as it absorbed top-flight executives of corporations into its executive committee, this strained feeling disappeared, with the Chamber adopting its own programs in the fields that properly belonged to it."

The executive committee and the staff became adept at obtaining bipartisan and popular support on measures before they were put to a vote. They almost invariably had good local press coverage, and they used this as a means of moving the programs forward. Henry J. Heinz II, vice-president of the Conference in 1966, in addressing the eightieth convention of the American Newspaper Publishers Association in New York City, credited Pittsburgh's newspapers with playing a major role in building community understanding and consensus:

Newspaper support was especially important to us in the early years of the program because we were doing something that had never been done before. I refer to the exercise of the right of eminent domain to condemn blighted private property, take it over, and resell it to other private interests. This was a new principle of law, and it was first tested in Pittsburgh. . . .

The point is, the exercise of this right, even under the most careful legal safeguards, could have been misunderstood. . . . The newspapers helped us to avoid that. They did it by informing the public in straight, factual news stories. They did it by molding public opinion through interpretation of facts in editorials and background stories written in the public interest.

Heinz added that each of the three daily papers assigned a full-time reporter to cover the Pittsburgh program, and that the reporters became knowledgeable specialists in community affairs.

They knew the details of the program, how all the pieces fitted together. This knowledge produced better stories, and it saved hundreds of hours of everyone's time. A rapport and a good working arrangement were established. We could go to those reporters with any problems we had in their field and count on getting sound advice. Sometimes they would even give us some information they had and we didn't.

Nineteen members of the executive committee of the Allegheny Conference meet in December 1956. From left to right they are (seated) Robert C. Downie, Carl B. Jansen, I. W. Wilson, Adolph W. Schmidt, William Penn Snyder III, Arthur B. Van Buskirk, Leland Hazard, James F. Hillman, Edward R. Weidlein; (standing) James M. Bovard, Lawrence C. Woods, Jr., William H. Rea, Leslie J. Reese, John A. Mayer, Oliver Kaufmann, John T. Ryan, Jr., George D. Lockhart, Henry L. Hillman, A. H. Burchfield, and Park Martin. (Ray Gallivan, Pittsburgh *Press*)

As the program continued, a remarkable thing happened. The reporters and editorial writers were themselves caught up in our work. They became affected by the same motivations and enthusiasm as the community planners. I wouldn't expect this of newspapermen in any other circumstances, and I imagine you would normally consider this over-identification with the subject of a story. But under the unique circumstances that prevailed, the press was in this unusual way all the more valuable to the Pittsburgh program.

Four of the reporters who covered the redevelopment beat, Heinz pointed out, later became planning administrators for Pittsburgh agencies.

The Point Park Committee was probably the most important committee of the Conference; it was certainly the most publicized. Reporters were always invited to committee meetings, and frequently their editors and publishers came with them. John Grove, assistant director of the Conference and secretary of the Park Committee, took care that everyone was well supplied with news releases, background stories, and photographs, and he tried to schedule meetings to accord with newspaper deadlines. Says one committeeman, "Every time we went to Harrisburg to get a major decision, we had a big spread in the Pittsburgh papers the day before that explained what we were doing and why it was needed. The gentlemen in the offices in Harrisburg had the stories laid out on the table before them, so that half our work had been done for us before we arrived." John Walker, Republican state senator and floor leader, went further. "The news stories," he said, "built up pressure for the legislation, even before the bills were introduced." There were long months of waiting when there was nothing much to write about, but Secretary Goddard followed a policy of maintaining public interest by awarding and announcing a number of small contracts at intervals instead of releasing them at one time or grouping them into a few large awards.

The Conference met with a problem in its early years that very nearly rendered it inutile. As Van Buskirk told the story: "The Bureau of Internal Revenue ruled that the Allegheny Conference was not a charitable or educational type of institution, but that it belonged taxwise to the chamber of commerce area. This meant that individuals, private foundations and so forth could not contribute and get a tax deduction. It was a very serious thing we faced because it was tax deduction money to a large extent that stood behind many of the things that we were doing and that we were planning. So we went to Mayor Lawrence, the Democrats then being in office in Washington, and we said, "We think this is a wrong ruling. It isn't just that we are hurt by it.'

"And Dave said, 'Well, let's go down to Washington.' And he called his close friend, the secretary of the treasury [John W. Snyder], and said that our little group would like to come down. I think three or four of us went. We went down there and we met in the secretary's office, who said, 'What can we do for you?' and Dave said, 'There's a perfectly dreadful situation. You're going to ruin all of the good things we're trying to do in Pittsburgh and which other cities are trying to do.' So we presented to him the work of the Conference, what it had already done, what it was planning to do and the lift the community was getting.

"The secretary of the treasury reached over and pushed a button and said, "Send in the general counsel of the Bureau of Internal Revenue," who appeared in a few minutes, and the secretary said to him, 'I want this ruling reversed. We in this administration are not standing for deterring the development of our cities.' Within a week, that bureau ruling was reversed."

Committee members are unanimous today in their conviction that their work, like that of earlier attempts, would have failed without the leadership of a powerful Conference and the capacity of its officers to make policy and take action. "There were hazards and threats," says one of the professionals, "that could have proved disastrous to the character of the park. The Conference and the committee were both wise enough to overcome the hazards and strong enough to throw back the threats."

The Point Park Committee was fortunate in that three able men who dominated the Allegheny Conference were also directly and deeply involved in the committee's work. Park Martin, as executive director of the Conference in the years 1945–1958, was present at all committee meetings. Arthur Van Buskirk, who served as president and then as chairman of the Conference in the years 1949–1953, headed the Park Committee from its inception until a few months before his death. Wallace Richards was secretary of the committee during its first six years.

Ralph Griswold describes how Park Martin conducted himself at meetings. "He was an important figure as a personality. And he was a very smart operator, in that he kept absolutely quiet and impersonal about the matter under consideration. He worked methodically and calmly, very calmly. He never entered into the preliminary discussions on either side, but would wait until both sides were hot under the collar, or perhaps had worked themselves into a fury. And then very calmly he would come out of his silence and state what he thought should be done. He would sum up all the arguments, though without saying so. He would sort out all the ideas that weren't good and come up with one that was really practical—a workable synthesis of different views. Then he would say, 'Why don't we do it this way?' and almost invariably he had the right answer.

"It was a marvellous gift, and it was largely responsible for our success in dealing with those state officials who sometimes went into tirades. 'By God, we're not going to do another God damned thing! Cancel all the contracts!'

(Laughter.) Park would sit there calmly and finally have them all on an even keel again, and we would proceed as though there hadn't been any controversy. This was true of all the factions that came into the picture. He was like a judge who listened to the arguments and then rendered a verdict. When we needed support or had a problem in Harrisburg, we always managed to take him along.

"He saved the day more than once for us in our own meetings. Van Buskirk would be on one side of an issue, maybe Kaufmann on another side, and Heinz on still another, all at each other's throats. But Park would smooth them down. He was a hallmark of good judgment in every meeting he attended."

Martin introduced a policy of never "front-running the public official." He explained: "The Conference does not have to be elected to anything. The public officials who were supporting the Conference's program did have to come up for reelection. We gave them all reasonable credit, sometimes even at the Conference's expense. Throughout my fourteen years as executive director of the Conference, we maintained this policy and never once was there a political corpse due to the Conference program."

When a *Fortune* editor and two photographers visited Pittsburgh in the fall of 1946 in search of a story, Martin took them to lunch "so that I could discuss what was happening in Pittsburgh with them. They were much inter-ested in the physical program, which they proposed to feature. To inquiries about the physical program, I replied, 'This is not the big story in Pittsburgh. The real story here is the new younger leadership which is now in Pittsburgh.' I pointed out that the day of the old rugged individualist was gone and that younger men were the leaders and active in support of the Conference and the program. . . . Evidently this argument prevailed, because when the *Fortune* article appeared in February of 1947, this was the main element in its story."

Another measure of Martin's capacities is seen in the way he handled the various groups who called at his office with suggestions, advice, or instructions on monuments they felt should be erected at the Point, for which they would supply the design and perhaps some of the cost. ("We have already selected the site.") The Point Park Committee had formally resolved and passed on April 29, 1953, a "Statement of Basic Policies," later approved by the state. It read:

1. Only those historic events and personalities that symbolize the significance of "The Point" and of Fort Duquesne and Fort Pitt, during the period it was serving as the frontier Bastion of Defense, will be given consideration in formulating the development program for Point Park.

2. No private memorials constituting tributes to individuals, groups, or organizations should be erected in the Park. Its theme must be dedicated to its important place in American history and to the spirit of the American pioneer prior to 1800. This

objective, it seems to us, can best be achieved by declining offers of memorials or assistance from individuals or organizations not related to the period prior to 1800.

Martin cited this policy to callers, and when they argued—as they generally did—that an exception should certainly be made for a cause so noble (patriotic) (religious) as theirs, he pointed out that such a splendid memorial (monument) (statue) (cross) deserved an even better location; it should be erected atop Mount Washington for all to see, overlooking Point Park. The projects generally died in transit from the Point to the mountain top.

Martin summed up his work in an interview in 1971: "One of the things I think you must give the Conference credit for—we were practical. We met the facts of life and did the things first that needed to be done, and the speed with which we did them is almost unbelievable. What was accomplished from 1945 until the time I left [in 1958] was almost unbelievable, and it's still going on."

In a newspaper article in 1960, Arthur Van Buskirk was given the title "The Philosopher of the Renaissance"; he had previously been called its "Anchor Man" and (even before his sixtieth birthday in 1956), its "Elder Statesman." To Jack Robin, he was the most intellectual of the businessmen involved in the Pittsburgh program. George Richardson remembers best that "he had a wonderful ability to get people to work together." Others have referred to his twinkling good humor.

Van Buskirk saw from the first that the Pittsburgh program should involve itself in things of the spirit—culture, education, the arts. But he was a realist, and he was convinced that physical regeneration of the city and the material benefits arising therefrom would have to precede any flowering of the spirit. "The physical things were of immediate importance at the beginning," he said in 1960. "In that day what we were planning was just an idea, and most people didn't believe it could ever work. It was only after we had begun with the physical that we were in a position to move into the cultural. Already we have made significant strides."

He preached the need for a new concept, a new cooperative relationship between industrial management and organized labor in which the two would work together. He said, "The thing that has drawn the eyes of the world to Pittsburgh has been the way the leaders of both industry and government have been able to work together for the good of the city, above either party or economic interest."

His friend Leland Hazard, who came to be a spokesman for the Conference on cultural matters, described Van Buskirk at work. "If a proposal sailed through the executive committee, we all knew he had either cleared it with R. K. [Mellon] or knew that he could. If Van said, 'Wel-l-l, let's think that one over,' we knew enough not to press. He was either uncertain himself or uncertain about R. K.'s reaction on the issue. This is not to say he was merely a messenger—far from it. He was not an *alter ego* for R. K. and he never pretended to be, nor would he guess in advance what his principal might think. . . . He was astute and imaginative in an operational way.

"The 39th floor at 525 William Penn Place— aerie of the Mellon establishment—was almost never mentioned. R. K.'s name was almost never mentioned—not even by the initials."

William Penn Snyder III says with a smile, "Arthur would sometimes get things done quickly by saying, 'The Mellon family would like to have it done that way.' I found out several times that the Mellon family had never heard of that particular matter and had taken no stand on it."

Leland Hazard said, "When the early physical revamping of the Golden Triangle, particularly the Point, was hanging in the balance, no prime minister ever employed the sovereign's power more ruthlessly than Van. When the famed collaboration between Richard Mellon and Mayor Lawrence was forming, Van was a municipal statesman far beyond the reach of any partisan thought or influence. . . . Mellon and Lawrence were a silent partnership; they seldom saw each other. Van was the intermediary between them."

In 1957, Van Buskirk, who had served as chief fund-raiser for Republicans in Pennsylva- nia, delivered a strong speech at the Schenley Hotel in support of David Lawrence, Democrat, in his campaign for reelection to an unprece- dented fourth term as mayor of Pittsburgh.

It is not known when Wallace Richards first met Richard Mellon, but it was presumably in 1937 in the office of the Regional Planning Association, of which Mellon was a member of its board and Richards its executive secretary. Richards "educated" Mellon in what he liked to call "applied civics," and when Mellon became president of the Planning Association in 1941, he saw in Richards certain qualities of daring and dramatic imagination he felt were valuable. The two men became closely associated; Rich- ards had an office next to Mellon's on "the thirty-ninth floor" to the end of his career.

It was an odd choice for a multimillionaire Republican banker to make, and one that does credit to his liberality and his good judgment. Richards, thirty-seven in 1941, had left Butler University to become a reporter, art critic, and foreign correspondent for the Indianapolis *News*. He wrote as a free-lance in Europe in 1931–1932 and then worked on publicity for a theatrical agency in New York City. (His clients included Ethel Barrymore, Eva Le Gallienne's ill-fated Civic Repertory Theater, Indiana's ex- hibit at the Century of Progress Exposition in Chicago in 1933–1934, and in Pittsburgh the reopening of Kaufmann Department Store's redesigned first floor, with murals by Board-

A prime mover in the Pittsburgh renewal program, Wallace Richards was a man whose flood of ideas was matched by his determination to drive his ideas to completion. With him are, from left to right, H. J. Heinz II, Richard K. Mellon, and John J. Kane. (Pittsburgh *Post-Gazette*)

man Robinson.) In 1934 he took a post with the Federal Resettlement Administration, serving as executive secretary of the Submarginal Land Program and in charge of Roosevelt's New Deal showpiece outside Washington, the Greenbelt housing project. Frederick Bigger introduced him to Arthur Braun and Howard Heinz, who in 1937, at Bigger's suggestion, offered him the post of executive secretary of the Regional Planning Association. According to James McClain, who was there at the time, Bigger wanted Richards to run the Planning Association in name only, while Bigger stayed in the background and gave the orders. Richards, however, "moved too fast" and was "too aggressive" for that arrangement, and Bigger one day showed him a list he had been keeping of Richards's activities he disapproved of. Richards agreed that the list was accurate but protested, "They were right and needed to be done." The friendship ended at that point. Richards kept the list and later showed it to McClain. Several years later Bigger (whose career had been eased by a comfortable inheritance) met McClain on the street and lamented, "The world has passed me by." Robert Pease recalls that among planning professionals ("we called ourselves 'hired hands' "), Bigger was known for the inordinate amount of time he spent "precising the plan." It was a practice Richards deplored, though to the end he always called Bigger "one of the great pioneers in the field of civic planning."

Richards, said Van Buskirk, was "an imaginative young fellow who had been rather close to Mrs. Roosevelt, and some people said he was 'New Dealish,' which was not supposed to be a desirable thing." He held money in contempt, had no fear or distrust of government controls, and was a nonorganization man, liberal in his views and cosmopolitan in his tastes, with a nice discrimination in literature and the arts. "Ideas," said Frank Hawkins, *Post-Gazette* editor, "poured out of him like water over the rocks at Fallingwater." He is credited with two for which Pittsburgh may be grateful. He conceived and sold to R. K. Mellon the idea of building Mellon Square in the block next to the Mellon Bank; and, in the words of William R. Oliver, "It was Wally who decided that the three-story apartment height on Fifth Avenue would be proper. . . . If the high buildings had gone up there, even with entire blocks around them, the shadows of those buildings would have fallen on the streets immediately to the north, which would be Castleman and Westminster and Kentucky, and those streets would have been ruined. The tall apartment concept would have been fatal to Shadyside."

There was a touch of flamboyance about Richards, reflected in part by the tailoring of his suits and by his continental haircut in a decade of conventional dress. On a visit with him to New Orleans, a colleague asked a nightclub waitress to name what each of them did for a living; she opined that Richards was a big-time gambler. Jack Robin, probably his closest professional friend in Pittsburgh, says it was not a bad guess, in the sense that Richards gambled on ideas and was not afraid to take big chances. Robin calls him a brilliant improvisor, a skilful organizer who could capture people's imagination. Mayor Lawrence said of him, "He had powers to dream and think up things that some of the more staid people couldn't grasp." Others use the words *driving, dynamic,* and *intense.* Park Martin called him "a supersalesman with a talent to influence the public and put across what he had in mind. A man of tremendous vitality." Leland Hazard, however, recalled that Park Martin complained more than once to him, "Wally is capable of talking down to people." Hazard added, "Wally's verve outweighed his imprudence and his inspirations overbalanced his arrogance. Planners have no choice but to be arrogant. They deal in the stuff of dreams and their nightmares are peopled with inert citizens. . . . When an unrelieved tension—or perhaps too many cigarettes—struck him down in his early fifties, I mourned a lost spiritual ally."

Don McNeil played penny-ante poker with Richards in a Friday night gathering of city-county engineers, planners, and suppliers, sometimes in the Regional Planning office in the Keystone Building on Fourth Avenue, and he retains strong memories of him. "He was the one who pulled us all together in the Pittsburgh program. He wanted to win. He wanted to be champion." Griswold corroborates his competi-tive spirit: "Anyone who played badminton with him, as I did, knew from the start that he was probably going to be beaten." John Grove, assistant director of the Allegheny Conference from 1952 on, calls him a perfect complement to Park Martin—one an engineer, the other a dreamer. Together they changed the Confer-ence from its start as a general discussion group under Dr. Doherty to a body whose aims were decisive action and visible results.

All his colleagues agree that Richards lived for results, and that delay, frustration, and fail-ure drove him to distraction. "His happiness," says McNeil, "was progress. He had to see a job getting done. I know that if we hadn't done the job in Pittsburgh he would have left. He was that type." Ralph Griswold speaks of working with planners in the 1930s who spent weeks and months on a project, presented it, and were not deeply concerned when nothing happened. "It was just a natural thing you had to expect. Wally, when he started something he felt was important and it didn't go through, became almost frenzied. His wife Rosemary said to us at dinner one night, 'You know, some time he's just going to blow up completely over one of these things.' "

With this drive, Richards worked too hard for too many hours in too many positions: execu-tive director of the Planning Association, secre-tary of the Conference's executive committee, secretary of the Point Park Committee, chair-man of the Parking Authority (which he

145

launched), and civic advisor to Richard Mellon. He was made director of Carnegie Museum in 1948 in the hope that he might reduce his work load, but he simply took it on as an added assignment. William Froelich, his associate at the Planning Association, later its director, recalls a conversation he had with Richards two or three months before he had his stroke. "Wally was the kind of person who couldn't say no to taking on additional jobs. He had his notebook—he kept his various meetings in a little notebook—and he recited to me the thirty-six separate assignments he had. I said, 'Wally, you can't *do* that. You've got to give some of this up.' 'Well,' he said, 'you're probably right, but I just don't know how.' "

Wallace Richards died in 1959 in his fifty-fourth year. His active work in Pittsburgh began in 1937 and ended on January 25, 1953—fewer than fifteen years. In that time he conceived great ideas for Pittsburgh, influenced people who had the power to put them into effect, and so set in motion forces that remade the city. He is now almost a legend in Pittsburgh: the stranger who came into the community, stayed a while, worked a miracle, and died for his work.

13

The Past, the Portal,
and the Bridge Under the Bridge

A historical and archeological salvage project was started at the Point on January 12, 1953. Dr. James L. Swauger, archeologist, curator of the Section of Man at Carnegie Museum, directed the operation, which was conducted during the excavation and grading work on the park's thirty-six acres. The team was responsible for three specific duties: (1) to collect all pre-1800 man-made objects; (2) to salvage bricks from the walls of Fort Pitt that would be inaccessible later because of planned highway construction; (3) to record gross fort features not previously discovered by archeological methods, and any previously discovered features, for comparison with known maps and plans of the fort complex. In carrying out these duties, the team maintained the written and photographic records customary in historical archeology. Swauger and his three associates kept daily journals in triplicate, and Lawrence Thurmond, of Old Economy, followed the

motor shovels, backhoes, loaders, power hammers, bulldozers, highlifts, clamshell buckets, and trucks about the area on foot, with authority to stop the machinery to protect artifacts. The contractor was protected by a "stop work" payment clause, and he and his men were both interested and cooperative. They were stopped only twice, briefly, during the ten months of their work.

The search for eighteenth-century artifacts was, in Dr. Swauger's words, a dismal and disappointing failure. Not one historical specimen, apart from structural elements of the fort, was found—no Indian material, no cannonballs, weapons, military equipment, tools, cut nails, bars of lead, kettles, or trade goods. A large part of the subsurface soil and probably artifacts as well had been removed in the excavations for numerous basements. The area had been ravished by fire and flood, churned by successive industrial and commercial developments, and then around 1900 largely covered with fill some eight to twelve feet deep. Many objects were found in the fill, but these were nothing but litter and rubbish of the late nineteenth and early twentieth centuries: broken crockery, glass, sewer pipes, machine-stitched shoes, piles of ashes, slag, cement, tarpaper, and a motorcycle license plate, all dating after 1880. (A small collection of such pieces was catalogued and stored at the Historical Society of Western Pennsylvania.) There was not a trace of Fort Duquesne, for the Emsworth Dam had raised the rivers some twenty feet, Fort Duquesne was now below the modern pool level, and archeological excavations quickly filled with water.

The archeologists had far better success in establishing the dimensions and boundaries of Fort Pitt. They worked with overlays of the maps of the fort made in 1761 by Lieutenants Bernard Ratzer and Elias Meyer, and with charts made in 1941–1943 by archeologists Eugene Murphy and Wesley A. Bliss for the city. Murphy and Bliss had worked in an area crowded by buildings, streets, and sidewalks, and they could not dig on private property, but they managed to sink thirty-five test pits, most of which revealed evidence of Fort Pitt. An oldtimer says, "I remember the thrill of looking down the pits to observe sections of the masonry fort walls and foundations exposed to view"; but because of lack of public interest, the pits were eventually filled in. Swauger's team dug new pits at two points along what had been Liberty Avenue, exposing standing portions of the fort's original brick and stone south wall, and a pit between Liberty and Penn that revealed a section of the inner wall that no one knew existed. Further excavation confirmed that the Ratzer and Meyer maps were accurate and that the Murphy-Bliss charts were "accurate within reason." The wall averaged eight to ten feet in width and was built in four "steps"— a foundation of roughly faced-dressed, light greenish-gray stone; a footer of carefully dressed stone; and two steps of wall built of orange, brown, and red hand-molded brick set in mortar in the English bond pattern. All parts were carefully laid; they were perfectly plumb and in a remarkable state of preservation after 192 years. The bricks were soft and easily broken, but the mortar, containing hair filler, was extremely hard. The entire Music bastion, pointing northeast, was uncovered, and the location of the other four bastions was firmly established: the Grenadier bastion (pointing southeast), Flag (south), Monongahela (southwest), and Ohio (northwest). Most of the bricks were salvaged, but there were fewer than expected (they had been taken early in the nineteenth century), and they could not be used, as had been hoped, in the planned reconstruction of the Monongahela bastion. The architect, however, was able to obtain bricks from modern kilns of the same size, color, and texture, almost indistinguishable from the originals.

An unexpected discovery in the archeological salvage work conducted in 1953 was the interior stockade wall of the north rampart of Fort Pitt. Chief archeologist James L. Swauger holds one of the elm and black oak posts, originally about fourteen feet long. Carnegie Museum Director M. Graham Netting and Carnegie Institute President James M. Bovard look on. (Carnegie Library, Pittsburgh)

The archeologists also uncovered evidence of the fort's parade ground, about two feet below the level of Liberty Avenue, and a line of stockade posts—palisade logs—on the "water" side of the fort. The total cost of the dig was less than $2,000, not counting $500 Carnegie Museum lost on the project. There was only one unhappy archeological accident. In making his rounds of the area, Charles Stotz was overjoyed to come upon a two-foot-high portion of the wall, with foundations intact, at an exterior corner of the Music Bastion. This contained "quoin stones," used at the external and internal corners of the bastions to avoid making special "shaped" brick at such locations. He laid them aside, asked the contractor's foreman to protect them until next morning, and departed to keep an engagement. When he returned next day, the quoin stones were gone, carried away with the masonry rubble. Fortunately, he had photographed and measured them, so that they served as a model for use in the design of the Monongahela bastion.

The newspapers had given front-page and feature coverage to the excavations, and this time public interest ran high. The archeologists were badgered by spectators and souvenir hunters who wanted bricks or stones from the fort walls. Some of them made off happily with bricks from street pavings, clearly stamped "Toronto" and "Pittsburgh Buffalo Co."; they are presumably built into patios and fireplaces and still identified as bricks from old Fort Pitt.* There were pleas to remove, preserve, and rebuild the stone foundation, but the state declined to pay the considerable costs, and a well-intentioned gentlelady withdrew her offer of $50,000 since it was impracticable to rebuild the whole fort—much of it would lie under the highway interchange.

When the last bricks were extracted and all possible knowledge gleaned on the structure of the fort, preparations were made to fill in the holes. Expressions of public dismay followed at burying forever what had so lately been uncovered, and on the recommendation of Dr. Oliver's Historical Advisory subcommittee, Point Park committeemen prudently reconsidered. They decided to preserve the scarp wall foundation adjacent to the original drawbridge entrance between the Grenadier and the Music bastions. Some 175 feet of this would be exposed in a depression at its original level, with its brick wall, partly restored, on top. What is more, a replica of the original drawbridge, leading over the moat to the main gate, would be installed. (The notches where the drawbridge had fitted into the masonry were clearly evident.) "This revised scheme,"

---

*A few genuine bricks were given to persons who had performed or were expected to perform special service on behalf of Point State Park. For the record, they carried the catalogue designation "PPP/number" on a yellow paint square, or were authenticated by a certificate signed by Swauger or Arthur M. Hayes, his assistant.

Griswold wrote to Oliver on April 21, 1953, "will give visitors an excellent view of the original fort wall and moat from the Grenadier to the Music Bastions. At the ends of this original section the wall will tie into a stone tracery of the fort outlining its complete location on the surface of the ground." Preservation of the wall, Van Buskirk wrote to Maurice Goddard on April 27, 1959, "will go a long way toward meeting criticism from the historians and many other citizens who feel that there should be some actual restoration of the original Fort Pitt in the Park."

The curtain wall was rebuilt as planned. It is marked by a bronze tablet and may be viewed from the entrance walk that leads into the park from Commonwealth Place and Liberty Avenue. The architect, however, had objected to the replica of the drawbridge, because it would be meaningless without building a section of the ramparts; they would stand about eighteen feet high and so block the view west through the interchange into the park. The drawbridge was scrapped. Stotz also felt that a straight entrance walk on the axis of the foundation would divide the sweeping approach area, and so he suggested two entrances, one from each end of Commonwealth Place, which would make wide curves and meet at the portal, where the full view of the fountain would break on the visitor. This design was adopted.

Other changes had been and would be made in the original 1945 design of the park. The round memorial building at the entrance and the deluxe restaurant were gone. Instead, a historical museum would be contained in the rebuilt Monongahela bastion abutting the highway wall. Early plans had called for a matching bastion on the Allegheny side, its interior to be solid earth, its top to be used as an automobile outlook over the park. This died when the state highway department refused to permit cars to leave and reenter the high-speed roadway, and when the architect and the Historical Advisory Committee objected to a bastion where no bastion had ever stood before. The plan to rebuild Fort Duquesne was also dropped because it, too, would have interrupted the long view to the fountain, and because, as an earth-and-timber structure, it would have to be rebuilt every decade or so and would be torn apart by any severe flooding. It was decided instead to mark the site with a tracery in stone, and to further mark the site with a bronze plaque showing the plan of Fort Duquesne in relief. The ideas of postwar architects and city planners who called for more open space and sweeping views were now becoming more popular. The nineteen-hundred-foot view along the axis of the park, from the southwest corner of the Hilton Hotel to the fountain, was recognized as an unusual and striking feature, and one that should not be sacrificed for an ersatz fort or a rebuilt drawbridge over a token moat.

At the April 29, 1953, meeting of the Park

Committee, William Rogers, a river transportation executive, suggested a change in the wharf along the Allegheny River. Not enough seating space, he said, was being provided for the aquatic displays and boat races that would presumably develop when the park was finished and in use. Having just seen the famous Water Gate along the Potomac River in Washington, he proposed that the slope wall along the Allegheny be changed to a stepped wall to provide some three thousand seats for spectators. There was some dismay at the heavy added cost and the need to redesign the wall, but Van Buskirk immediately saw the merit of the proposal and pushed it through. The Annandale granite quarry north of Butler, Pa., long closed and out of business, was reopened to provide the additional blocks that were needed.

A major change not visible to the lay public was made in the construction of the park's river walls and wharves. The normal method would have been to sink caissons in the river, pump out the water, build forms for a wall, and pour concrete. Michael Rapuano recommended a new technique that had been tried successfully in a few installations. The Park Committee studied these, gathered testimonials that the method was successful and economical, and in this way obtained authorization for its use at Point Park. Dravo Corporation engineers drove interlocking piles of sheet steel, one at a time, into the riverbed along the shore to the depth

where they "met refusal."* They cleared the earth and water behind this watertight wall and filled the area with gravel to within three feet of the top. Two-inch-diameter steel bars with huge turnbuckles led in some twenty feet from the wall to another set of piles that served as anchors. The turnbuckles were tightened and the bars were embedded in a three-foot slab of poured concrete.

The earth moving and grading were completed in the fall of 1953, and large areas were seeded with grass on a six-inch bed of topsoil. Griswold and Rapuano conducted a hopeful experiment to see if the excavated river muck would serve as topsoil. It would not. Too oily.

George Richardson's design for the "mixing interchange" connecting the two new bridges, the Penn-Lincoln Parkway, and the streets of the lower Triangle was finished in 1953. "We made a working model of the interchange," Griswold says, "because nobody except the designers could understand the damn thing, all the ins and outs and crossings. I consulted a professional display house, but their price was too high, so we built it ourselves in my office. It took the best part of three days, and we did a much more detailed and perfect job than I had expected. We packed it and the plans in a station wagon, and a group of us, including

---

*On both riverfronts the walls were built, with permission of the Department of the Army, fifty feet out into the rivers beyond the existing harbor line, thus substantially enlarging the whole Point area.

The river wall, wharf, and promenade were built by a new engineering method that eliminated the need for caissons. The three-foot-thick slab of concrete, laced with two-inch steel rods, will be poured over the gravel and locked by turnbuckles into inshore anchors. In the eighteenth century, the Point was some four hundred fifty feet shorter than it is today. (William Swain)

Van Buskirk, Park Martin, Bill Swain from my office, and Paul Ambler [State Highway Department], started out on a Monday evening for Harrisburg. We stopped overnight at Bedford and stayed up till midnight discussing the model and next day's meeting, all of us conveniently in one place and without interruptions, which was difficult to manage in Pittsburgh. We left next morning at eight and set up the model for a luncheon meeting with Governor Duff, Secretary Lewis, and Secretary Schmidt. We said, in effect, 'this is how it's going to look, and here is how it will work.' They approved it in principle and gave us some important, far-reaching decisions. It was a very successful trip."

There was one omission in the plans and the model. The sole land entrance to the park was to pass under the band of highways running north and south across the Point, connecting the two new bridges, and this entrance, now being called the portal, was not yet designed. At this time, after several years' absence, architect Charles Stotz reentered the scene; he and his brother Edward were commissioned by the state to design the portal.

It was an extremely difficult design problem, both in engineering and aesthetics. The band of overhead highway was one hundred sixty feet wide and only twenty-five feet high, with the south end somewhat higher than the north. There was fear, vociferously expressed, that the entrance through which the people passed from east to west under eight lanes of traffic would be like a tunnel. Speaking for his Point Park architectural subcommittee, Edgar Kaufmann called the elevated roadways "horrible looking structures" from the standpoint of park beauty; they would be a "Chinese wall" between the park proper to the west and the park plaza and the rest of the city to the east.

The clearance was so low, Stotz says in agreement, that it seemed impossible to develop a satisfactory solution. A rectangular passageway would look like a slot opening, a keyhole on its side; if it was widened, it would need a battery of pillars and would look like a railroad trestle. A normal arch would look like a culvert and would reveal only a glimpse of the park beyond.

Henry J. Heinz II, a member of the Park Committee, listened to a discussion of the problem. His company was building a research laboratory at the time in its factory complex across the Allegheny, and he volunteered the services of his architectural firm, Skidmore, Owings and Merrill. He suggested that Stotz talk with Gordon Bunshaft, the architect in charge. "I worked closely with Gordon," Stotz says, "and had a good experience with him. He recommended a very low, long, almost flat arch. That's a very difficult structure to build, because as an arch becomes flatter, the increased thrust at the spring line becomes critical. It could be done here because of new technology developed in prestressed reinforcing rods in the concrete structure."

Construction of the eight-lane portal, designed to connect the new Fort Pitt and Fort Duquesne bridges, began in 1961. Because of the complexity of the curves, arcs, and arches, a five-foot model of the portal was built first and the engineering drawings were taken from it. (Pittsburgh *Press*)

Aerial view of the Point in September 1969. The two old bridges are now subject of an intensive drive to save and use them as a kind of Pittsburgh Ponte Vecchio. The fountain cannot be built until they are removed, and the planting on most of the Monongahela side must wait until the long ramp to the Manchester Bridge is removed. (Harry Coughanour)

The design they developed was attractive and dramatic: a flat concrete rib arch with a span of 182 feet, a clearance height of less than 23 feet, a crest hardly more than 2 feet thick, and a clear, wide view to the park, fountain, rivers, and hills to the west. The portal had an interior hollow shell with three curved vaults, each 160 feet long, arching across and between four heavily reinforced ribs 40 feet apart, the ribs taking part in the overall arch action.

In the normal procedure, Stotz and Bunshaft would have given architectural working drawings of the portal to the Pennsylvania Department of Highways, but because of the irregular shape and the complexity of the vaults, this was impossible. Instead, they made a model five feet long in plexiglass. The department gave this to George Richardson, who studied it, advised that it was a structurally acceptable solution, and consented to use the model as the basis of his engineering drawings. He said of the portal in 1978, "It proved to be a beast to construct."

His structural design called for burying four huge rectangular concrete blocks at one end of the portal and four matching blocks at the other end, 180 feet apart. Each block held a twelve-ton hinge facing inward, and each "floated" on a slab of hardboard set on a two-inch layer of sand set on a twelve-inch layer of granular slag set on top of pilings. Each pair of blocks was tied tightly together by seventy-five tendons of eighteen-strand steel wire running underground across the portal—so tightly

that they stretched about eleven inches under tension. All this replaced the keystone in the normal arch; it bore the tremendous downward and outward thrust of the long, flat arch overhead, the hinges permitting a movement of several inches under pressure.

The structural blueprints were given to a contractor experienced in construction of ship's hulls. He had the concrete vault forms built of laminated tongue-and-groove timber on the west coast and then disassembled them and shipped them for reassembly in Pittsburgh. *Engineering News-Record* ran a three-page article on the Pittsburgh portal, "a most unusual structure . . . a gracefully arched monumental gateway to the park."*

*" 'Arch for Art's Sake' Bridge Will Serve a Double Function," November 1, 1962. For those interested in the technology of the construction, ENR reads: "Since the arch is so extremely flat . . . the engineers . . . were faced with exaggerated temperature stresses. Their solution was to make the arch three-hinged with the abutments held in place by four underground post-tensioned concrete ties (one for each rib). . . .

"Separate abutments for each rib [were] founded on steel H-beams driven to rock. . . . The underground members that tie the abutments of each rib together are each 177 feet long by 7.5 feet wide and 2.5 feet deep. Since the prestressing tendons extend through the abutments to the rear face, the actual distance between jacks is 225 feet. . . .

"Tying the ribs, shell and deck together are transverse diaphragms spaced about every 10 feet. These, with the ribs and longitudinal stiffeners that run along the crests of the arched shell between each rib, divide the interior of the bridge into closed cells. This cellular construction of arch, ribs and curved shell slabs acting as a unit is one of the bridge's unique features.

"Post-tensioning was by the Freyssinet system. The tensioning

The bridge-under-the-bridge looking east shows part of the reflecting pool, the ornamental "buckets" for lights (right), and the three ribbed arches. (Al Church, Allegheny Conference)

One lesser unsolved problem still remained. What treatment was to be given the immense flat area under the long, arching portal? Were visitors to cross this at random on entering the park—an area the size of six basketball courts? How would they be prevented from bumping their heads at the low ends of the long arch? The solution was ingenious and elegant. The whole area was made a shallow reflecting pool, eight inches deep, and an ornamental bridge with a slight camber or arc was designed to lead westward across the pool from the plaza to the park. Pedestrian traffic and service vehicles (up to ten tons) were thus gently led to the center of the portal arch, where the headroom was highest.

"We made the pedestrian bridge forty feet wide," Stotz says, "much wider than a normal walkway, simply to have it large in scale, in proportion to the portal. You'll notice those railings are great metal tubes supported by heavily anchored posts. I don't think you feel a confinement because of the low clearance beneath the vaults. It's part of the charm of it.

"One other problem was that the water would have to be drained in winter, and therefore the bottom of the pool had to be something of an interesting character. I specified the use of large cobblestones left in our rivers by the prehistoric glacial moraine, all about eight inches across and fairly uniform. They are laid in a concentric fish-scale pattern, a semicircular shape. The outer ring is formed of light-colored cobbles—which were easier to specify than to find. I think the pattern is interesting both with and without water.

"It was necessary, of course, to design a method of illuminating the vaults in the interior of the portal at night. In the daytime they receive reflected light. I worked with George Richardson on a system of overhead down-lights sunk in the vaults. They're not prominent in daytime, and at night they effectively light the walkway. To illuminate the vaults, we designed a great ornamental fluted bucket of masonry to stand at the bases of each of the three vaults. Six very strong lights are thrown up from these, to give an interesting play of light and shade on the overhead curved forms."

The plans for the portal were revealed at a meeting of the Point Park Committee on May 17, 1954, with the model prominently displayed. "The press photographers," Griswold wrote in his diary, "came in droves. The meeting proceeded promptly and smoothly with no major uprisings. Everyone, and Schmidt in particular, was pleased with the Portal, and the historians were again placated."

Van Buskirk made a statement: "The 'Gate-

job was, in fact, one of the last that Mr. [Eugene] Freyssinet supervised personally before his death. Each tie member contains 75 tendons of eighteen 0.196 inch diameter wires each. When the concrete reached a strength of 4,500 pounds per square inch, the tendons were jacked to an average tension of 65,000 pounds, enough to keep some tension on the tie member and prevent cracking after the bridge load is applied. The tie members were two-coated with waterproof paint before being buried."

A fishscale design of carefully graded river stones appears on each side of the portal bridge and around the fountain at the Point. The pattern looks good under water and without it. (Pittsburgh *Press*)

The portal looking west toward the fountain. The 160-foot arched span with a flat crown only a little more than two feet thick was accomplished by tying the members together by buried tendons prestressed to a tension of 65,000 pounds. (Thomas E. Morgan, Advertising & Public Relations)

way Portal' will be something unique. It will afford visitors entering the park a spectacular view of the picturesque forks of the Ohio River, plus the proposed fountain at the Point itself." Public response was favorable, and satisfaction was expressed that the interchange, as finally approved, would take up only twelve acres in all, leaving twenty-four acres for the park and the park plaza. Nine years later, when the interchange and portal had been completed, an editorial in the Pittsburgh *Post-Gazette* rendered a verdict:

Ah, the Portal Bridge

We have been among those concerned about the new portal bridge in Point Park. We were worried as the plan unfolded that this new bridge across the park would be a wall rather than a portal to the point, an obstacle rather than an invitation to the historic area.

But the other day, it being too hot to concentrate on the weighty world of editorial writing, we sauntered over to view the new portal span more closely and to get an idea of the approach to the point through its curving arch.

We want to report to our readers that our fears are dispelled. This portal is handsome, a flowing band of concrete that reminds us of the use of reinforced concrete by such masters as Yamasaki in his science building at the Seattle World's Fair and Saarinen in the TWA terminal at Idlewild Airport.

The portal will furnish an attractive entrance to the rest of Point Park, a framework for the vista which will greet pedestrians walking toward the junction of the rivers.

We congratulate the Point Park Committee, the State Highway Department and the designers. If there had to be a highway across the Point Park development, they at least have made the best of it.

14

The Museum in
the Bastion

Through the next ten years, 1954–1963, Point State Park seemed to move sluggishly, almost in slow motion. There was some progress, but always in the face of delays, impediments, and frustrations. In 1954 the lower portion of the masonry wall of the Music bastion and the adjoining curtain walls were opened permanently to public view. The wharves and river walls were completed in 1955, and now it was possible to make a promenade around the entire Point. The two ancient overhead bridges still crowded down on the open area and blocked the unbroken vista, but this uninterrupted half-mile stretch, the longest section of improved waterfront in western Pennsylvania, was nevertheless a contribution to conservation unequalled at that time in urban renewal in this country. Pittsburghers had access once again to the rivers that had made their city great.

Four more years passed with work progressing but no major piece completed. The Grenadier bastion was finished in 1959. This is a solid structure (without interior space) that abuts the interchange on its eastern side and stands next to the parking lot across from the Pittsburgh Press Building. It was designed and supervised by John Renner while his partner, Ralph Griswold, was working in Athens on the Agora planting.* The Maintenance Building was completed about the same time. Though an architect, Stotz was firm in his conviction that there should be few buildings in the park, and those few as inconspicuous as possible. He placed the Maintenance Building in the only site in the park that provided complete concealment; it nestles under the highway, providing offices, storage space, truck garage, and quarters for maintenance and security people.

*Charles Stotz, who did not serve as Renner's consultant on the bastion, says that Grenadier bastion is the correct identification, though it has always been known (erroneously) as the Flag bastion. The site of the original Flag bastion lies under the approach to Fort Pitt Bridge.

On June 19, 1959, the new double-deck Fort Pitt Bridge was dedicated and opened for limited use, and the old Point Bridge was closed. Four more years passed. The entrance into the park, the portal, was completed. Point Bridge still stood, rusting away, because the state and the county could not agree on who should pay how much to have it demolished. A revanchist movement sprang up to retain the old bridge, and the longer it stood unused, the stronger the movement grew to save it.

The park, in the meantime, was being used. People made their way around the machinery and stacks of material, ate their lunches on the park benches, began to drop fishing lines into the rivers, occasionally coming up with a carp or catfish; children practised their gyrations with hoola hoops. The park was spruced up to serve as the site of the city's two-hundredth birthday party in 1958–1959, and while the celebration was something less than a smashing success, it did draw scores of thousands of people into the new park. All but a few of the most confident planners had always shared a nagging doubt and fear: Who would use the park? Would anyone take the trouble to go there? The early tentative returns seemed to suggest that people would use the park and that, even without the attractions of the planned museum and fountain, they would take the trouble to go there in considerable numbers.

The park's sister development, Gateway Center, progressed at a faster pace. The first office buildings—three cruciform structures clad in stainless steel—were completed by the end of 1953. They were at once recognized as serious, though not fatal, blunders. They were designed by a committee—by a consulting board of design, with no principal architect, that met every Monday at Equitable's headquarters in New York. The buildings had only their surroundings to redeem their unimaginative dullness and lack of originality. Ralph Demmler recalls, "Government restrictions during the Korean War made it impossible to get the nickel-alloyed stainless steel that Equitable had planned to use for the skin of the buildings. Admiral Ben Moreell, then president of J & L Steel, said that chrome-alloyed steel could be used but that Equitable might end up owning 'towers of rust.' A delegation of us went to Washington and tried to convince the bureaucracy to allow us to use nickel steel. We failed. In another leap of faith, Equitable decided to go ahead with chrome."

The architecture that followed was more successful: the State Office Building in 1957; the Bell Telephone Building, 1958; the golden Hilton Hotel, 1959; Gateway Four, 1960; the IBM Building, 1963; Gateway Towers (luxury apartments), 1964; the Westinghouse Building, 1970. Two pleasant landscaped plazas were built: one, designed by Clarke, Rapuano, and Holleran, to the north around the earlier Gateway Center buildings; the other, designed by Simonds and Simonds, lying to the south over a 750-car parking garage below street level. The two plazas and a number of the new buildings were connected by a pedestrian tunnel. The Pittsburgh Press Building, one of the two structures left standing after the clearing (the other was the city's Public Safety Building), removed the Scripps-Howard Lighthouse from its roof and took on a new exterior design. To the south, across the Monongahela from the Point, the Fort Pitt Tunnels under Mount Washington were opened in 1960. To the north, across the Allegheny from the Point, the eighty-four-acre Three Rivers Stadium was completed in 1970, and with it a small stretch of north-shore riverfront improvement.

One of the happy developments in building Point Park was Charles Stotz's speculation in 1953 that the Monongahela bastion at the southwest end of the portal might be more than a reconstructed relic of Fort Pitt. It could also possibly serve as a structure holding a Point Park museum. To be sure, it would be a unique and difficult design problem. Build a concrete box of most irregular shape on military plans 192 years old. Face it with brick in the eighteenth-century manner. Give it a watertight concrete roof twenty inches thick. Cover that with four feet of earth topped with natural sod. Place thereon a sentries' walk, gun platforms, and military embrasures with cannon. Within this archaic structure place a modern museum. Give it an inconspicuous, modest entrance.*

Stotz drew an isometric cutaway view of the museum showing the interior arrangements and displayed and described it at the eleventh meeting of the Point Park Committee on April 29, 1953. Not much happened on the museum project for the next ten years. He displayed and described the drawing again at the thirteenth meeting on May 17, 1954, and again at the fourteenth meeting on April 26, 1956, and again at the fifteenth meeting on June 9, 1959, and again at the sixteenth meeting on December 5, 1960—each time with additions, deletions, revisions, and refinements on his original concept.

• The Park Committee approved the museum project as proposed in February 1957 and appointed a bastion subcommittee.

• Stotz persuaded Dr. Goddard in 1958 to bring Dr. Sylvester K. Stevens and the Pennsylvania Historical and Museum Commission into the park project for the first time. Goddard asked Stevens to assume responsibility for the planning and operation of the museum, acting only in an advisory capacity until the state found the money to build it.

• Stotz appointed an advisory committee to give him guidance on the design of the museum and its contents.

*The original Mongahela bastion was a solid earth structure, but in the modern reconstruction its outer walls are faced with brick, in a manner identical with the original Music and Flag bastions on the inland or eastern side of the fort.

The museum is housed inside a reconstruction of the Monongahela Bastion of Fort Pitt. Four feet of soil and grass top a concrete roof twenty inches thick. (Pittsburgh *Press*)

• Van Buskirk set a program in motion to solicit private gifts for furnishing the museum, starting with $25,000 from the Richard King Mellon Foundation. Stanton Belfour, who had succeeded Dr. Oliver as head of the Historical Advisory Committee, volunteered the services of the Pittsburgh Foundation as trustee of gifts of money; the Historical Society of Western Pennsylvania served as custodian of historical pieces.

• In October 1958, Stotz made a detailed progress report on the museum with recommendations. The name should be the Fort Pitt Museum. In accordance with Conference Resolution 201, the spread of time covered by the museum should terminate at the year 1800. No memorials should be erected in the building beyond those considered pertinent to the museum. The museum format, he said, "should be in the nature of pictorial and graphic exhibits amplified by life-size rooms. The limitations of space preclude any normal type of museum housing great variety and quantities of artifacts and similar museum material. Since the period covered by this museum is precisely defined, the picture book method of depicting and explaining events and structures at the Point area is entirely feasible. This treatment will provide school children and others interested in a correct but not heavily documented story of the district." The Park Committee approved the recommendations.

• On April 1, 1959, the Park Committee was told there were no funds allocated for building the bastion museum in any specific state budget.

• The Buhl Foundation gave the Point Park Committee a grant to build a large model of Fort Pitt, to the scale of ten feet to one inch, for permanent display in the museum. Stotz designed it, using documents he found in the Royal Library at Windsor Castle and in the map rooms of the Public Record Office and the British Museum.

• Special permission was wrested from officials in the Department of Highways in Harrisburg and the Public Roads Administration in Washington to place the Maintenance Building and storage yards under the interstate highway. (It is believed to be the only such authorization ever given; it entailed rigid regulations on storage of gasoline and oil.)

• Stotz was formally commissioned by the state to design the museum interior and its exhibits. Contracts were signed. In 1964, ground was broken and work actually started on construction of Pittsburgh's first historical museum.

During these ten years, the Point Park Committee and the state were negotiating with the Fort Pitt Society of the Daughters of the American Revolution on the status of the Blockhouse and the caretaker's lodge, which now stood near the museum on a small island of private property surrounded by a state park.

In 1892 the Pennsylvania Railroad, needing the space for a warehouse, had intended to dispose of the old Blockhouse. The Pittsburgh chapter of the DAR organized and led a protest movement to save it. The railroad compromised and offered to move it intact to Schenley Park. The DAR protested the harder. The railroad began condemnation proceedings. The ladies of the DAR marched on the state capitol and had a law passed that prohibited the railroad from using condemnation proceedings against patriotic shrines. The railroad admitted defeat and withdrew.

At that point, Mary Elizabeth Schenley, a DAR member, bought the Blockhouse and on March 15, 1894, deeded it to the Pittsburgh chapter. Since its bylaws did not permit the DAR to own private property, it formed the Fort Pitt Society to receive the deed. The society had maintained the building for public use ever since, charging no admission, selling souvenirs to meet expenses, and holding board meetings there five times a year. In 1909 they planted a number of trees on their property as a memorial to the early pioneers.

The Point Park Committee and the state now proposed to complete this rescue of a historic shrine. The state was willing to accept the property as a gift from the Fort Pitt Society and to preserve it as part of Point State Park. They would give it needed repairs and professional rehabilitation, restore the interior to what it had been in 1764, open the second floor, and install a scholarly push-button lecture on the history and significance of the structure. The souvenir counter, of course, would be removed. The caretaker's lodge, built in the 1890s, would be demolished. The grass would be replaced by English ivy. The trees would be removed, in accord with the decision that growth in the park should be limited to what was native to western Pennsylvania and present before 1800. These trees were ginkgos, an ancient oriental tree first brought to North America from Europe by William Hamilton and Thomas Jefferson in 1807. They would be replaced by full-grown indigenous trees.

This offer was conveyed to the DAR in the autumn of 1953. To their surprise, state officials and Point Park committeemen met with a response not unlike that directed at Pennsylvania Railroad malefactors sixty-two years earlier. Somehow the rumor had spread that the real intention of the state and the Park Committee was to demolish the Blockhouse, or at least to move it out of the way to another area. The 525 women of the local DAR sprang into action to effect a second rescue of the structure. They retained James Marsh as their lawyer, and through him they let it be known that they did not intend to give, sell, or in any other way relinquish their rights in what had become a sacred trust.

An exchange of views followed. To settle once and for all the rumors of improper intent, a passage from the *Report of the Study Committee on Historical Significance of the Point Park Committee,* April 18, 1946, was cited: "Your Committee desires to recommend that Bouquet's Redoubt (The Blockhouse), be left in its present location," and the action of the full Point Park Committee at its third meeting on the same date:

MOTION: THAT THE POINT PARK COMMITTEE OF THE ALLEGHENY CONFERENCE ON COMMUNITY DEVELOPMENT RECOMMENDS THAT IN THE PREPARATION OF OFFICIAL PLANS FOR A PARK AT THE POINT BOUQUET'S REDOUBT (THE BLOCKHOUSE) BE LEFT IN ITS PRESENT LOCATION. . . . MOTION APPROVED

The state explained that it must own the property for three reasons: It could not legally repair, rehabilitate, or maintain privately owned property; a corner of the DAR property overlapped the Monongahela bastion; and since the state owned all the other land in the park, it would not be proper for a private group to own a piece in the center. The state would agree, however, that after the transfer of the property the members of the DAR could manage and control the Blockhouse and sell souvenirs. The ladies, however, were adamant on the basic point of ownership.

On orders of Samuel S. Lewis, secretary of the Department of Forests and Waters, the state retreated again. Representatives of both sides met in the Blockhouse in May 1954. The meeting opened with a prayer. The state, "in recognition of the part the Society has played in conserving the Blockhouse property," offered to leave ownership, maintenance, and control of the Blockhouse with the Fort Pitt Society. It would, moreover, give the society the exclusive use, without charge, of a room in the bastion museum designated "Fort Pitt Society Headquarters," subject only to the requirement that the society "permit use of said room at reasonable times by other responsible parties" approved by the state. In return, the society was to permit certain physical changes, including demolition of the caretaker's lodge, replacement of the ginkgo trees, and transfer of ownership to the state of the land on which the lodge stood "without any cash consideration."

The ladies were still adamant. The Blockhouse, they said, needed twenty-four-hour attention, and if the caretaker's lodge was torn down, a new one should be built to replace it. If they agreed to use a room in the museum for their headquarters, it should be locked when they were not using it. They rejected any proposal to remove the trees they had planted. They were disturbed that there was to be no street running to their Blockhouse, as there had been before, and no parking space beside it—no one would walk the long distance through the park to see the Blockhouse. In the language of a lawyer's report on the meeting, "the conversations did not reach the state of agreement." The Point Park Committee gamely passed a resolution on May 17, 1954:

BE IT RESOLVED: THAT THE POINT PARK COMMITTEE EXPRESS, AND IT DOES HEREBY EXPRESS, ITS SINCERE APPRECIATION TO THE OFFICERS OF THE FORT PITT

The last certified eighteenth-century building in Pittsburgh was originally one of five redoubts built in 1764 by Colonel Henry Bouquet at strategic points outside the walls of the fort. This, the so-called Blockhouse, had not yet been built at the time of the Indians' six-week siege in Pontiac's War. (Clyde Hare)

The Blockhouse here stands at its original grade, some twelve feet below the level of the built-up industrial jungle around it. The long Pennsylvania Railroad warehouse and freight station, above, stretches off to the right. (Allegheny Conference)

SOCIETY OF THE DAUGHTERS OF THE AMERICAN REVOLU-
TION FOR THEIR AID, INTEREST, AND COOPERATION IN
THE DEVELOPMENT OF A PROPOSAL RELATING TO THE
BLOCKHOUSE PROPERTY AND IN CONFORMITY WITH THE
FINAL PLANS NOW BEING PREPARED.

The exchange of views ended; the impasse continued for the next six years.

Negotiations were revived with a meeting in December 1960. State and Park Committee representatives repeated their 1954 offer. They pointed out the enticing advantage of what they proposed: "With demolition of the caretaker's house and regrading and fencing, the Block-house would be given its original prominence, greater public attention, and more effectual protection. The caretaker could still perform his function in the prescribed hours without living there, as the building would be under the surveillance of park guards day and night." The ladies were not convinced.

Other meetings followed. State and Commit-tee people were dismayed to find a different group of women at each meeting, to whom the situation had to be explained from the begin-ning, and who were unaware of, and indiffer-ent to, commitments made by their predeces-sors. On December 5, 1960, February 14, 1961, and January 9, 1962, Van Buskirk raised the threat of condemnation by the right of eminent domain, though he and Secretary Goddard felt that David Lawrence, as mayor before 1959 and as governor afterward, would not permit it, or would permit condemnation of only the land that lay within the limits of the bastion museum. (The three men knew that the DAR could exploit a court case to its own advantage, and that the law's delay would run into years.) At a meeting on September 11, 1962, on being asked to cover ground he had covered many times before, Ralph Griswold announced angrily that he would never attend another meeting with DAR representatives (he never did), and he advised that the meetings should be ended.

Agreement was reached and a document—composed in 1953 by Theodore Hazlett and revised many times—was signed on June 25, 1963. The Fort Pitt Society retained ownership of the Blockhouse and of the land extending to the iron fence that enclosed it—a lot ninety by one hundred feet in size. It kept control over the operations of the Blockhouse, including the exclusive sale of Blockhouse souvenirs. It deeded over to the state the caretaker's lodge and the ninety-by-twenty-foot corridor on which it stood, for which it received $50,000 paid in trust to the society. The lodge was not to be demolished until the bastion museum was completed. If the society ever sold its property, it would have to sell to the state. The one ginkgo tree on the caretaker's lot was cut down; the others were to be left standing. (They are still standing.) The Blockhouse caretaker was given a desk in the museum and a window was built in the wall through which he might view his charge.

The president of the Fort Pitt Society was

quoted in the newspapers: "We are really delighted with the contract. You might call it a compromise, but we feel victorious. We plan to use the $50,000 to maintain the Blockhouse and do some additional landscaping." Brass markers were placed around the Blockhouse with the words "Not deeded."

Thirteen years later, on November 11, 1976, the Fort Pitt Society, the Blockhouse, and the latest Battle of the Blockhouse were the subject of a by-lined feature story on the women's page of the Pittsburgh *Post-Gazette*. It marked the birth of a new and probably undying legend:

The Blockhouse's latest flirtation with demolition was when plans were submitted to convert the land at the junction of the three rivers into a park, which meant the Blockhouse would have to be condemned.

Members of the DAR again went to bat for the endangered fort to preserve its legendary value according to Mrs. Schenley's intentions. And again the Blockhouse was saved for future generations.

Thus is error compounded and misinformation perpetuated.

"I was amazed," Charles Stotz says, "when I began the actual interior design of the museum and saw how very much space we had to work with." Visitors shared his amazement when the museum was dedicated in an outdoor ceremony on June 30, 1969, and opened to the public. (Part of the museum, showing a few temporary exhibits, had been open at intervals beginning on July 4, 1967.) Just beyond the turnstile they walked into a large hall named for William Pitt, whose bust looked down from a niche and whose coat of arms (specially prepared and authenticated by the College of Arms in London) appeared in one of seven mosaic panels in the floor. At the far end was a curved white wall approximately thirteen by fifty-six feet in size, where a painting, a mural on canvas, was to be placed. A round raised area sixteen feet across occupied the center of Memorial Hall. It held the principal feature of the museum: a large model of Fort Pitt, based on eighteenth-century military plans and records and showing in accurate detail the structure, soldiers, animals, outbuildings, river craft, and the whole area of the Point. The visitor picked up one of the battery of earphones, leaned comfortably on a wide, solid railing, and listened to a taped narration on the construction, history, and significance of the largest and most costly British stronghold on the western frontier. Lights flashed on and off at appropriate places on the model at appropriate times during the talk. (The model was built by Holiday Displays of Pittsburgh from scale drawings prepared by Stotz.)

Visitors could then turn left into an eighty-four-seat, sloping auditorium with a projection booth, where they were oriented on what they were about to see. They then walked through a chronological sequence of almost seventy separate exhibits, displays, dioramas, and scale models, imaginatively constructed using the

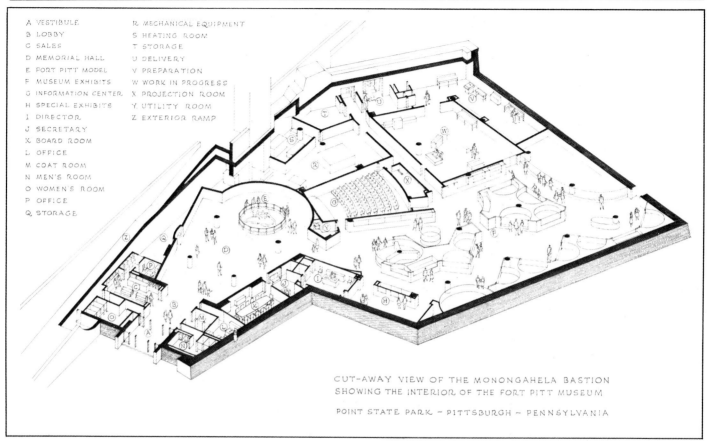

A VESTIBULE
B LOBBY
C SALES
D MEMORIAL HALL
E FORT PITT MODEL
F MUSEUM EXHIBITS
G INFORMATION CENTER
H SPECIAL EXHIBITS
I DIRECTOR
J SECRETARY
K BOARD ROOM
L OFFICE
M COAT ROOM
N MEN'S ROOM
O WOMEN'S ROOM
P OFFICE
Q STORAGE

R MECHANICAL EQUIPMENT
S HEATING ROOM
T STORAGE
U DELIVERY
V PREPARATION
W WORK IN PROGRESS
X PROJECTION ROOM
Y UTILITY ROOM
Z EXTERIOR RAMP

CUT-AWAY VIEW OF THE MONONGAHELA BASTION
SHOWING THE INTERIOR OF THE FORT PITT MUSEUM

POINT STATE PARK – PITTSBURGH – PENNSYLVANIA

A cutaway view of the Monongahela Bastion shows the interior plan of the Fort Pitt
Museum. (Charles M. Stotz)

A beautifully detailed scale model of Fort Pitt stands in the museum's William Penn Memorial Hall. Visitors pick up earphones and, guided by on-and-off lights, hear a description of the fort, its garrison, and its history in two wars. The well is sixteen feet across. The bust in the background is that of William Pitt, earl of Chatham. (Paul Russell)

latest museum techniques, that showed the history of the second half of the eighteenth century in elucidative, understandable, digestible segments—in Stotz's "picture book method." Each segment had a written explication in readable type; some had a push-button spoken commentary; a few had continuous rear slide projection. The series began with a theme exhibit: a case that showed individual life-size figures of an Indian warrior, a French soldier, and a British soldier, and displayed Stotz's much-quoted introductory statement on the exhibits:

From their seats of power in Paris and London two foreign nations contested for the land beyond the mountains in the New World.

The native owner of this land, the Indian, was now an ally, now an enemy, but always the tragic figure in the unequal struggle.

All three were victors in their time, all losers in the end.

The sequence of exhibits continued with the incursion of the French in 1749, George Washington at the Point in 1753, the French capture of the Point, Washington's surrender at Fort Necessity, Braddock's defeat, Forbes at the Point amid the charred ruins of Fort Duquesne, and Bouquet's victory at Bushy Run. Interspersed among these were animated maps; exhibits of tools, weapons, and furniture; and dioramas of frontier trades—printing, boatbuilding, glass-making, charcoal, iron-making, a gristmill.

The tour de force was a display of four life-size rooms. The first was a walk-in log cabin with an earth floor—a trading post complete with a trader, an Indian selling skins and furs, and authentic properties, including a stuffed mouse in a corner. This was followed by a very lifelike group of three soldiers passing the time in their six-bunk barracks room; another group at work in an underground artillery casemate; and a parlor of a typical upper-class, western Pennsylvania home as it might have appeared before 1800. There was no glass protecting these four rooms; the onlookers felt themselves a part of the scene, and two or three times a week someone would claim that he could actually *smell* the unwashed soldiers in the barracks.

In his work on the Fort Pitt Museum, Charles Stotz performed what may be a unique one-man accomplishment in the annals of American museums, at least since the time of Charles Willson Peale. He researched, designed, and supervised the construction of the building. He developed the rationale and story line of its exhibits. He designed the exhibits and the cases that held them. He wrote the text that accompanied each exhibit and in several instances recorded (anonymously) the text he had written. He then wrote a 120-page book, *Point of Empire,* on the museum.

"I built up the series of subjects and then wrote as condensed a narrative as I could manage on each of them, which then became

The trader's cabin is one of four lifelike habitat rooms in the museum. The figure at the right is a young spectator. (Pittsburgh *Press*)

the captions. I don't know of any more grueling problem than to condense history into caption form. Braddock's defeat in forty words. And I wanted to have the assurance that this material would not be lost. I was determined to have a complete published account of it, so that the original would be a matter of record. *Point of Empire* is really a book of captions and photographs or drawings of the exhibits they relate to. It was first published serially in the magazine of the Historical Society of Western Pennsylvania, which then published the parts as a book. The safest place to record anything is in a book. Once it's published in a cover, you have credibility and a permanent record."

The Fort Pitt Museum won critical acclaim and public favor from the start. A Pittsburgh *Press* reporter on opening day called the exhibits masterpieces, the boat-building diorama a monument to perfection, and the museum a historical jewel. Visitors came in large numbers—a thousand people on a summer Sunday afternoon and ten school groups on a spring day were not uncommon; attendance was lower during the winter, lowest in January and February. A volunteer support group, the Fort Pitt Museum Associates, organized itself to mount a program of entertainment, lectures, educational activities, and community involvement. Then in June 1972, disaster struck. Hurricane Agnes generated a flood that rose five feet in two hours and exceeded the esti-

mate of the highest possible water level. (The eight flood-control dams and reservoirs on the headwaters of Pittsburgh's rivers held the flood twelve feet below what it otherwise would have been. Without the dams, the flood would have been worse than the forty-six foot record flood stage of 1936.) Point Park and the floor of the museum lay under four feet of water. Because of concern for just this contingency, Stotz had designed the exhibit cases in such a way that they could be rolled out to the truck entrance, the backs opened, and the contents carried away. But as commonly happens with major floods, the warning came too late to obtain the necessary trucks, except for a few furnished by Carnegie Museum. There was no negligence or inefficiency on part of the museum staff.

Most of the artifacts, antiques, and documents were trucked or hand-carried away, but some were lost, and there was damage to the museum's floor, walls, roof, and heating and water systems. Repairs took two years and cost almost $150,000. The museum reopened on May 19, 1974.

The other misfortune that struck the museum in these years concerned the choice of an artist to paint the mural for the thirteen-by-fifty-six-foot curved wall in William Pitt Memorial Hall. The Park Committee considered four muralists and chose Harry Jackson, a forty-year-old sculptor and painter. Jackson had had a moderate success as an abstract artist in the

A devastating flood caused in June 1972 by Hurricane Agnes exceeded all expectations; it crested at 35.82 feet, 10 feet over flood stage, with 4 feet of water in the museum itself. Most possessions were saved, but damage cost almost $150,000.

1950s, but, in a reversal of the usual procedure, he then became a "cowboy artist" and turned to traditional, representational paintings and sculptures (*The Cowboy's Meditation, Ropin', The Range Burial*) in the style of Frederick Remington. With these, and with promotion by a prominent New York gallery, he was creating a small stir in the art world. In Pittsburgh in 1964 he agreed to paint a three-panel "heroic" mural titled *River, Road, and Point* for $60,000, delivery to be in the fall of 1967. The work was to be a gift from the Richard King Mellon Foundation to the state, as were the seven small mosaic panels Jackson was to make for the floor of the hall. Jackson was enthusiastic about the mural. "I am overjoyed at the prospect of this commission," he said. "It and I were absolutely made for each other."

In 1966 he came from his studio near Lucca, Italy, and installed the mosaics in colored tile: the coat of arms of William Pitt and representations of the Indian, the soldier, the missionary, the settler, the trader-trapper, and the riverman. In Pittsburgh again in May 1967, he showed his completed sketches for the mural to the Park Committee. Griswold was the one committee member who distrusted Jackson and had voted against giving him the commission, but he found his 1967 presentation "impressive and highly successful. Everyone was pleased with the historical accuracy, imaginative composition and skillful drawing and coloring."

On the strength of the sketches Jackson was paid the second of the three promised $20,000 installments. About this time he proceeded to set up a foundry in his studio near Lucca and employed a crew of casters to turn out his bronze sculptures in quantity at $10,000 to $15,000 each. In 1971 he exhibited twelve of his bronzes and nine drawings in the museum's special exhibition room and discussed the possibility of placing small bronzes for sale in the gift shop.

Years passed, and there was no mural. Griswold (and later Stotz and Hazlett) visited the artist in Italy. Griswold reported back: "I concluded that bronzes were his main interest and our mural was a second-string matter. I think he was afraid of doing the mural. His interest was in the west, and here he was required to do a prescribed historic subject in which he had no personal interest whatever. He had had one major success at a Smithsonian Institution show with the critics, and now he was afraid of what the critics would say about his museum mural."

The Allegheny Conference took five of Jackson's bronzes as collateral for his $40,000 obligation on the missing mural. A museum official says today that the piece is still in Italy, still only three-fourths finished. In September 1976, however, a United Press International article stated that the mural was completed, but "Jackson said he has changed his mind about the original plan of installing it in the Fort Pitt Museum in Pittsburgh because of the danger of flooding. Jackson said a public building on higher ground would be a more suitable place." (The panels, of course, could have been easily and quickly hand-carried to high ground on the threat of a flood.) Today the great curved wall in the Fort Pitt Museum serves as a backdrop for displays, and it holds a set of large, handsome paintings on the theme "The American Pioneer" by Nat Youngblood, Pittsburgh *Press* art director. They were given to the museum in 1976 by the *Press* as a Bicentennial present to the people of Pittsburgh.

The Park Committee and the Allegheny Conference had had an earlier misfire, though a less costly one, in attempting to bring sculptural beauty to the park. Van Buskirk appointed a subcommittee to consider the propriety of erecting a monumental statue in the park as a symbol of Pittsburgh. When the state declined to pay for a competition among sculptors, the subcommittee asked four museum directors to name outstanding sculptors qualified to produce such a work. They named fifteen. These were approached, and some responded. Carl Milles submitted a model: three dancing maidens in his incomparable style. William Zorach came to Pittsburgh to inspect the site. Ivan Mestrovic submitted a line of warriors pulling bows carved on soapstone. Jacob Lipschitz sent a square cake of white soap with some scratches on it. Heinz Warneke designed a rugged, striding, bare-chested pio-

neer. The subcommittee recommended that Warneke be given the commission.

Warneke was head of the department of sculpture at the Corcoran School of Art in Washington; he was an able sculptor noted for his good stone work and his ability to handle one of the most difficult of sculptural problems, that of producing pieces on a massive scale. His pioneer man, sixteen feet tall, of granite, was to stand on a nine-foot bronze base, backed by a soaring, twisting pylon fifty-one feet high. This was to be erected at the end of the long semicircular walk leading to the left side of the portal.

The subcommittee's recommendation was revealed and Warneke's model unveiled on December 6, 1960. Ralph Brem, having done some historical research for a *Press* column, observed, "Everytime somebody wants to put up a statue in Pittsburgh somebody else wants to put up an argument." He was right on this occasion. The artistic community and the press launched an attack on December 7; the statue was called, among other things, "pseudo-classic," "outmoded," "post-office art," "sentimental and obvious," "an eyesore," "unfortunate," "an abomination," and "Russian heroic." The newspapers were filled with indignant letters, most of them in opposition to the statue. The five hundred members of the Associated Artists passed a resolution of condemnation. Gordon Washburn, director of fine arts at Carnegie Institute, was *horribly* embarrassed and

Pioneer man, sixteen feet tall, standing on a nine-foot base under a soaring masonry pylon fifty-one feet high, was to have stood on the east or city side of the portal. Maurice K. Goddard, secretary of forests and waters, the state official in charge of building Point State Park, here examines the model of Heinz Warneke's statue. The project was killed by public protest and the newspaper appellation, "Russian heroic." (Pittsburgh *Post-Gazette*)

let it be known that *he* had not listed Warneke among *his* recommended sculptors. Warneke responded to the onslaught:

The monument will be able to be seen from all over the city. And it will be understood.

But if the people want me to kick an old automobile to pieces and weld it together and call it "Pittsburgh," I'll be only too happy to do it. It's very easy.

At a committee meeting on December 13, Van Buskirk, appalled at the public outcry, suggested that they ignore the whole matter in the hope that it would die a natural death. On July 25, 1962, the committee resolved "to postpone any further action on sculpture indefinitely." Charles Stotz says, "We just decided that sculpture was a potential source of trouble and, after all, not vital to the project. We were delighted to be free of sculpture." "It is obvious," Griswold wrote in his journal, "that the Warneke figure is dead. I am not sorry." The conference paid Warneke a $1200 fee from its private resources, and no more was heard for a while of sculpture in Point State Park.

15

A Tale of
Two Bridges

Point State Park was four-fifths completed in 1969, but in that year work virtually stopped. Everything had been done at the Point that could be done as long as the two old bridges remained standing. The last phase—the final landscaping, the opening up and leveling of the lower Point, the completion of the walks, the construction of the fountain—these had to wait until the old Point Bridge and the older Manchester Bridge were demolished.

The Park Committee struggled unsuccessfully through much of the 1960s to have the Point Bridge razed, but it ran head-on against a surprising new development. This was a movement that began as a small effort to save and use first the Point Bridge and later the Manchester Bridge, and then grew into a belated but vociferous attack on the whole park as conceived, designed, and carried out.

The Point Bridge, owned by Allegheny County, had been ready for demolition ten years earlier when the new Fort Pitt Bridge was opened a thousand feet up the Monongahela in June 1959. The old bridge was left standing, however, barricaded and empty, because of two complicated legal controversies. The first involved trolley tracks—the tracks on Point Bridge, some in the Triangle, and six miles of unused tracks in five West End communities. These communities opposed the planned change to buses until the Pittsburgh Railways Company agreed to dig up its rails and repave the street, or at least the right-of-way. The company wanted simply to abandon the rails without further obligation.

After eighteen months of disputatious delay on this issue, the Pennsylvania Public Utility Commission made a ruling. John Grove, secretary of the Park Committee, wrote in August 1961 to David Lawrence (now governor of the state), to Park Martin (now state secretary of Highways) and to other appropriate persons:

The Allegheny wharf was well under way in 1964. The height of the cut-off end of the Manchester Bridge, looming some thirty feet overhead, was one of many obstacles to its proposed use as a platform for a restaurant, hotel, library, art gallery, and shops. (John R. Shrader)

"The settlement of the dispute over the removal of the streetcar tracks in the Point and in the West End municipalities has paved the way for the . . . next phase in the Park's development— namely, the demolition of the Point Bridge." But by now the two majority members of the Board of County Commissioners were expressing reluctance to pay for removing the old bridge. They took bids in May 1962, threw out the low bid ($391,589) on a technicality, declared that they could find no record that their predecessors had promised to remove the bridge, and suggested a simple solution: Let the state do it.

Six years passed. Secretary Goddard pleaded with the commissioners to remove their bridge and in September 1968 threatened to divert state money from Point Park to other state projects. In the meantime, voices had been saying as early as 1962 that the old bridge should be saved, used, and fitted into the city's plan for a mass transit system. The bridge was narrow and single-deck, and the turns at the ends were almost right-angled. The district's leading automobile club called it an eyesore and a traffic hazard and called for its demolition. Traffic engineers pointed out that the reopening would cause more problems than it would solve. But the proposal was backed by some influential people as long as the bridge stood.

The state capitulated in August 1969: It agreed to assume the cost of removing the Point Bridge and its massive ramps (at a figure some $200,000 higher than the bid of 1962) in a trade-off for some county help on a projected state road at the County Airport.

The battle to save the Manchester Bridge was quite another story. Those who opposed its demolition were different from those who had tried and failed to save the Point Bridge. They were artists and architects, not politicians; they waged a fiercer fight; and the reasons they gave for their rescue operation had nothing to do with trolley tracks and buses, nor with the use of the bridge in a mass transit system, nor with the question of who would pay to remove it. This group wanted to save the bridge as an architectural treasure, as a valuable public facility, and to use it to contain buildings that they felt would draw people into the park. Since the Manchester Bridge was to be saved, they decided to save the Point Bridge as well. To do this they demanded that Point State Park be redesigned.

The Manchester Bridge, built in 1915, belonged to the city of Pittsburgh. From the first it had been understood that the state would pay to demolish it as soon as the Fort Duquesne Bridge was completed. The new bridge was built in 1963, but there were delays and disputes concerning its northern connections, and for six embarrassing years it stood idle and unused, known as the "Bridge to Nowhere." When the first traffic finally crossed it to the North Side on October 17, 1969, the city closed the Manchester Bridge and the state let a $2.6

million contract to Dravo Corporation to remove both old bridges and their ramps. Labor problems, however, delayed the work for fifteen months. It was in this period that the movement to save both bridges reached its peak.

The first proposal to preserve the Manchester Bridge had surfaced on April 6, 1967, when six architects, sculptors, and painters calling themselves Group STL ("Stop, Think, Look"), some of them connected with Carnegie-Mellon University, issued a manifesto in a tabloid newspaper named *The Point*. In it they called for "a moratorium on present plans" for the park, objected to "urban space that is dead," opposed a fountain at the Point as "an inadequate symbol," and prescribed, among other things, that the two old bridges be converted into platforms holding pedestrian walkways and a commercial and cultural center. Pittsburgh newspapers and broadcasters welcomed a bit of high-level intellectual controversy in a continuing story where there had been none before, and the protesters were given good news coverage.

Other voices joined the campaign of the STL. A Pittsburgh architect, one who "has lectured on architecture around the world," and his partner, a Pittsburgh business consultant, produced a somewhat more specific plan. They looked on the two old bridges as "abandoned facilities offering great potential." On the Point Bridge they wished to see a 350-room motel and an industrial museum. On the Manchester Bridge they would place a public library, an art gallery, a restaurant, and a shopping mall. They would link the Duquesne Incline, the Point Bridge, the Manchester Bridge, the Park, Three Rivers Stadium, and Allegheny Center on the North Side with what they called a "people mover"—a kind of monorail or moving sidewalk attached to the sides (or the bottoms or perhaps the tops) of the bridges. The monorail would also run in two lines from the tip of the Point to the eastern end of the park, presumably across the greensward and through the Gateway Portal. There would be a heliport under the south end of the Point Bridge and a marina at the park end, with elevator connections to the hotel and the museum. The architect said the bridges could support the weight of the buildings "with some minor repairs." The project, he added, should be privately financed by stock sales to the public. When asked to estimate the possible cost of such an undertaking, he replied, "If you have the idea and the potential, the money is incidental."

A young man engaged in graduate research in housing and transportation at Carnegie-Mellon University entered the fray in November 1969 and was given a feature story in one of the dailies, with his picture. He called for an international architectural competition for plans to convert the Manchester Bridge into a modern American Ponte Vecchio. He felt sure that any technical difficulties could be overcome. To help the project, he intended to get a court injunction to prevent demolition of the bridges.

Donald Miller, art critic of the *Post-Gazette*, wrote of "the surprising range of people" who supported the young graduate researcher's ideas, and he named the president of Carnegie Institute, the director of the Museum of Art, the chairman of the department of architecture at Carnegie-Mellon University, the director of the American Wind Symphony (which performed at the park), the member of congress from the Twenty-seventh Pennsylvania District, and Local 1271 of the United Steel Workers of America, whose members hoped to be able to walk or ride across the bridges from the South Side to Three Rivers Stadium. A Pennsylvania legislator introduced a resolution in the house to save the bridges. The director of research of the Pittsburgh History and Landmarks Foundation lamented that the Manchester Bridge "could have been given a new lease on life had there been anyone around with enough imagination or good sense to use it properly." The Stadium Authority opposed the idea, but the graduate researcher announced, "I expect to win the Authority's full support . . . as soon as they grasp the broader aspects of the problem."

The drive to save the bridges was inevitably broadened to include an attack on the concept and design of the park itself. The criticism was neither gentle nor polite. Group STL declared that it was acting in desperation, "because we firmly believe that a life-time of dreams are being made a mockery of by allowing Point State Park to be finished as an anticlimactic whimper, an insipid monument to a lost opportunity. . . . To presume to build fake forts and pointless worn-out symbols, such as the talked-about fountain, is ludicrous." STL called for a world sculpture exposition to be held in the park every three years, without specifying who was to put up the money. The young graduate researcher called the park "a sterile cemetery to the past" and declared that the city had made a mistake in giving the land to the state in the first place. The executive director of the Pittsburgh Council for the Arts was convinced that the park without the bridges would appeal primarily to tourists, and that "a more meaningful concept would be people participation—all people." The architect who had lectured around the world declared on the city's leading talk show that no successful park had ever been built with a dead end.* An industrialist wrote, "A fountain that would lie idle for at least seven months in the year . . . should have no part in this historic shrine, as it would be both incongruous and inane."

A number of the complainants pounded hard on one theme: The idea of open space and a vista to the west may have been valid in 1945, when it was adopted, but it was now obsolete.

*The Boboli Gardens in Florence and Villa d'Este in Tivoli, near Rome, among others, are "dead end" parks, entered and left by a single entrance.

One said: "The 1945 plan . . . fails to recognize the dramatic environmental changes in these 25 years and to adapt to today." Another: "A person is legally dead after seven years, but the Point plans have been dying for over twenty. The whole impact of urban planning has changed in that time. The Point plans aren't good enough. They are dull and inadequate. We must rethink for the future."

The temper of the time was changing, and criticism of the park design in the 1960s, whether right or wrong, was to be expected. It was given impetus by widespread public dissatisfaction with three major developments elsewhere in the city. These were the Allegheny Center project on the North Side, the East Liberty renewal, and the Lower Hill District development. In the Hill, houses had been leveled and the inhabitants dispersed, replaced by tall buildings and a Civic Arena, the five-acre retractable dome of which was called by Roy Lubove, in *Twentieth Century Pittsburgh*, "a disaster."

The Point Park committeemen winced and suffered under the attacks on their work. They suffered the more because they had carried on an intelligent, continuing program of informing and educating the public, and because the attacks came, unexpectedly, long after the plans had been approved, after many changes and revisions, by all parties concerned, and only when the park was nearly completed. Despite an ambitious and sustained educational effort by the Park Committee, Pittsburghers sometimes showed a surprising lack of knowledge about what was being done at the Point. Proposals they made in the 1960s and early 1970s seemed to indicate that they thought the work had just started, with not much settled and less accomplished. Park committeemen were jolted when friends and acquaintances said cheerfully, "Let me tell you what I think you should do about the park," or, "You don't mean to say you're going to put a fountain down there!"

Such a lack of knowledge was to be expected among the general public on a project that had extended over two decades, with long waits between completed contracts. But the committeemen were surprised to find a lack of hard factual information among the professionals who in 1967 began to criticize their work. These critics seemed to assume that the Park Committee had the resources, power, and authority to impose any decision or change they wished or were told to make, and to do so without regard to the views of a dozen other concerned federal, state, and city bodies. Several architects were perhaps unaware that three other architects and three landscape architects had been and were legally under contract to complete the design and construction of the park. These critics seemed also not to know the true condition of the Manchester Bridge. They ignored or were unaware of one crucially important fact: that the permit issued by the secretary of the army for the construction of the new Fort Pitt Bridge, dated September 12, 1958, provided that within one year after it was opened to traffic, the old Manchester Bridge and its pier in the middle of the Allegheny had to be removed, as it was a navigation hazard in obstructing river traffic.

For the most part, the committeemen suffered in silence. They wrote out lengthy rebuttals to the charges and sent them to each other, but they tried to follow a policy of avoiding controversy and of not making a public response. When Oliver Kaufmann, a Conference member, wrote to Van Buskirk in November 1968 proposing drastic changes in the design of the park, Van Buskirk answered in a private letter: "It is the unanimous opinion of the Point Park Committee of the Allegheny Conference that the design plan for Point State Park is final and definitive and that any scheme to change or alter the plan materially in any way would be disastrous.

"As you will recall, the Point Park Committee approved the final plan only after considerable study by urban designers and engineers. It was then adopted by the Commonwealth of Pennsylvania as the official plan.

"The approved plan has been carried to the point where four-fifths of the park has been completed and funds to finish the project have now been appropriated by the Commonwealth in accordance with the plan."

The executive committee of the Pittsburgh chapter of the American Institute of Architects gave support to the conference on January 28, 1970, when it reaffirmed its approval of the design concept. The Park Committee prepared several fact sheets for the information of "those who have sought to save the old bridges" and sent them to Secretary Goddard, but these were not used or released to the public. They made these points:

• that in none of the proposals to save and use the bridges was any mention made of the practical problems of heating, plumbing, lighting, and sewage services, nor of meeting fire and safety codes of the city and state.

• that except for the thoroughly impractical monorail, there was no explanation of how people were to get to and from the bridge ends, especially at night, and more especially in winter, nor of how they were to be lifted and lowered some thirty feet to and from the level of the Manchester Bridge in the park.

• that neither bridge was a distinguished structure of its kind. The buildings proposed to be put on the bridges would have to be totally enclosed against the weather, which would conceal the tracery of the truss and arch members, thus robbing the bridges of what little aesthetic appeal they had.

• that the original design for the park had been continuously revised and refined since 1945 "to produce a park worthy of a modern city."

• that these designs had periodically been reviewed and approved by eleven federal, state, and city authorities (the names listed).

190

▪ that the favorable public response to the design of the park and the extensive use of the park since its substantial completion (1,059,494 visitors in 1969)—both of these points ignored by the critics—"has justified the conception of a beautiful open space, so rare in modern cities."

Actually, there was never at any time a real danger that Point Park could be drastically redesigned, and the park committeemen knew this. "But it was frustrating," Stotz says. "In a conversation one day, Van and I wondered if we would live to see the park completed. Poor Van never made it." But they both knew that it would be completed, and completed as planned.

For one thing, the state owned and was building the park, and the two men in charge, Governor Lawrence and Secretary Goddard, understood what was being done and would resist any effort to change direction. In 1967, at the time of the first STL blast, Goddard made a rare public statement in defense of the park. "It is," he said, "a magnificent plan for a park. What could be better than a fountain? The plans for the park are an old decision. It is not designed to be an art center. I see no reason to change it now."

For another, the Point Park architects knew that the rusting Manchester Bridge was in extremely bad condition and that putting it into shape to hold up a shopping center, a public library, an art gallery, and a restaurant would be prohibitively expensive. As a matter of fact,

the bridge turned out to be in even worse condition than they had thought. Louis R. Fosner, architect in the firm of Stotz, Hess, MacLachlan and Fosner, tells of a visit to the bridge on the day the demolition started. "I was called down, and believe me, I looked at the structure itself, the rusted out structural members, and it was frightening. There was no life left in the bridge. It was not safe to *walk* across, let alone drive across it, or build a city on it."

The commitment to the Corps of Engineers to raze the Manchester Bridge and clear the channel, moreover, was irrevocable, short of an act of Congress. The pier in the middle of the Allegheny had been like a bone in the engineers' throat. Now the piers of the old and the new bridge were not in line, and thus there was an additional navigational hazard. Manchester Bridge and its pier had to go.

A fourth factor favoring the committee and its park as planned was the support from the press. Having given publicity and pictures to the opposition, the newspapers now analyzed their ideas and dismissed them as wrong and bad. Ralph Brem, managing editor of the *Press*, wrote on the STL program in October 1967:

Talk of the Manchester Bridge as a walkway to the Stadium is simply nonsense. A look at the Stadium site plan will show homeplate just about where the Manchester Bridge touches down on the north bank of the Allegheny River. . . .

As for the Point Bridge, once the ground beneath it is cut down for beautifying the tip of the

Golden Triangle, the old span wouldn't have a pier to stand on.

And even if the Point Bridge stayed, it would take a tremendous flight of stairs to fit it to the park level.

Thus the bridges should go if the tip itself is to become the focal point it deserves.

And in a second article the next day:

As artists the group should know what the change of one major element can mean to any overall picture, especially when the canvas is four-fifths complete. . . . Any carpetbagging city planner or artist can come through here and look down his nose at what has been done, forgetting that much of it was done before anyone else in the nation even dared to try.

The *Post-Gazette* delivered the coup de grace with an editorial on November 4, 1969:

It is incredible that at this late date serious attention should be given to johnny-come-lately schemes for preservation and commercializing the Manchester Bridge and thereby destroying the park's noble concept. We simply cannot believe that responsible public officials would allow such a thing to happen.

It was known all along that the old bridges had to go. That stage in the park construction has been reached and contracts for their demolition have been let. If there is any regret over the removal of these bridges, it involves only the delay which makes it costlier to take them down now than had it been done earlier.

The sooner the old bridges are down and Point Park is completed, the better. We have waited more than long enough for that welcome day when we can enjoy an unimpeded view of that monumental sweep down the river that greeted the eyes of this area's first visitors.

The park's planners and architects, finally, were fortified in their conviction that their concept was the progressive one—that their park design, with trees and grass, with landscaped open space and a sweeping vista, and with physical contact with the rivers, was quite in tune with "the dramatic environmental changes" and would be welcomed by the generations to come.

Work on removing the bridge approaches and ramps began early in November 1969, even while the controversy was continuing. A forty-six-man crew began demolition of the bridges themselves the following April. The single-span Point Bridge was first. It was dismantled by the reverse cantilever method, the sections being removed piece by piece in steps reversing those used in its construction. In September the crew planted RDX explosive charges under the stripped-down south span of the Manchester Bridge and dropped it into the river. When the skeletal structure had been hoisted by derrick, cut apart and removed, the other span was blown and the center pier was taken away.

On April 22, 1970, Ralph Griswold wrote in his diary: "They have actually started demolishing the Point bridges. This is one of the happiest days in my life."

The Manchester Bridge came down at last in September 1970. After the deck, railing, and fittings had been removed, the two spans were blown up three weeks apart in order to keep a river channel clear. Each span was then hoisted by a floating crane, cut apart by torches, and carried away in barges for scrap iron. The stone pier was dismantled to a depth nineteen feet below the river surface. (Allegheny Conference)

The barren apex of the Point, the foundation of its river wall and wharf in place, the old bridges gone, is now clear for the last major element of the park, the fountain. (Pittsburgh *Post-Gazette*)

On July 14 he and his wife Dorothy came to Pittsburgh on their fiftieth wedding anniversary. He wrote: "Breakfast in our room overlooking the park. Tears filled my eyes as I looked down on the park with old bridges half gone. Even now you can visualize the sweeping view of the rivers."

One week later the American Institute of Steel Construction named Fort Duquesne Bridge as one of the most beautiful bridges opened to traffic in 1969. The jurors called it "an imaginative solution to a complicated and difficult design problem." The designers, they said, "have used considerable ingenuity to create a structure that, despite its massiveness, projects a light and airy appearance."

16

The Monumental
Column

When Ralph Griswold and Charles Stotz made their first design of Point Park in 1945, they began with a sketch of a fountain. Now, in March 1972, with the old bridges and their ramps finally cleared away, work started on the last project to be built, the last thing needed to complete the park: the fountain.

The first sketch showed the fountain as the focal point of the park, three streams meeting in the middle from a triangular position, representing the confluence of the rivers. "When Mike Rapuano saw it," Griswold recalls, "he said, 'That's a good idea, but I think we want more dignity than that. Let's make it round instead of triangular, and one big squirt instead of three small ones.' So we redesigned it that way. We never conceived it as an ornamental fountain. In fact, we never called it a fountain, but rather, a monumental column, which is exactly what it is.

"The original idea," Griswold continues, "was to pump water directly out of the rivers at the Point and literally stand it on end as a dramatization of the rivers' dynamic influence on the history of the city. But engineers have the habit of taking the romance out of such ideas, and for mechanical and sanitary reasons they ruled that the water would have to have a treatment plant. So we made a compromise and decided to use already filtered city water—to catch it in a basin when it fell and recirculate it over and over again. That's why we designed the basin. It was ridiculed as a superfluous 'reflecting pool,' but that criticism was pointless. How can a pool reflect anything when its surface is being constantly agitated by water falling back down on it?"

Other critics charged that it was illogical and unimaginative to create a fountain at the confluence of existing bodies of water. In response, Griswold and Stotz cited the unchallenged success of the great fountain in Lake Geneva, where, rising from the surface of the water several hundred feet from the shore line, it had attracted admirers for many years. Another criticism frequently expressed, notably in letters to the editor, was that the strong wind at the Point would drench everyone near the fountain, or in the park, or in the Golden Triangle, with spray. Says Griswold, "I checked the wind velocity at the Point regularly during two summers, and I was amazed to find that it was so low that on most days people would be able to stand fairly close to a fountain, even at full height, without getting wet. Of course, we always intended to use a control and an automatic override system to adjust the height of the column to the force of the wind."

"We decided on a single spout," Charles Stotz says, "because of the high scale of the Point area. With thirty-six acres, the broad rivers, the mountains, we had to make something large enough to hold that scale. The fountain had to be big—an aquatic symbol commensurate in size with the significance of the rivers in the history of the nation."

Griswold continues the story: "Actually, in the scale we drew it, we wanted the fountain to be 150 feet, to fit the scale of the round pool, which was 200 feet in diameter. That's just a little under one acre. If you took the square, it would be an acre. The question was, could we physically make a column of water 150 feet high? We got the opinion of hydraulic engineers in New York, and they said, 'No, it cannot be higher than seventy-five feet.'

"In the meantime I went to Longwood Gardens, the du Pont establishment at Winterthur, Delaware, and when I saw that fountain going up, it looked to me like more than 75 feet. I went to the operator and I asked, 'How high is that?' He said, 'That's about 125 feet, but we can make it go higher.'

"Well, I went back to Van Buskirk and I said, 'This information about not being able to go over 75 feet from those consultants in New York, it's b—— s——. I wish you would go to see the fountain at Longwood Gardens.' So we organized a tour: Van Buskirk, Park Martin, Mike Rapuano, Charlie Stotz, George Ketchum, and I, and the engineering consultant from New York. This was on July 29, 1953. We made an appointment with du Pont's staff. We all met at Wilmington and were the guests at dinner that evening of the New York consultant. There was a theatrical performance after dinner on that water stage, Sigmund Romberg's *The New Moon*, and then the fountain display. We went over to the control room for the fountain, and Pierre du Pont joined us there.

"They played the fountain like an organ, with all kinds of combinations of colors. When they turned on the big jet, everybody gasped with its beauty. I spoke to the operator. [Griswold imitated the drawl of a rustic hayseed.] 'How high is that fountain?' The operator said 'That's only 125 feet, but if you push this button, it goes up to 150.' And zoom! up she went to 150 feet. The consultant had an embarrassed look on his face. [Laughter.] I said, 'Who designed this fountain for you?' There was a kind of hush for a moment, and then the operator said, 'Mr. du Pont did it.' [Laughter.] Well, that was settled from then on—no more nonsense about 75 feet. It was to be at least 150. That was set as the goal.

"Our engineers still wanted proof that it could be done, so we conducted an experiment with the help of the Pittsburgh Fire Department. One day in April 1954 they showed up on the Monongahela wharf at the foot of Wood Street with their hoses, pumpers, different sizes of nozzles, the fire boat, and gauges to measure pressure. We had an engineer there with an instrument to measure the height. People gathered around to watch. They didn't know what was going on, but they gathered. We reached one hundred feet."

After the plans for the 150-foot fountain had been drawn and approved, Park Martin made a new proposal: Why not manufacture artificial ice in the basin and use it for an all-weather skating rink, from September to May? The idea was discussed. Opponents cited three objections. The basin was certainly large enough for skating, but the winter wind at the Point was so strong that it might blow the skaters right off the rink. A structure would have to be built nearby where visitors could change their skates and warm themselves. And machinery to freeze the water would have to be installed, housed,

and serviced. Despite these objections, skating was approved, and at considerable expense the fountain was redesigned with equipment for artificial refrigeration. A temporary building was designed for warmth and changing skates—one that would be put up in the autumn and removed each spring.

Enthusiasm for having a skating rink at the Point died when the state totaled the cost estimates—the high cost of the freezing equipment and of maintaining it and the shelter. At the sixteenth meeting of the Point Park Committee, on November 19, 1963, the members, on the urging of the state, reconsidered and rescinded the decision to have artificial refrigeration and ice skating at the Point. The minute reads simply, "It was originally thought a good idea to have outdoor skating. . . . Now with skating facilities in North and South Parks and the Civic Arena, it seems inappropriate to have these facilities at the Point also." The blueprints were redrawn again.

The "peacock tails" around the base of the fountain, Griswold says, were Van Buskirk's idea. He was also very strong for a whole gamut of colors—red, blue, green, purple—and so a group made another trip to Longwood Gardens to study what they were doing with color. Louis R. Fosner, who was to succeed his partner, Charles Stotz, as designer and chief architect of the fountain, describes the trip. "Longwood Gardens made us realize we should only use white and amber light. The other colors dissipate at a certain height, and you don't get much of an effect. Certainly they would not be effective in a 150-foot column. We saw at the Gardens that there was no response from the audience on the reds and blues, but the minute the white and the gold came on, they ohhh'd and ahhh'd. There's something exciting about the gold and the brightness of the white. If you play the reds and blues, you have to have something like a 'dancing waters' program. We never intended anything of that nature. There is a magnificence about a tall column of water in its total height and power, and you don't make that amount of water dance." Griswold says, "Van held out for a rainbow of colors, but at the next committee meeting Park Martin voted for amber and white, and that's the way it was built."

Another major change was made in the source of the water that fed the fountain. Since 1893, office buildings in the Golden Triangle had tapped pure artesian well water for their drinking fountains and later for air-conditioning machinery. Someone asked the question: Was there perhaps enough of that water to supply the park fountain? Geological experts were called in. Their answers were encouraging.

They told of a great underground "river" that flows under the Golden Triangle, generally on the same course as the Allegheny and the Ohio rivers, starting above Warren and surfacing near Beaver, where rock ledges force it into visible streams. It runs in a channel formed by the Wisconsin Glacial Flow, which was an enormous sheet of ice that some seventy thousand years ago pushed southward over the northern United States. It filled the river valleys of southwestern Pennsylvania with gravel deposits as deep as three hundred feet, and in so doing it reversed the flow of rivers north of Kentucky, including the Allegheny, that had flowed north into the Great Lakes, turning them southward to empty instead into the Mississippi River system. When the glacier receded, the Pittsburgh area was exposed as a flat plain at the approximate level of its highest present terraces. Erosion and water courses then cut away the soil, sand, and gravel to form today's valleys and rivers. (Allegheny County produces more hard gravel and sharp sands than any other county in the United States.) The valleys and the rivers, however, did not cut all the way down through the gravel deposits to reach the bed of the Wisconsin glacier. A drift of gravel from fifteen to thirty-five feet thick remained in place and uncovered, its width in Allegheny County extending from a half-mile to more than a mile. It is through this gravel that "Pittsburgh's Fourth River" runs. Where the Allegheny or the Ohio flows directly above it, the two streams are kept apart by a layer of clay—that is, by the seal of silt and washed clay that forms the bed of the surface stream. The underground river flows through the gravel deposit at the rate of from five to six feet a day. Its purity, temperature and chemical content bear no relationship to that of the surface rivers. It does not increase in volume or rate of flow in time of heavy rains.

Lou Fosner says, "We were told that our best chance of hitting water was to drill on the Allegheny side of the park, where we would strike the underground river at 125 to 150 feet. Well, we committed a blunder, one of those mistakes that make you look like a genius. We sank a test well on the wrong side, the Monongahela side, and we hit water on the first shot at 57 feet.

"It was wonderful water. We ran a twenty-four-hour test, and we got 700 gallons a minute, more than a million gallons a day, which is phenomenal. Self-flowing, and as far as we could tell, forever. A constant year-around temperature of fifty to fifty-two degrees. As pure as anyone could ask for. No suspended matter, no need for filtration treatment, no chemicals in the water, no corrosion in the system, no deposits on the pipes, no packing around the joints on your machinery."

After the fifty-seven-foot well was drilled and a flow rate established, a cylindrical carbon steel casing twenty-six inches in diameter was lowered to contain the walls of the well. A 100,000-gallon reservoir was built to receive this water, and the pump house was built on top of the reservoir. The water was vacuum-suctioned from the reservoir to the three 250-horsepower pumps, then to the hub of the fountain through a three-foot diameter pump. The entire system holds more than one million gallons.

The normal construction method for the hub of the fountain and basin would have been to lay down a spread footing solid enough to hold the weight of the structure and then to build on top of that. The engineering for the Point fountain however, was quite different. "Our problem," Fosner says, "was not sinking, but rising. We knew we would have some positive upward pressure from our glacial flow, and that the pressure would be much stronger when the rivers were at flood stage. We had to tie the fountain down, so that it and the 200-foot diameter basin would not pop up and start floating down the Ohio like a giant saucer. So we put in slip piles. These were large-chamber steel pipes, caissons driven down sixty feet, 130 of them. When they were in place we filled them with concrete. Then we fastened the fountain and the basin to them by a ring of reinforced concrete, which forms the floor of the fountain. We are also able, when there is a flood condition, to fill a tunnel with water to provide additional weight and anchorage for holding the whole structure in place."

The pump house and the operating machinery were originally to have been placed underground, below river level, in a water-tight structure. But after the serious flood in the summer of 1972, the state ordered the pump house to be placed above ground. Once more the working drawings were revised. They had called for two comfort stations, one on each side of the park, each built with a low profile so as

This is the hub, the motive power, of the fountain: three 250-horsepower pumps for the monumental column, three 75-horsepower pumps for smaller jets. Workmen are here cleaning the nozzles. (Andy Starnes, Pittsburgh *Press*)

not to obstruct the view. These were consolidated into one station on the Allegheny side, and a pump building of the same exterior design was erected in the vacated space on the Monongahela side. Fosner says, "The building is absolutely waterproof in flood time. It is built like a submarine. We have an underground view window. We have doors built like submarine bulkheads. The whole pump building, with all the working machinery, is sealed off from flood water. The Point would have to be inundated twenty-four feet above the level of the window before there would be any seepage into the pump room. The only possible damage to the fountain and its components would be from the physical impact of something like a runaway barge. There's no way, of course, we could protect ourselves from that sort of thing."

The fountain was completed and ready for a test run in June 1974. It cost $1 million— one-third of the work done at the apex of the park. (The total cost of the park, exclusive of highway connections, was about $17 million.) The shallow ornamental basin of the fountain is 200 feet in diameter, with a rim of Indiana limestone and an immense floor of river pebbles set in a fish-scale pattern like that of the pool in the portal. The hub of the fountain, a 22-foot bronze casting with twelve nozzles, weighs nine tons.

The fountain was operated manually in the test, and it worked perfectly. Three 250-horsepower water pumps shot a stream 150 feet straight up, one of the three filling out the center of a column that measured five feet in diameter and weighed seventy-four tons. Three smaller pumps created a low-level play of peacock tails. It was a hot, windless day, and the assembled spectators commented on the cooling effect of the fountain over a large area. The water flowed as planned in a closed-loop system back to the reservoir, ready for recirculation; relatively little make-up water was needed to replace that lost in aeration.

Compressed Air Magazine, which had a reporter present, described the scene in language not commonly found in technical journals: The fountain "is a striking moving monument of enchanting beauty."

Lou Fosner says of the project on which he worked for much of twenty years: "Success is normally measured in public acceptance, and by this standard the fountain was a success—the public accepted it immediately, from the day of that first test run. Once it started up, people had a better understanding of what we were trying to accomplish with the open-space concept in an in-town park. The fountain went a long way toward eliminating any desire to fill the park with monuments, statues, sculpture—objects that would make it look like a graveyard.

"We've had requests from a number of newspapers to hold an international contest for an altitude record. That sounds undignified, and it will probably never happen—but if it did, I think that under the right conditions we could win it. We've already reached 320 feet without any problem. The fountain was never intended for that, of course, and aesthetically it's designed for 150 feet. But we have the capability. We operate now under normal conditions as high as 200 feet plus, when the wind has velocity of less than four miles an hour.

"I've never seen anything to match the number and variety of comments and questions on how the fountain works and what it does. Everybody has his own theories, opinions, and statistics. Well, that shows they're thinking, and that's fine. There are a good many misconceptions about the fountain, but we have always felt the public is entitled to its own ideas on what it does and can do. We never interfere and tell them they're wrong. Some people think the underground river is a huge cavern with a rushing stream. As far as I am concerned, if they're using their imagination a bit, why should I contradict them? I would hate to disillusion them.

"A number of people always assured us that as soon as a big convention hit town, they would have fun by filling the fountain with bubble bath and detergent. I hated to tell them, when I had to, that it would require about five hundred 55-gallon drums to make any impression in that volume of water.

"Everyone who writes about the fountain says it is operated by a computer. Well, we have a Selsin anemometer, a wind gauge, on top of the pump house, and we send the reading on wind velocity down to our console, and when the wind kicks up, it automatically lowers the height of the column. The console includes dimmer equipment, such as you find on a dimmer board in any theater. The only thing automatic about it is that we have a magnetic tape programmed for what we want the fountain to do. For example, we have a day cycle on the tape and a night cycle. But there's no such thing as a computer down there.

"A reporter from one of the papers told me the fountain was operated by a computer. I asked him where he had heard that. He said that everyone knew it, and he asked me to describe how the computer worked. I explained that there was no computer and told him about the console. He said, 'Mr. Fosner, to you it's a console; to me it's a computer.' And that's the way it appeared. [Laughter.] It's a much better story with a computer.

"My only disappointment in the fountain is that it has been operating on a schedule from 10 A.M. to 10 P.M. and not continuously. I've heard complaints from people who say, 'I come across the bridge at nine o'clock every morning and I don't see the fountain. What's the matter with it?'

"This city doesn't shut down at 10 P.M. We don't turn off the advertising signs at 10 P.M. I think the people would like to see the fountain in operation at one o'clock from Mount Oliver or the North Hills.

"Actually, the energy costs are much less per

One of the largest man-made geysers in the world rises for the first time against the illuminated Three Rivers Stadium on July 23, 1974. On a calm day, 6,000 gallons a minute are driven 150 feet or more straight up. Pure water is taken from Pittsburgh's "fourth river," which flows 54 feet underground. (Thomas E. Morgan, Advertising & Public Relations)

hour, when it runs continuously. One reason for this is that the first fifteen minutes—the start-up—takes seven times as much power as when the fountain is in regular operation. Another reason is that we have installed a capacitor, which takes the excess surge of electricity and stores it in a bank instead of wasting it. Then it is sent back for use as required, without going through the meter again. Today, in the fall of 1978, it is costing $15 an hour to operate the fountain twelve hours a day—a total of $180. But the one start-up at 10 A.M. costs $1200, making a total of $1380. Continuous twenty-four-hour operation would always cost $15 an hour after the initial start-up, without the daily demand charge. To that we would have to add the cost of additional manpower for supervision.*

"Can the state afford round-the-clock operation? I don't think the decision should be made solely on the basis of how much it costs. We don't support the arts that way, or other features that make Pittsburgh an attractive city. But if cost was the only consideration, I do think the additional people attracted to Penn-

*During the summer of 1980 the schedule was extended, and the fountain operated from 10 A.M. to midnight.

sylvania to see one of the fine sights of America would more than pay the added cost.

"I believe that Pittsburgh and Pennsylvania are not making full use of one of their most valuable assets. The fountain is—or could be—widely recognized as one of the greatest landmarks of any city in the world. Possibly greater than the St. Louis arch, the Seattle tower, the San Francisco Bay bridge or the Top of the Mark. I've seen the famous fountain at Geneva that attracts people from all over the world, and compared to ours it's absolutely sexless. Ours has life, with its constantly changing pattern of water seen close up. It excites everyone.

"We have at the Point a feature that could be as famous as any of those. Restaurants on Mount Washington could be world-famous for one of the most dramatic views anywhere, but just when the dessert is served, the lights go out at the Point. I think we're not properly exploiting the fountain as the focal point of the city of Pittsburgh, as one of the great sights of Pennsylvania, and as an American landmark. If we did, more people would come to see it. But to accomplish this, we must operate the fountain continuously from early spring to late fall—yes, even all year long. Winter should not be a deterrent."

17

The Planting of
the Point

To a naturalist, a nurseryman, and a landscape architect, Point State Park is a kind of historic arboretum—an example of authentic flora of the colonial period. It was also a difficult design problem. Here were thirty-six acres that had lately been an asphalt jungle with no significant natural growth, none of it as much as fifty years old, and almost no topsoil. The area was to be stripped bare and regraded to a new level. It was to be planted with trees, shrubs, and flowers suitable for a public park, but solely with botanical species that were present or might have been present in 1753. There were few records of the flora in western Pennsylvania in the colonial period. The park was bisected by an elevated high-speed highway 160 feet across, which had to be screened in part and muffled by the planting. The landscaping was to leave a clear, open vista the full length of the park to the Ohio River. It had also to follow specifications set forth in a General State Authority

contract that was almost an inch thick, calling for 117,170 plants that ranged from large, scarce specimen trees to small wildflowers. Finally, the work was to be done in stages, over a period of several decades.

The landscape architects began by consulting the one great authority on the plant ecology of western Pennsylvania, Dr. O. E. Jennings, director emeritus of Carnegie Museum and author of *Wildflowers of Western Pennsylvania*. Margaret Winters, a member of the Griswold firm, spent hours with Dr. Jennings drawing up a list of plants that were both suitable to the park design and historically correct.

A preliminary planting was done in 1953, before the entire park was cleared for final construction. It consisted of some two hundred trees, including thirty-eight sugar maples, forty flowering dogwoods, seventy-eight hawthorns, one American beech, several honey locusts, eight hemlocks, and three American elms. (The elms later became infected with Dutch elm blight and had to be replaced by honey locusts.) Large trees with good heads were planted for the immediate effect they produced. Specifications called for the beech to be from six to eight inches in diameter and between twenty and twenty-five feet tall; the elms were to be from eight to ten inches in diameter and thirty to forty feet tall. The other trees were from two to three inches in diameter and between eight and ten feet tall.*

The first major problem lay in finding trees that would meet the specifications. Julian Whitener, garden editor of the Pittsburgh *Press,* wrote about this search in 1965:

Teams of tree hunters visited nurseries and tree farms, spotting and marking the best. But the final decision was always made by Mr. Griswold, architect in charge.

"I climbed hills I didn't believe existed in Pennsylvania, trying to find the right beeches," Mr. Griswold explained. "After all these years of logging and of using other trees in landscaping, the American beech is not common."

---

*Diameter was measured by calipers at four feet above the soil line. General State Authority specifications called for the trees to be placed in prepared pockets at least twelve inches wider and six inches deeper than the burlapped balls of root and soil. The bottom of each pocket had to have at least four inches of topsoil and well-rotted manure in equal parts. Backfill for the pockets had four parts topsoil, one part manure, and one part humus. Each tree was fed with a 5-10-10 fertilizer worked into the soil. Water rings—a dike of soil to hold water in the root area—were to be maintained around each tree until final acceptance by the state.

The one bad misfire in the planting program happened at the elevated terrace just beyond the highway on the Allegheny side of the park. Forest soil was trucked in to create a natural woodland area. This "token forest" was separated from the open meadow by flat natural rocks hauled in from Pennsylvania woodlands and laid informally as a ledge to retain a level one foot above that of the lawn. The kinds of trees planted here, intermingled with shrubs and wildflowers, would require loose, woodsy soil, which would discourage visitors from entering this rock ledge and rough planting.

It was intended to delay the interplanting of wildflowers until the trees had matured enough to provide the necessary shade, and then to plant them in five planting seasons over a two-and-a-half-year period. The state Department of Property and Supplies, however, overruled the strategy of delaying the planting. The wildflowers were planted (partridgeberry, wintergreen *Lycopodium,* spring beauty, wild phlox, bloodroot, wild ginger, Indian turnip, sweet cicely, black snakeroot, wild grape, and bittersweet), exposed to sunlight, and, except for a small patch of volunteer Virginia cowslips, were overcome by weeds. Consequently, unsightly weeds and flowers were turned under and the area seeded with grass, contrary to the designer's intention. This was wrong horticulturally, aesthetically, and practically, since the grass was difficult to maintain and was completely inconsistent with the proposed woodland character. Only a small part of the wildflower ground cover has since been replanted, though the natural shade for it now exists and the soil is still suitable for such growth. Some two thousand wild strawberries—a beautiful and tough ground cover that spreads prolifically and cannot be harmed by people picking its berries—were planted in 1967 in the beds above the rock ledge along the meadow side of the wooded area. In the meantime, the woodland soil has produced quite a few volunteer native trees and shrubs. But subsequent use of the park by masses of people interested chiefly in entertainment has made the concept of naturalistic ground cover impractical. Nature, however, is having her way.

There is a noticeable "unbalanced maturity" in the two forested areas that extend along each river shore to the fountain. This has happened because it was impossible in the 1960s to phase the planting properly with the construction of the new bridges, with the result that the Allegheny side of the park could be and was planted some six years earlier than the Monongahela side. It is estimated that fifteen years will pass before the foliage and growth of the two sides appear to be equal.

Imagine that you are visiting Point State Park for the first time and that you have an interest in planting and landscape design. You will stand for a time on Commonwealth Place at the eastern edge of the park, which is marked by several bronze plaques commemorating historic events, a row of pin oaks, and some comfortable benches. You will look over a grass-covered replica of the ramparts and most of Fort Pitt in an uninterrupted vista to the fountain and the Ohio River. You take one of the curving walkways into the park, following the bordering hedges of American hornbeam underplanted with myrtle. Beyond the hedge is a hillside forested with American beech and other native trees. On each near side of the portal, plantings of evergreen trees screen the highway interchange and its ramps and frame the portal opening. The eight-foot-tall hornbeam hedges and wooded slopes lower the traffic sounds. Sweetgum, shagbark hickory, honeylocust, cucumber, dogwood, and hawthorn trees, underplanted with elderberry, laurel, viburnum, and spice bush, are among the native Pennsylvania trees. In this nonhistoric part of the park next to the modern city, some exotic plants such as Japanese yew and Hall's honeysuckle have been planted for practical reasons.

Beyond the portal, in the western half of the park, you choose one of the walks that connect the main points of interest, always gravitating toward the apex of the triangle. You observe that down each side of the park is a plantation of trees and shrubs, thickest on the Allegheny side, that encloses the central meadow and frames the view of the fountain. You take the left-hand or south walkway past the museum and the blockhouse. The walk leads through the trees between the meadow on the right and the promenade along the shore of the Monongehela on the left. There are some two hundred benches (cypress wood, specially designed) in the park, arranged in conversational groups. There are no Keep Off the Grass signs.

You continue to the fountain, which is operating at 150 feet, and go around it to the very tip of the Point. One writer has said you will feel almost as though you were at the prow of a ship as you stand with rivers on three sides of you and watch towboats and pleasure craft virtually at water level. You return part of the way through the meadow, observing the stone blocks that trace the original shoreline of the Point, some 450 feet east of where it is today. You observe the tracery that outlines the site of Fort Duquesne and study the flat bronze relief map that describes, in French, that fort. You turn left to the Allegheny side and continue upriver along the promenade, past the step-wall riverside bleachers, and turn into a woodland path that leads to a raised overlook terrace that commands a panoramic view of the park, the fountain, the rivers, and the hills. Gilbert Love, in a column for the *Press* written as early as 1968, marvelled at the naturalness of the scene there:

You stroll to the top of the artificial observation hill, noting that the mountain laurel along its sides seems to have had a good year. More interesting is a walkway through a small woods. Its trees seem to have been here always, although planted only a few years ago. Birds are lunching on the berries and seeds of vine and shrub. A cricket leaps across the asphalt walk. You raise your eyes to the tops of the Gateway buildings to make sure you're still in the heart of a great city.

Frederick Law Olmsted, who in 1910 pleaded with Pittsburgh "to rise to its opportunity and nobly form the Point into a great monument," would surely have been pleased to see what you have seen.

Plant Species Planted in Point State Park in 1965

TREES

23 American Beech *(Fagus grandifolia)*
370 American Hornbeam *(Carpinus caroliniana)*
7 Black Tupelo *(Nyssa sylvatica)*
28 Canada Hemlock *(Tsuga canadensis)*
10 Cockspur Thorn *(Crataegus crusgalli)*
59 Flowering Dogwood *(Cornus florida)*
5 Honeylocust *(Gleditsia triacanthos)*
3 Littleleaf Linden *(Tilia Cordata)*
4 Moraine Locust *(Gleditsia triacanthos inermis "Moraine")*
351 Native existing Hawthorn *(Crataegus)* varieties
13 Pin Oak *(Quercus palustris)*
4 Red Maple *(Acer rubrum)*
18 Red Oak *(Quercus borealis)*
2 Scarlet Oak *Quercus coccinea)*
33 Sugar Maple *(Acer saccharum)*
18 Sweetgum *(Liquidambar styraciflua)*
7 Tulip Tree *(Liriodendron tulipifera)*
4 White Oak *(Quercus alba)*
13 Wild Sweet Crabapple *(Malus coronaria)*

SHRUBS AND VINES

410 American Bittersweet *(Celastrus scandens)*
120 Common Witchhazel *(Hammamelis virginiana)*
4,230 Hall's Japanese Honeysuckle *(Lonicera japonica halliana)**
7,240 Hardy English Ivy *(Hedera helix baltica)*
25 Japanese Yew *(Taxus cuspidata)**
1,180 Mountain laurel *(Kalmia latifolia)*
520 Pinxterbloom Azalea *(Rhododendron nudiflorum)*
2,830 Lowbush Blueberry *(Vaccinium augustifolium laevifolium)*
90 Spice Bush *(Lindera benzoin)*

HERBACEOUS PLANTS

99,580 Common Periwinkle *(Vinca minor)*

*Planted in the nonhistoric area.

18

After 1974

Ralph Griswold wrote in his diary on April 10, 1966, "Time will prove this to be one of the great historic parks." Seven years later, on June 11, 1973, he wrote: "It is going to be one of the most spectacular parks in America." Does the record so far indicate that he was right or rhetorical?

Some critics held in the 1950s that the park lacked the necessary "attractions" and would be little used, except perhaps by vagrants; in this sense they labeled the park a project for the improvement of the poor. The Point Park Committee and key state officials gambled on the validity of the Griswold-Stotz basic concept: that people would welcome, use, and cherish an in-town park without such "attractions." They held that people young and old would find and make their own entertainment in a park free from traffic and enclosed dramatically by water, trees, and sky; that they would stroll along the edge of the river and look at the current, the boats, the water-skiers, and the fishermen; that

they would sit on a bench and contemplate their souls or sit on the grass and hold a picnic, or play games. They would observe the birds, the foliage, the kite fliers, and the play of the fountain; watch the children and the young people at play. Who was right? After the first few years, how has the park turned out?

In at least one measurable respect the park has turned out well. The engineering was sound and the construction solid. (Such matters are generally taken for granted, but we have learned in late years that they should not be.) The fountain works on command and it has stayed rooted in place in times of high water. The half-mile U-turn of wharf, anchored twenty-five years ago by a new technique, does not reveal so much as a hairline crack. The long spun-out arch of the portal has not collapsed or sagged under the pounding of billions of tons of traffic.

The park, moreover, has been kept clear of cenotaphs, statues, markers and memorials to

The Royal American Regiment before 1775 was a regular unit of the British army, paid by King George but recruited, trained, and stationed in the American colonies. The resurrected regiment, its equipment, uniforms, and arms correct to the smallest detail, drills, makes music, and fires its cannon at the park almost every summer Sunday afternoon. (Pittsburgh *Press*)

various causes. There is a forgivable exception; a small bronze plaque was set in place in June 1975. At its dedication, Ralph Brem, managing editor of the Pittsburgh *Press,* wrote a fine passage in a column titled "Renewal Collapse Hurts City":

So, they put up the plaque to Dave Lawrence, pointing out that he was born right around the spot Point Park now occupies.

As plaques go, it will eventually get old and crusty.

Even if future generations read it, they won't be able to appreciate the work and dedication captured in those brief lines. For they won't be able to see that barrel-chested, white-haired, broadly smiling man charging up the Boulevard of the Allies, into the wind, his hat brim turned back, hands thrust deep into his coat pockets.

In fact, none of us will see his like again.*

There was some worry when Ralph Griswold doggedly fought off attempts to place a waist-high iron railing the length of the wharf, but in twenty-five years no one has fallen into the water and drowned.

Hardly anyone laments the absence of the monstrous Point bridges, or even remembers the fierce battle that was waged to save and use them. Some people, however, including some of the original Point Park committeemen, do regret that the plan to have ice skating on the basin in winter was dropped.

*David L. Lawrence died in 1966 in the midst of a political rally being held on the stage of Pittsburgh's Syria Mosque.

In 1976 the Highway Users Federation, Washington, D.C., cited the park as an example of superior urban design. It passes, the federation said, a huge volume of traffic without disturbing the pedestrians enjoying its facilities. The vehicle noise is relatively muffled by good design. The highway overpass is an attractive entrance to the park. In Washington in July 1980, the American Society of Landscape Architects chose Point Park from 131 entries for a national honor award, citing it "for mastery and originality in landscape architecture."

The Pittsburgh *Press* ran a picture layout titled "The Perfect Triangle" on July 10, 1977, and it said, "The Point has proven itself the perfect site for a park. . . . It has become a giant playground for the young and young-at-heart. Life's beat slows to the patient pace of the passing rivers. Tensions relax as cascading waters from a mammoth fountain wipe out the noises of downtown."

David Lewis, a planning-minded Pittsburgh architect, said in May 1976, "Point State Park is rightly being taken over by the people, but not necessarily by strollers and those interested in Point history as originally envisaged. The young take over there on weekends with touch football or festivals of all kinds. Very little encourages them. There is no pavilion, no place for the elderly, and ice cream vendors are not allowed in. What's happening in the park is occurring in spite of it." In the last recorded blast against the park by an architect, Mr. Lewis called for admission of ice-cream vendors, provided their stands were well designed.

As for the adjoining Gateway Center complex, all its building sites are filled, 25,000 people are working where 4000 were working before, and rehabilitation is extending itself eastward along its edges.

A visiting New York *Times* reporter wrote in April 1977, "In all urban America there may be no more dramatic spectacle than the wonderland that bursts suddenly into view as one emerges from the Fort Pitt Tunnel and sees downtown Pittsburgh, glittering across the Monongahela River." Harry Coughanour, professional news photographer, agreed. He said, "Pittsburgh, condensed into a triangle and tipped by a gleaming fountain, is one of the most photogenic of all cities."

Frank Hawkins, editor of the *Post-Gazette*, did not agree with the *Times* reporter's qualified praise. "There is no more dramatic urban view in the world," he said, "than the one from Mount Washington, with the possible exception of a few coastal cities. . . . Of all the inland cities I have seen around the world, none has a view to surpass that of Pittsburgh." Hawkins had written earlier: "For the downtown office worker who enjoys a lunch-time stroll, there is no more inviting place than Point State Park. . . . The park is . . . a natural setting of major historical significance. As one strolls its walks, he or she can enjoy the flora indigenous to Western Pennsylvania. . . . In this tranquil

setting people of all ages frolic or sun bathe on the broad expanses of grass or relax in the shade of the trees, only minutes from the heart of the city's commerce.

"There are even squirrels and rabbits in the park but how they were introduced into what only a few years ago was a concrete jungle no one seems to know."

Donald Miller called the fountain "splendid and larger in reality than expected. . . . It is not just a memorial to the past. . . . It is a dynamic salute to the present. Even if an old esthetic idea, the fountain does not fail to impress." A *Post-Gazette* editorial, in delivering a weighty pronouncement on the problems of Big Steel in Pittsburgh (May 19, 1976), tossed off a revealing line. United States Steel, it said, should stay in Pittsburgh, for it is an integral part of the community, "like the fountain at the Point, the Pirates and the Steelers."

Fort Pitt Museum has attracted a good attendance in the warm months, and throughout the school year it is visited by a daily pullulation of school children. It suffered a setback in June, 1978, when the state felt obliged to charge a $1.50 admission fee for casual visitors, but it has recovered; yearly attendance has increased slightly over its 100,000 annual average. The director has mounted a series of exhibits of art, antiques and artifacts that have had a good press and have given good reason to make return visits. Performances of a uniformed company of Colonial troops, armed with and firing muskets, the Royal Americans, have become a Park institution.

There was an unpleasantness on Labor Day 1974 when a promoter held a rock music concert in the park, using amplifiers that could be heard up and down the river valleys. More than sixty thousand fans took over the area, and they did not behave as older people think younger people should behave. There was minor damage to the shrubbery and the fountain pipes. The Coast Guard used a public address system to ask the participants not to jump off Fort Duquesne Bridge. The washrooms could not handle such a large crowd, which led to what one official called "obscene behavior." There was pot smoking and booze. ("Beer cans. My God, you should see the beer cans!") The neighbors complained. The long-range remedy was simple: No more rock music concerts of unmanageable size in the park. Ever.

There was more serious unpleasantness throughout 1976 and 1977, when criminals began to work the park, especially muggers and pickpockets. The thirty-six acres were being patrolled by a private security agency under contract with the state; the patrolmen were mostly unarmed and they had no powers of arrest. The city police were asked to help on an emergency basis. On a September evening in 1976 a plainclothes city detective sitting on a bench in a stakeout was shot in the back and seriously wounded. Pittsburgh had seen a revival of its downtown night life with the opening of Heinz Hall, and it had developed an enviable national reputation as one of the few large cities in America whose downtown streets were relatively safe at night. (The Cleveland *Plain Dealer* sent a newsman to Pittsburgh in April 1973 to report on how it was done.) Now the reputation was blemished, and decisive steps had to be taken. Point Park, a *Post-Gazette* editorial said, "is the crowning glory of Pittsburgh's urban redevelopment program. Its safety must be secured for every citizen who wishes to enjoy its beauty at any time."

The city agreed to police the park for the state and assigned armed patrolmen in two-man teams, each with walkie-talkies, one man with a police dog. The results were good. There were only three violent crimes in the summer of 1978—muggings—and one of those ended in the apprehension and conviction of the mugger. Says the police inspector in charge, "The park has been turned around. It has been returned to the people, and we're going to keep it that way."

To some observers, Point State Park is seen at its very best on a pleasant weekday midafternoon when a few hundred people have the place to themselves, with a kind of public privacy. A courting couple; a mother spending relaxed hours while her small children play in safety. An elderly couple seated on the overlook, watching the river. Students from the nearby college throwing frisbees. Two boys with

The park invites the young. (Pittsburgh *Post-Gazette*)

The park invites the old. (Kent Badger, Pittsburgh *Press*)

fishing poles, a jogger, a serious young lady headed for the museum, an unshaven vagrant dozing on a bench.

To others, the park best justifies itself on a Sunday or a holiday when it is thronged with people, and especially when they have gathered to see a planned program. The Children's Folk Fair, with strolling minstrels, booths with ethnic food, ethnic dances by the renowned Duquesne University Tamburitzans, hour-long free rides on the paddlewheel Gateway Clipper. A water show with an exhibition by Army parachutists dropping on a target. A performance of the Wind Symphony on its moored barge, conducted by Robert Boudreau. A drill session by King George's colonial regulars, the Royal Americans. By this standard, the park had its largest crowd and its most moving experience on July 4, 1976, on the nation's two hundredth birthday.

Probably the park's most varied and exciting festival was the Three Rivers Regatta held in July 1978. (The weather was bad in 1979.) Twenty-one local groups and associations participated in the first of what is planned as an annual affair. The two-day program included an underwater escape act of the Houdini type ("bound with chains and sealed in a packing crate with eight padlocks," etc.); craft exhibitions and ethnic food stands; demonstrations of precision jet formation flying by a U.S. Air Force unit; exhibitions of hang-glider flying and waterskiing; a fishing contest for children;

a parade of towboats and barges; a towboat pushing contest; races by eight classes of speed and pleasure boats; a race of model sailboats; and as a main feature a 2.2-mile race between old-fashioned sternwheel paddleboats (actually driven by diesel engines with screws). In addition to the thousands gathered at the Point, spectators watched from the bridges, the office buildings, the opposite banks of the rivers, Grandview Avenue on Mount Washington, and from their own pleasure craft. (Allegheny County has more than twenty thousand registered boaters.)

The author of this history of Point State Park was with one of the builders of the park on a Saturday afternoon in summer—a friend who was "present at the creation." We walked from Commonwealth Place down the sweeping curved walk to the portal and to the sudden, dramatic view of the open meadow, always surprisingly large. There were hundreds of people. My friend said, "No matter what proposals we used to make about the fountain, the overlook, the promenades, the museum, there were always those who asked, every time, 'Who's going to go down there, anyway?' It was impossible to convince them that people would go there just for the pleasure of being there. I wish I could bring back some who are dead and show them this. They still wouldn't believe it, I imagine. I wish even more that I could bring back the departed leaders we worked with:

A worrisome question asked by the early planners is answered: Would anybody really use the park? (Morris Berman, Pittsburgh *Post-Gazette*)

Richard Mellon, Arthur Van Buskirk, Davey Lawrence, Wally Richards, Park Martin, and some others. They deserved to see this."

I told him of an inscription I had seen in London in October 1977, over the interior of the north door of St. Paul's Cathedral. It was carved under the name of Christopher Wren, put there by his son, and it said: *Si monumentum requiris circumspice.* For the absent builders of Point State Park, I paraphrased it to read: If you would see their monument, look about.

Such is the history of the park at Pittsburgh's Point, conceived by Mayor McClintock early in the nineteenth century, begun in 1945, completed in 1974, and flourishing in 1980. It was and is the prize exhibit of the city's regeneration and rebirth. The Gateway Center developers came because the park was to be there, and the Renaissance followed.

The planners, the technicians, and the men of power and property placed primary emphasis on physical renewal, on building and rebuilding, on material things. Some said that they placed too much emphasis there, but the results indicate that they knew what they were doing. The survivors say today that they could not have succeeded if they had followed any other course. These were knowledgeable and dedicated men. They felt that in producing material improvements they were meeting social needs as well as civic responsibilities. Business leaders like Arthur Van Buskirk, Edgar

Kaufmann, H. J. Heinz II, Lawrence Woods, Adolph Schmidt, Leland Hazard, Ralph Demmler, William Penn Snyder III, and Henry Hillman needed instruction from no one on the importance of social welfare or the significance of cultural development. Nor did the professionals like Wallace Richards, Ralph Griswold, Charles Stotz, John Robin, John Grove, Robert Pease, Stanton Belfour, or Theodore Hazlett. Their first goal was to lay the material base on which the work and health and spirit of the whole city might develop.

That was the hope, expressed from time to time on the record. What has been happening since 1974 has come fairly close to what the planners envisioned. The material, physical, visible developments are continuing, now again, after a pause, at a somewhat accelerated pace. At the same time, Pittsburgh, the industrial giant, is showing a different face. There was a notable flowering of cultural and social activities in the 1970s—of arts and crafts, music, dance, poetry readings, ethnic festivals and community programs, educational television (in which Pittsburgh was the pioneer), the restoration of historic buildings and sound neighborhoods, participating and spectator sports. Pittsburgh is unusual in that its downtown streets are often crowded at night the year around. As long ago as 1971, in one of its last weekly editorials, the old *Life* magazine wrote, "If there are ways to turn the inner city neighborhood around, Pittsburgh may be the first city to find them. . . .

The region now has a rebuilt heart that offers identity to even the most far-flung suburbanite. The heart beat is getting stronger." In the autumn of 1978, Jack Smith, writing in the Philadelphia *Enquirer,* said:

There is . . . the feeling that, whatever Pittsburgh has accomplished, it has done it on its own. . . . As the excitement and stimulation of cities like New York City become more and more synonymous with instability, Pittsburgh, with its tightly knit leadership and cohesive neighborhoods, becomes, from afar, at least, the object of wonder for municipal governments and voters alike. . . . If, indeed, America is, as a multitude of media signals tell us, yearning to get down to basics, Pittsburgh is the city that can give us all lessons in how it is done.

Perhaps a new measure in approbation came in *Sports Illustrated,* December 1979, when Frank Deford called Pittsburgh "a heterosexual's San Francisco."

The new younger leaders of the Allegheny Conference and its associated organizations like to stress one point: that Pittsburgh is an unfinished, continuing story. They emphasize that some of the key proposals of the original planners—the Crosstown Boulevard, for example, or the North Shore Waterfront development, or the high-speed boulevard to the heart of East Liberty, or the development of the city's green hillsides and steep slope areas—have not yet been built, or are not yet finished. Where there is still decay and ugliness, they say, "Wait. Look again in five years, ten years." They feel

that the city's performance in the next decade and a half could possibly surpass that of the great years 1945–1960.

The 1979 report of the Allegheny Conference, issued in June 1980, dwells on the danger that external problems in an age of uncertainty "will delay, diminish and distort the community's private and public goals as they are now targeted and its future opportunities as they are now perceived." Economic, political, and social problems—notably inflation and unemployment—are causing hardships in 1980. There is trouble in some of the county's older industrial boroughs. But the Conference report records an extraordinary surge of major new projects under way or with firm commitments. One plan is an $18.5 million development of both shores of the Allegheny River extending continuously two and a half miles upstream from the Point to form a River Edge Park. This will include and incorporate Point State Park's thirty-six acres. The prospect is that this will become a national park under the administration of the National Park Service.

"What is happening," the Conference report reads, "is that Pittsburgh is overcoming the constraints of its urban geography: the steep hills, the broad rivers, the narrow flatlands. There is an opportunity for the first time in the City's history to treat central Pittsburgh—the heartland of the urban region—as an integrated whole. This means that the Triangle, instead of being separated in form and function from its adjacent and complementary areas, can be meshed with them into a superbly strong city center." The city's slope areas and hillsides "could be converted . . . into a network of woodland which would interlace the City, creating new values along its borders and new amenities for the whole community."

In the meantime, there is the Point, known to man for some twenty thousand years, and there is Point Park, created in the past thirty. Hugh Henry Brackenridge described the setting beautifully, and his description is as fitting today as it was when he wrote it in 1786:

There is not a more delightful spot under heaven to spend any of the summer months than at this place. . . . Here we have the town and the country together. How pleasant it is in a summer evening to walk out upon these grounds, the smooth green surface of the earth, and the woodland shade softening the late fervid beams of the sun; how pleasant by a chrystal fountain . . . with the rivers and the plains beneath.

Acknowledgments

I am deeply indebted to those persons, named in the Bibliographic Essay, who consented to give me in extended interviews their experiences and opinions in working on Point State Park. I wish to express my gratitude to them, with special thanks to those who turned over their records to me.

Nine persons read the entire manuscript; five others read those chapters or passages with which they were specifically involved. I am grateful for their corrections and suggestions, many of which I adopted. I must make it clear, however, that the reading in no way signifies their approval of or control over what appears here in print. The responsibility for any errors and for views expressed (other than those in actual or implied quotation marks) is entirely mine. This is additionally true because most of the readers received the pages in typescript rather than in galley sheets, and so they may not have seen material I added to the final version given to the publisher. Historical research is a continuing process and changes and corrections are normally made up to the moment when the author reluctantly signs and releases the final page proofs. To paraphrase F. Scott Fitzgerald: A book is never completed; it is only abandoned.

I also thank those institutions that allowed me to draw upon their picture files: Carnegie Library, the Allegheny Conference, the Fort Pitt Museum, the Pittsburgh *Post-Gazette*, the Pittsburgh *Press*, and Griswold and Associates.

I am happy to acknowledge my indebtedness to Patrick Horsbrugh, professor of architecture at Notre Dame, for allowing me to quote in chapter 5 long passages from his book, *Pittsburgh Perceived*, and from his article in *Landscape Architecture*, "Contrast in Urban Design."

I wish to thank Anton V. Long of Naples, New York, for permission to quote a passage from his father's *Pittsburgh Memoranda;* the late Leland Hazard for permission to quote from his autobiography, *Attorney for the Situation;* and Ralph H. Demmler for permission to quote from his history of Reed, Smith, Shaw & McClay.

It is difficult to express adequately the gratitude I feel toward the late Theodore Lyle Hazlett, Jr. It was a privilege to work with this remarkable man, to be associated with him most closely during the last six months of his life, when with patience, courage, and forbearance he worked with me on this manuscript. Having labored for some twenty years to rebuild Pittsburgh's physical base, he had then used his considerable influence, with some success, to bring a cultural renaissance to this city. He thus became a prime mover of good new things that have happened to and in the city, among which I pray that this book may in some degree be considered as one. I am profoundly pleased, for him much more than for myself, that, in my last meeting with him, Ted Hazlett expressed a lawyer's measured approbation of the work he had initiated.

Notes

The notes are keyed, first, to the text by page number and a phrase from the matter being identified, and then directly to the source, or to a short title of a work that is given in full in the Bibliography. Sources given in the text will not be repeated here; a full citation will be found in the Bibliography. The following abbreviations are used:

ACCD   Allegheny Conference on Community Development
POHP   Pittsburgh Renaissance Oral History Program
PPC   Point Park Committee
PRPA   Pittsburgh Regional Planning Association
PSP   Point State Park

Preface

xiv   The person who died two months after my interview with him was Michael Rapuano, partner in the New York firm of landscape architects and engineers, Clarke, Rapuano and Holleran.

Chapter 1. "A Clear View to the West"

4   The insurance company was the Equitable Life Assurance Society and its chairman was J. Henry Smith. The president of the Fort Pitt Chapter of the Daughters of the American Revolution was Mrs. Mynard McConnell. The aged Son of the American Revolution was A. G. Trimble.

4, 6   The professional who was not present at the dedication ceremony was Ralph E. Griswold. His letter, dated August 23, 1974, was written to John J. Grove, assistant director of the Allegheny Conference. The director of the Fort Pitt Museum was Rex T. Lohmann. Ernest P. Kline was the lieutenant governor.

6   The subject of Haniel Long's poem was Fred Demmler, a promising Pittsburgh artist, a painter, who was wounded in action at Olsene, Belgium, on October 31, 1918, and died on November 2. He had been a pupil of Willa Cather at Allegheny High School.

8   The planner who could not believe it had happened was Ralph E. Griswold, who wrote the comment in his diary on July 22, 1974.

Chapter 2. The Significance of the Point

9   The resident historian was Dr. John W. Oliver, chairman of the History Department, University of Pittsburgh.

11   The commander-in-chief of New France was the Marquis de la Galissoniere. His letter appears in Stevens-Kent, *Wilderness Chronicles*, p. 27.

20   Bouquet to Anne Willing. *Pennsylvania Magazine*, III, p. 135.

20   The dispatch of the unnamed correspondent in the *Pennsylvania Gazette* appears in Cleland, p. 225.

26   Lowoughqua's oration appears in Downes, *Council Fires*, p. 122.

28   On the British sentiment for returning Canada to France, see Alberts, *Stobo*, pp. 292–93, 390.

Chapter 3. The Point as Part of Pittsburgh, 1800–1914

29   Griswold on Pittsburgh as French capital. Griswold interview; Griswold, "From Fort Pitt to Point Park."

32   Mayor McClintock's proposal for a Point park. "General Description: Point Park Development Study," p. 1.

33   Lawrence a Shabbas goy. Source of this information is Anna G. Greenberg, widow of Dr. Joseph H. Greenberg, registered pharmacist; they so employed young Lawrence early in this century when they lived on Reedsdale Street.

33   Buildings at the Point in 1902. Weir, *Report,* pp. 126–27.

36   "Hell with the lid taken off." Parton, "Pittsburgh in 1866," p. 10. This is the correct wording.

37   Attractions at Exposition Hall. Stotz interview.

37   Pittsburgh's first Renaissance. Alberts, *The Good Provider,* pp. 189–90.

37   Bituminous honey. Griswold, "Wright Was Wrong," p. 209.

37   Court's 1910 ruling on smoke control. Auerbach, "Pattern of Leadership," p. 32.

39   Olmsted's recommendations. Olmsted, *Pittsburgh.*

40   Failure of Municipal Art Commission. Lubove, *Twentieth Century Pittsburgh,* pp. 56–57.

Chapter 4. The Seeds of the Renaissance

42   Municipal Planning Association founded. *Prelude to the Future,* pp. 6–11.

42   Senator Reed's resolution. Oliver, "The Point Memorial," p. 33.

43   Bell-Lee proposal. Ibid. p. 32–35; *Post-Gazette,* July 30, 1945.

43   Planning Association revived. *Prelude to the Future,* p. 16.

43   Historical Society committee and dinner. Stotz interview; Weir, *Report,* pp. 1–4; *Bulletin-Index,* March 24, 1938; program pamphlet for the dinner.

45   1938 meeting with National Park Service. "The Point Problem," pp. 10–12; Griswold interview.

46   Moses recommendations. Moses, *Arterial Plan; Prelude,* pp. 17–19; Lubove, *Twentieth Century Pittsburgh,* pp. 103–05; *Bulletin-Index,* November 23, 1939, July 11, 1940.

55   PRPA's Pitt Parkway and Golden Triangle committees. Lubove, *Twentieth Century Pittsburgh,* p. 105; *Bulletin-Index,* July 11, 1940.

55   Chamber of Commerce Golden Triangle Division. Lubove, *Twentieth Century Pittsburgh,* p. 105; *Bulletin-Index,* November 2, 1939.

55   All planning groups agreed. Lubove, *Twentieth Century Pittsburgh,* pp. 104–05.

55   Scully appointed Point Park Commission. Weir, *Report;* Lubove, *Twentieth Century Pittsburgh,* p. 112; *Bulletin-Index,* March 24, 1938.

56   City Council's 1941 Smoke Ordinance. Lubove, *Twentieth Century Pittsburgh,* pp. 114–16; *Bulletin-Index,* February 13, June 26, 1941.

56   St. Louis learned about smoke control. I heard this in 1942 from David H. Kurtzman, who was with the group that visited St. Louis. The Mellon Institute did conduct a smoke control research program for St. Louis.

Chapter 5. "The Prodigious City"

57   Arthur Rooney on Pittsburgh smoke. *Sports Illustrated,* December 24/31, 1979, p. 39.

58   *Wall Street Journal* survey, "Our Big Cities Today and Tomorrow," 1944.

58   Arthur V. Davis intended to move. Magee, POHP.

58   Storm Jameson on Pittsburgh. New York *Times Magazine,* March 27, 1949.

Chapter 6. The League of Yes-and-No People

64   "Colleagues around the Duquesne Club." *Time* erred in making Edgar Kaufmann a member of the Duquesne Club.

64   *Reader's Digest* version. Steinberg, 84–85.

66   State official's call on Richards. McClain, POHP.

66   Gow, visit from Richards. Gow, POHP.

66   Washington breakfast meeting. Lawrence, "Rebirth," pp. 381–82.

66   Weidlein version. Weidlein, POHP.

67   First ACCD meetings. ACCD Minutes, May 24, June 29, 1943; Lubove, *Twentieth Century Pittsburgh*, pp. 108–09.

68   June 29 luncheon meeting. Gow, POHP.

68   Momentous decision. Schmidt, POHP; Gow, POHB; Pease to author in conversation, October 11, 1978.

68   Chicago *Tribune* story. Kurtzman, POHP.

69   R. K. Mellon thought of moving. George Bloom in a note to the author via Thomas W. Corbett and T. L. Hazlett, Jr.

70   Early design work on park. I have based the account of these early developments on ACCD and PPC minutes; on PRPA's October 1, 1945, Development Study, and on my interviews with Griswold, Stotz, and Richardson.

76   Mellon discussed Point Park with Governor Martin. Braun, POHP. It has been said (Lowe, *Cities*, p. 130) that Arthur Van Buskirk went to Pennsylvania's Republican governor and told him that when Allegheny County received its fair share of state funds for highways and the park, the community's business leaders would have more money for the party.

77   Announcement of park was to embarrass Lawrence. Lawrence, "Rebirth," p. 419; Robin interview; Robin, POHP. Several dozen Republicans deny this.

77   J. J. Kane believed in ACCD program. Martin, POHP; Robin interview. Robin attested: "I never liked Kane, and he never liked me, but you must give him credit. Kane was the first one really to perceive that there was some affinity of interest between the Democratic officeholders and the Republican business community."

77   Robin's advice to Lawrence. Robin interview; Robin, POHP. Lawrence's Republican opponent was Robert N. Waddell, an insurance broker.

Chapter 7. "Our Mission as Keepers of the Gate"

79   ACCD meeting on park. ACCD minutes, November 14, 1945; Pittsburgh *Press, Post-Gazette*, November 15, 1945.

84   Richards's visit to Van Buskirk. Van Buskirk, POHP.

85   First meeting of Point Park Committee. PPC minutes, December 27, 1945.

85   Hazard on character of Van Buskirk. Hazard, "Wanted: A Van Buskirk."

86   Richards's call to Griswold on Wabash fire. Griswold interview and diary.

86   Lawrence declared end of World War II. Lawrence, "Rebirth," p. 386.

87   Committee trip to New York. Lawrence, "Rebirth," p. 432; Van Buskirk, POHP; Hazlett interview.

88   Lawrence's self-appointment illegal. Robin, POHP.

89   Edgar Kaufmann role. Lubove, *Twentieth Century Pittsburgh*, pp. 130; Hazlett interview; Froelich interview; Van Buskirk, POHP; Hazard, *Attorney*, pp. 221–22, 246.

Chapter 8. "Cantilever Development in Automobile Scale"

This chapter is based on Frank Lloyd Wright's six-page presentation prepared for the Allegheny Conference; my interviews with Griswold, Richardson, and Robin; Griswold, "Wright was Wrong"; Pittsburgh *Press*, January 29, 1961, January 6, 1969; Felix, "Wright for Fairyland."

Chapter 9. The Authority to Develop

I have based this chapter on my interviews with Robin, Hazlett, Demmler, and Corbett; Lawrence, "Rebirth," pp. 430–39; *ACCD Presents*, p. 7; Van Buskirk, POHP; Auerbach, "Pattern of Leadership," pp. 85, 87; Demmler, *First Century*, pp. 165–69.

101   State legislators did not grasp. Lowe, *Cities*, p. 139.

101   Van Buskirk had his own candidate. Auerbach, "Pattern of Leadership," p. 87.

102   Equitable preferred office buildings. Martin, "Narrative," p. 14; Lowe, *Cities*, p. 140.

102   Visit to Equitable in New York. Hazlett interview; Lubove, *Twentieth Century Pittsburgh*, p. 122–123.

103   First URA debt in the United States. George C. Burgwin III, POHP. Burgwin was Hazlett's law partner at the time. Most of the Redevelopment Authority bonds were bought by Pittsburgh foundations.

106   "All trains . . . at one time." This was said by Robert J. Dodds, Sr. Demmler, *First Century*, p. 167.

106   Nothing stronger than coffee. Ibid.

107   Giesey on URA's risk. Giesey, POHP.

Chapter 10. "The Action Stage": Demolition and Design

110   No blasting permitted. Swain interview.

110   Bridge design. Rapuano interview; Richardson interview, work journal, documents, and correspondence.

120   Van Buskirk, "Something in sight." Swetnam, "Philosopher."

Chapter 11. Leaves from a Journal of These Days

Ralph Griswold's diaries are in the possession of the company he founded, Griswold, Winters, Swain & Mullin. Typed extracts bearing on Point Park, totaling 117 pages, are at the Historical Society of Western Pennsylvania.

Chapter 12. The Conference and the Committee

129   Lowe on Pittsburgh accomplishment. Lowe, *Cities*, pp. 110, 111, 116, 117, 163.

130   Schmidt on leadership. Schmidt, *The Pittsburgh Story.*

130   Hazard on character of R. K. Mellon. Hazard, *Attorney*, pp. 218, 231–34, 236; Hazard, POHP.

132   McClain on Mellon. McClain, POHP.

132   P. Martin: Mellon attended meetings. Martin, POHP.

132   Gow: Mellon seldom attended. Gow, POHP.

132   Martin persuaded Mellon to be identified. Martin, POHP.

132   Mellon called Appleton on smoke. Paul Block, POHP.

133   Mellon responsible for leases. Martin, POHP.

133   "More reactive than creative." Cusick, POHP.

133   Too much credit given Mellon. Gow, POHP.

133   "Nothing could have been accomplished." Hazard, POHP.

133   Lawrence on Mellon leadership. Lawrence, "Rebirth," 386.

133   Mellon and Lawrence relationship. Robin, interview; Robin POHP; Van Buskirk, POHP; Giesey, POHP. Kane's emissary to Park Martin was George Kelly, public relations man for the Democrats, later director of parks.

134   Character of David Lawrence. Robin, interview; Robin, POHP.

135   Invitation to join executive committee. Hazard, *Attorney*, p. 235.

135   Makeup of executive committee. Auerbach, "Pattern of Leadership," pp. 41, 44.

138   Harrisburg always had news stories. Griswold interview.

138   News stories built up pressure. Walker, POHP.

138   Goddard philosophy on letting contracts. Goddard interview.

138   ACCD and Internal Revenue Service. Van Buskirk, POHP.

139   Character of Park Martin. Griswold, Grove, and Froehlich interviews; Martin, "Narrative," pp. 7, 8, 16, 64. Martin was paid $12,000 a year at the Conference; he had received $7,500 from the city.

141   Park Martin summed up. Martin, POHP.

141 Character of Van Buskirk. Hazard, *Attorney*, pp. 233, 235–36; Hazard, "Wanted: A Van Buskirk"; Robin, Richardson, and Snyder interviews; Swetnam, "Philosopher."

142 Van Buskirk supported Lawrence for mayor. Giesey, POHP. Jack Robin says that no Mellon financial contributions were ever made to Lawrence's campaigns.

142 Character of Wallace Richards. Griswold, Robin, Froelich, and McNeil interviews; Hazard, *Attorney*, pp. 238–40; Oresman, "Pittsburgh Spark Plug"; Van Buskirk, POHP; McClain, POHP; Froelich, POHP lecture; Pease to author. Van Buskirk sometimes called Richards "our wounded soldier."

144 Bigger had a comfortable inheritance. Froelich, POHP.

144 "Ideas poured out of him." Hawkins, POHP.

144 Richards thought of Mellon Square. McClain, POHP.

144 Richards set height of buildings. William R. Oliver, POHP.

Chapter 13. The Past, the Portal, and the Bridge under the Bridge

147 Archeology at the Point. Weir, *Report*; Bliss, *Archeological Report*; Swauger-Hayes, *Historical Archeology*; Swauger, work journal, correspondence, and other papers; Stotz interview; Stotz, *Drums*, 158–59.

148 The old timer fascinated by the early archeological pits was Charles Stotz. Stotz interview.

152 Construction of river wall. Griswold and Rapuano interviews; Griswold, "From Fort Pitt to Point Park," 199, 200.

154 The Portal. Griswold, Stotz and Richardson interviews; *Engineering News Record*, "Arch for Art's Sake"; Brem, "Portal Bridge"; minutes of PPC meetings; *Post-Gazette* editorial, July 5, 1963.

Chapter 14. The Museum in the Bastion

164 Three buildings designed by a committee. Robin interview.

167 Blockhouse and the DAR. Griswold, Stotz, and Goddard

interviews; Griswold diary; continuing articles in the three Pittsburgh daily newspapers.

173 The museum. Stotz interview; Stotz, *The Model of Fort Pitt, Point of Empire,* and "Point State Park"; Wintermantel, "History."

178 Jackson mural. Stotz and Griswold interviews; Griswold diary; Stearns, "American Frontier"; Brem, "How to Paint a Mural," "Fine 'Italian Hand'," and "Cowboy Artist"; PPC minutes, May 22, 1967.

181 Park sculpture project. Stotz and Griswold interviews; Griswold, diary; Seidenberg, "Point Park Sculpture"; PPC minutes, October 21, November 24, 1953, May 17, 1954, June 19, 1959; ACCD file, "Sculpture."

Chapter 15. A Tale of Two Bridges

The chapter is based on my interviews with Stotz, Griswold, and Fosner; the Griswold diary; Stotz's letter to Goddard, February 4, 1970; Ralph Brem and Donald Miller articles as cited in the text and the Bibliography; and continuing newspaper stories.

186 Goddard threatened to divert money. Pittsburgh *Press*, September 16, 1968.

187 Group STL. *Pittsburgh Point,* April 6, 1967; Donald Miller, Ralph Brem, works cited.

188 Pennsylvania legislator. Donald O. Bair, who on February 3, 1970, introduced House Resolution No. 174.

188 Director of Landmarks. James D. Van Trump to editor of the Pittsburgh *Post-Gazette*, August 25, 1970. In January 1975 in *Landscape Architecture* he wrote, "The Fountain, looking like a citified Old Faithful, was notably spectacular and a welcome addition to a remarkable cityscape."

188 "Acting in desperation." Pittsburgh *Post-Gazette*, October 2, 1967.

188 Executive director, Pittsburgh Council. Louis D. Waldman, letter to the Pittsburgh *Press*, November 7, 1969.

188   Leading talk show. Marie Torre, KDKA, January 12, 1970.

188   Idea of design obsolete. Leon A. Arkus, letter to the Pittsburgh *Press*, July 17, 1970.

Chapter 16. The Monumental Column

I have based this chapter on my interviews with Lou Fosner, Stotz, and Griswold. Other sources are the Griswold diary; Ireton, "$3 Million"; Spatter, "City's Hidden River"; Hawkins, "Big Fountain"; Miller, "Fountain in Point Park"; Swetnam, "The Unnamed River"; and "Fountain Focal Point."

Chapter 17. The Planting at the Point

The chapter is based on the Griswold interview and diary; the Swain interview; ACCD, "Preliminary Report on Landscape Development"; Gilbert Love, "Through the Arch" and "Stroll in a Park"; Whitener "Point Park Planting"; Winters, "Primeval Planting"; Griswold letters to Van Buskirk, May 8 and 12, 1967; Griswold report to Point Park Committee, June 8, 1967.

209   Like standing at prow of a ship. Love, "City's Point Sharper."

Chapter 18. After 1974.

213   Brem on Lawrence. Pittsburgh *Press*, June 23, 1975. There was a move in the autumn of 1970 to rename Point State Park the "David L. Lawrence Memorial Park," and House Bill 2546 was entered into the state assembly to that end. Van Buskirk and Goddard killed the move by persuasively declaring that Lawrence would have opposed it. They later headed off a move to name the fountain for R. K. Mellon. (ACCD correspondence file.)

213   Lewis on ice-cream vendors. Miller, "Architect Calls People."

214   Coughanour on photogenic Pittsburgh. So quoted in various articles and verified in conversation with the author.

214   Hawkins, "No more dramatic view." Pittsburgh *Post-Gazette*, April 21, 1977.

214   "Fountain more splendid." Miller, "Fountain in Point Park."

220   *Life* magazine editorial. October 29, 1971.

221   Philadelphia *Enquirer* columnist. Jack Smith, "What is This Thing Called Pittsburgh?" November 5, 1978.

222   Brackenridge, "not a more delightful spot." Newlin, *Life and Writings*, p. 72.

Bibliographical Essay

Most of the sources I used in writing this work are primary and unpublished. They include interviews and correspondence with persons deeply involved in the Pittsburgh rehabilitation program and the design and building of Point State Park; the letters they and their colleagues wrote and the work journals they kept in the years 1937–1974; the minutes of the committees they served on; the documentary reports that were made by and for those committees; and the other archival material found in the filing cabinets of the people and the organizations principally involved.

The research began with, and is to a large extent based on, interviews I conducted with the following sixteen men.

Thomas W. Corbett, deputy attorney general on assignment to the Pennsylvania Department of Forests and Waters, who represented the state in acquisition of land for the park.

Ralph Demmler, attorney for Reed, Smith, Shaw and McClay, which represented the Equitable Life Assurance Society in redeveloping Gateway Center.

Louis R. Fosner, a member of, later a partner in, the architectural firm of Stotz, Hess, MacLachlan and Fosner, who was in charge of redesign of the park fountain.

William R. B. Froelich, chief planning engineer of the Pittsburgh Regional Planning Association, later its executive director.

Maurice K. Goddard, secretary for twenty-four years (1955–1978) of the Pennsylvania Department of Forests

and Waters (later Environmental Resources), the agency that built Point State Park.

Ralph E. Griswold, landscape architect, who was the prime design contractor for the park from its inception. I spent three days taping an interview with him in Williamsburg, Virginia, in the course of which he gave me 117 typed pages of extracts from his work diary pertaining to the park.

John J. Grove, assistant director of the Allegheny Conference on Community Development, secretary of the Point Park Committee, and the state's supervisor in operation and maintenance of the completed park.

Theodore L. Hazlett, Jr., counsel to the Allegheny Conference and the Urban Redevelopment Authority and last chairman of the Point Park Committee. He gave me his complete files on the park.

Donald M. McNeil, traffic engineer, one of the four participants in the preliminary design of the park in 1945. He made the traffic studies necessary for designing the bridges and the highway interchange.

Michael Rapuano, landscape architect, whose New York firm entered into a "joint venture" with Griswold and Associates in design of the park.

George S. Richardson, civil engineer, who supervised construction of the park portal and designed and supervised construction of the Fort Pitt and Fort Duquesne bridges and their approaches. He gave me plans, records and correspondence.

John P. Robin, the first executive director of the Urban Redevelopment Authority, which initiated the Gateway Center project adjoining the park.

William Penn Snyder III, industrialist, in charge of coordinating the work of the different agencies involved, later chairman of the Allegheny Conference.

Charles M. Stotz, architect, who worked with Griswold on the original design of the park and on its many modifications. He designed and supervised construction of the Fort Pitt Museum and collaborated on design of the park portal. Charles Stotz gave me all his records on the park and the museum, including correspondence and minutes books back to 1937.

William G. Swain, landscape architect, associated with the firm of Griswold, Winters, Swain & Mullin, later president of the successor firm, GWSM, Inc.

James L. Swauger, associate director of Carnegie Museum, in charge of the archeological salvage work at the Point. Dr. Swauger lent me his complete files on the work done there.

All the interviews were taped except those with Snyder, Demmler, Hazlett, and Swauger. The cassettes, the transcriptions, and all the documentary material supplied me, or copies thereof, are now in the archives of the Historical Society of Western Pennsylvania. In a few instances the material quoted in print may differ from the tape because of emendations made by the person interviewed.

I also drew on the unpublished interviews and lectures, some ninety-five in number, of the Pittsburgh Renaissance Oral History Project. These were financed by the Buhl Foundation and managed by the University of Pittsburgh as part of the Stanton Belfour Oral History Collection, with Dr. David H. Kurtzman as project director and sometime interviewer. The interviews were on the Pittsburgh redevelopment program as a whole, with relatively little information on the park as such, but they included conversations with several principal figures who had died before I began work in 1975. The interviews with Walter Giesey, J. Steele Gow, Park H. Martin, James McClain, Robert B. Pease, Arthur Van Buskirk, and Edward R. Weidlein were especially useful. Transcriptions of the

interviews and lectures may be found in the Pennsylvania Room of the Carnegie Library and in the Archives of Industrial Society at Pitt's Hillman Library.

The minutes books of the Allegheny Conference, the Point Park Committee, and their various subcommittees are of essential importance as a source of information. Since the minutes touch on virtually every aspect of the park's development, since they are readily accessible at the Historical Society, and since their content may be easily extracted under the appropriate dates, I have cited the minutes as a source only where the information is of special significance.

There are too many magazine articles on the Pittsburgh Renaissance to list in their entirety; I have included those I believe to be the most important. I have listed a number of newspaper articles quoted or referred to in my text, mostly from the Pittsburgh *Press* and the *Post-Gazette*. The special value of these articles to this book lies in their expression and reflection of opinion on the park during the thirty years in which it was being designed, built, publicized, attacked, and defended. Where I know it, the author's name is given.

I give supporting sources for only a few of the statements made on the early history of this region, the city, and the Point, since the facts for the most part are well known. The bibliography for the role of Western Pennsylvania in the years 1749–1800 is enormous and readily accessible elsewhere. I have drawn on it in writing chapter two, but I list only those works from which I have quoted. I offer the following suggestions on this period for the reader who wishes further information. The twelve volumes produced in the 1930s and early 1940s in a three-way collaboration of the Buhl Foundation, the Historical Society of Western Pennsylvania, and the University of Pittsburgh Press, then under the editorship of Lawrence E. Erwin, are outstanding and are, moreover, still in print. For the French-British conflict in Western Pennsylvania, *The French Invasion of Western Pennsylvania* by Donald H. Kent (Harrisburg: The Pennsylvania Historical and Museum Commission, 1954) and *Wilderness Chronicles of Northwestern Pennsylvania,* edited by Donald H. Kent and S. K. Stevens (Harrisburg: Pennsylvania Historical Commission, 1941) are valuable and digestible source books. *Defense in the Wilderness* by Charles M. Stotz (Pittsburgh: Historical Society of Western Pennsylvania, 1958) is strong on the military aspects of the period. A reader or writer seeking original and fresh material would do well to study Fernand Grenier's *Papiers Contrecoeur et autres Documents Concernant le Conflit Anglo-Française sur l'Ohio de 1745 à 1756* (Quebec: Les Presses Universitaires Laval, 1952), which, regrettably and inexplicably, has never been published in English.

For Washington's role, see Douglas Southall Freeman, *George Washington: A Biography* (New York: Scribner's, 1948), especially volumes 1 and 2. For Braddock's expedition, Lee McCardell's *Ill-Starred General* (Pittsburgh: University of Pittsburgh Press, 1958) and a recent work, Paul L. Kopperman's *Braddock at the Monongahela* (Pittsburgh: University of Pittsburgh Press, 1977). For the Bushy Run engagement in 1763, Niles Anderson's *The Battle of Bushy Run* (Harrisburg: Pennsylvania Historical and Museum Commission, 1966). For Bouquet's 1764 expedition, Edward G. Williams's recent work *Bouquet's March to the Ohio* (Pittsburgh: The Historical Society of Western Pennsylvania, 1975), which is based on the original documents.

The best history of Pittsburgh is still Leland D. Baldwin's *Pittsburgh: The Story of a City* (Pittsburgh: University of Pittsburgh Press, 1937), though it is inadequate on events after the Civil War and, of course, has nothing on developments since 1937. Stefan Lorant's *Pittsburgh: The Story of an American City* is a valuable if imperfect 608-page history told in text, pictures, and picture captions.

I should like to acknowledge my indebtedness to Roy Lubove's *Twentieth Century Pittsburgh,* a unique book among the works about modern Pittsburgh, and to Arnold J. Auerbach's Ph.D. dissertation, "The Pattern of Community Leadership in Urban Redevelopment: A Pittsburgh Profile." Jeanne R. Lowe's *Cities in a Race Against Time* has a useful and readable chapter on Pittsburgh, "The New Coalition: Pittsburgh Action Formula Saves a City"; it also has a monumental howler on page 139 in stating that Thomas J. [I] Parkinson, "president of the railroad which then owned the Wabash facilities, set off to New York" to persuade the president of the Equitable Life Assurance Society, "a personal friend of Parkinson," to undertake Pittsburgh's Gateway Center development.

I have drawn on one chapter of Lorant's *Pittsburgh,* "Rebirth, by David L. Lawrence, as Told to John P. Robin and Stefan Lorant," in writing about the early years of the Pittsburgh Renaissance. The reader should be apprized, however, that Robin protested in a lecture delivered on November 13, 1972, "There is no true account, to my knowledge, of what Pittsburgh did and how and why it did it. The published materials were oversimplified, platitudinous and very often inaccurate. I would especially warn you against Lorant's *Pittsburgh: The Story of a City.* There's a chapter in it which carries my name as co-author, to which I would have made very violent objections had I been in this country when it was being prepared for final publication."

I read two books expectantly when they appeared simultaneously in 1978: David E. Koskoff's *The Mellons: The Chronicle of America's Richest Family* (New York: Crowell, 1978), and Burton Hersh's *The Mellon Family: A Fortune in History* (New York: William Morrow, 1978). I still find it remarkable that neither author produced one new fact, one original idea, or one interesting phrase about the Pittsburgh redevelopment program initiated by R. K. Mellon—a feat which I should have thought difficult. Koskoff devotes 4 pages to the subject in a 463-page book. Hersh gives 8 pages out of 640 and, among other errors, misdates Wallace Richards's incapacitating stroke by some five years.

The second half of Leland Hazard's *Attorney for the Situation* gives a lively, original, and quite frank appraisal of developments in Pittsburgh after 1938, with shrewd assessments of the characters of those involved.

A selected list of articles, books, and documents used in writing this book follows.

Alberts, Robert C. *The Most Extraordinary Adventures of Major Robert Stobo.* Boston: Houghton Mifflin, 1965.
———. *The Good Provider: H. J. Heinz and His 57 Varieties.* Boston: Houghton Mifflin, 1973.
Allan, William. " 'Eiffel' Tower Urged at Point State Park." Pittsburgh *Press,* July 24, 1961.
Allegheny Conference on Community Development. *Point Park Development Study.* Report prepared for the governor of Pennsylvania by Griswold, Stotz, Richardson, and McNeil, November 14, 1945.
———. *Digest,* six numbers, 1945–1947.
———. *Pittsburgh—Challenge and Response.* Pittsburgh, 1947.
———. *Point State Park: Preliminary Report on Landscape Development.* A report prepared for the state by Ralph Griswold & Associates and Clarke & Rapuano, Inc., July 1952.
———. *The Allegheny Conference on Community Development Presents . . .* Pittsburgh, 1956.
" 'Arch for Art's Sake' Bridge Will Serve a Double Function." *Engineering News Record,* November 1, 1962, pp. 30–32.
Atcheson, Richard. "Pittsburgh: The Smoke Clears." *Show,* February, 1964, pp. 27–34.
Auerbach, Arnold J. "The Pattern of Community Leadership in Urban Redevelopment: A Pittsburgh Profile." Ph.D. diss., University of Pittsburgh, 1960.
Bernhard, Andrew. "Allegheny Conference Entitled to Take a Bow." *Pittsburgh Post-Gazette,* October 11, 1954.
Bigger, Frederick. "Analysis and Recommendations re Proposals for Triangle Improvement Submitted to the Planning Commission." Pittsburgh, June 28, 1938.
Bliss, Wesley L. *Archeological Report on Fort Pitt and Fort Duquesne.* Prepared for the Point Park Commission, 1942–1943.
Brem, Ralph. "Portal Bridge—Something Different—To Rise from Maze of Steel at Point." Pittsburgh *Press,* July 8, 1962.
———. "Cowboy Artist Commissioned for Fort Pitt Mural." Pittsburgh *Press,* October 14, 1964.
———. "Fine 'Italian Hand' of Yankee Cowboy." Pittsburgh *Press,* February 27, 1966.
———. "Architects, Artists Challenge Point State Park Plans." Pittsburgh *Press,* October 2, 1967.
———. "Park Critics 'Cry Before They're Hurt.' " Pittsburgh *Press,* October 23, 1967.
———. "Fountain is Fountain? Not in New State Park." Pittsburgh *Press,* October 24, 1967.
———. "How to Paint Mural on Wall Not Yet Built." Pittsburgh *Press,* October 17, 1974.
———. "Renewal Collapse Hurts City." Pittsburgh *Press,* June 23, 1975.
Bulletin-Index Magazine (Pittsburgh). Unsigned articles in the issues of March 24, 1938, pp. 6–7; November 2, 1939, pp. 6–7; November 23, 1939, p. 6; July 11, 1940, pp. 6–7; February 13, 1941, p. 6; June 26, 1941, p. 6; and September 25, 1948, p. 9.
"The City: Will Its Beauty Be Lost?" *Pittsburgh Point,* April 6, 1967, pp. 1, 4.
Cleland, Hugh. *George Washington in the Ohio Valley.* Pittsburgh: University of Pittsburgh Press, 1955.
Conrad, Will C. "Unity Helps Pittsburgh Build New Heart from Rotted Core." Milwaukee *Journal,* September 9, 1951.
Deford, Frank. "Roses and Donuts." *Sports Illustrated,* December 6, 1979, pp. 98–112.
Demmler, Ralph H. *The First Century of an Institution: Reed, Smith, Shaw and McClay.* Pittsburgh, 1977. Privately Printed.
Dickey, Robert, III. "The Other Side of the Giant." A special report, an eight-page advertising insert, on Pittsburgh in *The Saturday Review and World,* August 24, 1974, Part II.
Doherty, Robert H. "The Pittsburgh of Tomorrow." *Greater Pittsburgh,* March 1947.

Downes, Randolph C. *Council Fires on the Upper Ohio.* Pittsburgh: University of Pittsburgh Press, 1940. Reissued 1969.

English, Neal. "The Golden Triangle." *Masonry, the Magazine for the Masonry Industry,* October 1975, p. 6.

Felix, David. "Wright for 'Fairyland' at Point Park." Pittsburgh *Sun-Telegraph,* May 5, 1949.

"Fountain Focal Point." *Compressed Air Magazine,* November 1974, pp. 8–11.

"From Urgency to Action: The Story Behind Pittsburgh's Renaissance." In *Pittsburgh Quote,* Tenth Anniversary Issue, 1965.

"General Description: Point Park Development Study." Pittsburgh Regional Planning Association, November 14, 1945.

Griswold, Ralph E. "From Fort Pitt to Point Park: A Turning Point in the Physical Planning of Pittsburgh." *Landscape Architecture,* July 1956, pp. 193–202.

———. "Wright Was Wrong." *Landscape Architecture,* April 1963, pp. 209–14.

Hawkins, Frank. "Lawrence of Pittsburgh: Boss of the Mellon Patch." *Harper's,* August 1956, pp. 55–61.

———. "Big Fountain to Cap Glory of Point Park." Pittsburgh *Post-Gazette,* June 20, 1974.

Hazard, Leland. "Wanted: A Van Buskirk to Blow the Bugle." *Post-Gazette,* August 30, 1974.

———. *Attorney for the Situation.* Pittsburgh: Carnegie-Mellon University Press, 1975. An autobiography.

Heinz, H. J., II. "Newspaper Leadership in Community Action." Address given at the eightieth convention of the American Newspaper Publishers Association, New York, April 27, 1966. Mimeographed.

Horsbrugh, Patrick. *Pittsburgh Perceived: A Critical Review of Form, Features and Feasibilities of the Prodigious City.* Pittsburgh: City Planning Commission, 1963.

———. "Contrast in Urban Design." *Landscape Architecture,* April 1963, pp. 196–201.

Ireton, Gabriel. "$3 Million Pumped into Park Fountain." Pittsburgh *Post-Gazette,* November 19, 1973.

Lawrence, David L. "Rebirth, As Told to John P. Robin and Stefan Lorant." In Stefan Lorant, *Pittsburgh: The Story of an American City.* New York: Doubleday, 1964. Chapter 10.

Long, Haniel. *Pittsburgh Memoranda.* Santa Fe: Writers Editions, 1935.

Lorant, Stefan. *Pittsburgh: The Story of an American City.* New York: Doubleday, 1964. Author's edition, "revised, enlarged and updated," 1975.

Love, Gilbert. "Through the Arch." Pittsburgh *Press,* October 1, 1963.

———. "City Makes a Point for History." *Pittsburgh Press,* November 23, 1966.

———. "Stroll in a Park." Pittsburgh *Press,* October 24, 1968.

———. "City's Point Sharper Than Ever." Pittsburgh *Press,* July 28, 1974.

Lowe, Jeanne R. *Cities in a Race with Time.* New York: Random House, 1967. Chapter 3, "The New Coalition: Pittsburgh's Action Formula Saves a City."

———. "Rebuilding Cities and Politics." *Nation,* February 8, 1958.

Lubove, Roy. *Twentieth Century Pittsburgh: Government, Business, and Environmental Change.* New York: John Wiley, 1969.

McCaffery, Mary K. "Tutor Pittsburgh—Steel City Plans New Lesson in Shaking Off Old Civic Shabbiness." *Wall Street Journal,* February 24, 1953.

Magee, Edward. "Pittsburgh: A City That Almost Died." Address to the Annual National Conference, Controllers Institute of America, October 27, 1959. Mimeographed.

Martin, Park. "Narrative of the Allegheny Conference on Community Development and the Pittsburgh Renaissance, 1943–1958." Manuscript, 1964, 70 pp.

Mellon, Richard King. "Management's Responsibility to the Community." An address given at the Wharton School of Finance and Commerce, Philadelphia, November 16, 1953.

Miller, Donald. "Sculptor Envisions Pedestrian Mall." Pittsburgh *Post-Gazette,* November 1, 1969.

———. "Two Point Bridges Could Hold a Motel, Gallery." Pittsburgh *Post-Gazette,* December 13, 1969.

———. "Architect Rebuilds Nation's History." Pittsburgh *Post-Gazette,* July 21, 1972. An article on Charles M. Stotz.

———. "Fountain in Point Park Better Than Expected." Pittsburgh *Post-Gazette,* September 6, 1974.

———. "Architect Calls People Key to Urban Design." Pittsburgh *Post-Gazette,* May 28, 1976.

Moses, Robert. *Arterial Plan for Pittsburgh.* Pittsburgh: Pittsburgh Regional Planning Association, 1939.

"Mr. Mellon's Patch." *Time,* October 3, 1949, pp. 11–14. A cover story.

Murphy, Charles J. V. "The Mellons of Pittsburgh." *Fortune,* October 1967, p. 121; November 1967, p. 159.

Nelson, Robert Colby. "Renaissance in Pittsburgh." *Christian Science Monitor,* May 9, 1961.

Newlin, Claude Milton, ed. *The Life and Writings of Hugh Henry Brackenridge.* Princeton: Princeton University Press, 1932.

Nicklin, Philip H. *A Pleasant Peregrination Through the Prettiest Parts of Pennsylvania, Performed by Peregrine Prolix.* Philadelphia, 1836.

Oliver, John W. "The Point Memorial." *Pittsburgh Record,* October 1930, pp. 33–35.

———. "Historical Significance of Point Park, Pittsburgh, Pennsylvania." An address given on the occasion of the demolition ceremony, May 18, 1950.

Olmsted, Frederick Law. *Pittsburgh: Main Thoroughfares and the Downtown District. Improvements Necessary to Meet the City's Present and Future Needs.* Pittsburgh: Pittsburgh Civic Commission, 1911.

Oresman, Donald. "Pittsburgh Spark Plug." Pittsburgh *Press,* September 30, 1951. An article on Wallace Richards.

Parton, James. "Pittsburgh in 1866." In *Pittsburgh,* ed. Roy Lubove. New York: New Viewpoints, 1976. An anthology of articles and extracts on Pittsburgh.

Perry, George Sessions. "The Cities of America: Pittsburgh." *Saturday Evening Post,* August 3, 1946, p. 14.

"Pittsburgh Begins to Rebuild." *Progress,* January 1939, pp. 10–12. Published by the Pittsburgh Regional Planning Association.

"Pittsburgh Comes Out of the Fog." *Newsweek,* September 26, 1949, pp. 25–29.

Pittsburgh Point, vol. 1, no. 23, April 6, 1967.

"Pittsburgh Rebuilds." *Fortune,* June 1952, p. 90.

"Pittsburgh Sets a Precedent by Bold Planning, Major Building." *Engineering News Record,* Special Report, November 19, 1959, pp. 54–78.

"Pittsburgh's New Powers." *Fortune,* February 1947, p. 69. This unsigned article was written by Lawrence P. Lessing, a staff writer for *Fortune* who had been an editor of the Pittsburgh *Bulletin-Index* in the 1930s.

"The Point Problem." *Progress,* January 1939, pp. 10–12. Published by the Pittsburgh Regional Planning Association.

Prelude to the Future. Pittsburgh: Pittsburgh Regional Planning Association, 1968.

Price, Gwilym A. "What We Did—What We Learned—in Rebuilding Pittsburgh." Address given at a Businessmen's Luncheon, Dallas, Texas, May 11, 1960. Mimeographed.

Richards, Wallace. "Pittsburgh's Thrilling Renaissance." *American City,* July 1950, p. 155.

Schmidt, Adolph. *The Pittsburgh Story.* Address before the International Press Institute, University of Pittsburgh, April 19, 1958.

Schriftgiesser. "The Pittsburgh Story." *Atlantic Monthly,* May 1951, pp. 66–69.

Schubert, Jane Gary. "A Man and His City." A biography of Frederick Bigger produced as a seminar paper in social studies, Carnegie-Mellon University, 1971.

Seidenberg, Mel. "Point Park Sculpture Seen 'for the Birds.'" Pittsburgh *Post-Gazette,* December 11, 1960.

Shames, Sally Olean. "David L. Lawrence, Mayor of Pittsburgh: Development of a Political Leader." Ph.D. diss., University of Pittsburgh, 1958.

Smith, Jack. "What is This Thing Called Pittsburgh?" Philadelphia *Inquirer,* November 5, 1978.

Smith, James. *Scoouwa: James Smith's Indian Captivity Narrative.* Columbus, Ohio: Ohio Historical Society, 1978.

Spatter, Sam. "Builder Uses City's Hidden River." Pittsburgh *Press,* August 25, 1974.

Stearns, Bob. "The American Frontier in Bronze." Pittsburgh *Press,* May 13, 1979.

Steinberg, Alfred. "The New City Called Pittsburgh." *Reader's Digest,* May 1955, pp. 83–86. Condensed from *National Municipal Review,* March 1955.

Stotz, Charles M. *Defense in the Wilderness.* Part 2 of *Drums in the Forest.* Pittsburgh: Historical Society of Western Pennsylvania, 1958.

———. "Point State Park: Birth Place of Pittsburgh." *Carnegie Magazine,* January 1964, pp. 15–20.

———. *The Model of Fort Pitt: A Description and Brief Account of Britain's Greatest American Stronghold.* Pittsburgh: Fort Pitt Museum, 1970.

———. *Point of Empire: Conflict at the Forks of the Ohio.* Pittsburgh: Historical Society of Western Pennsylvania, 1970.

Stryker, Roy, and Seidenberg, Mel. *A Pittsburgh Album, Revised for Bicentennial U.S.A.* Pittsburgh: *Post-Gazette* and Herbick and Held, 1975.

Stuart, Roger. "The Many-Sided Mr. Stotz." Pittsburgh *Press,* June 23, 1968.

Swauger, James L. "Excavations at the Flag Bastion of Fort Pitt, 1958–1959." *Pennsylvania Archeologist,* December 1960, pp. 111–15.

Swauger, James L., and Hayes, Arthur M. *Historic Archeology at at Fort Pitt, 1953.* Anthropological Series No. 4. Point Park Committee of the Allegheny Conference on Community Development, 1959, pp. 247–73.

Swetnam, George. "Philosopher of the Renaissance." Pittsburgh *Press,* January 3, 1960. An article on Arthur Van Buskirk.

———. "The Unnamed River." Pittsburgh *Press,* August 22, 1965.

Van Buskirk, Arthur B. "What Business Has Learned About Rebuilding a City." Address before the Committee on Economic Development, May 29, 1958. Mimeographed.

Van Trump, James D. "Pittsburgh Points to the Great Fountain." *Landscape Architecture,* January 1975, pp. 59–63.

Weir, Fred W. "Report of Point Park Commission." Pittsburgh, December 31, 1943.

Whitener, Julian. "Point Park Planting Returns to Primeval." Pittsburgh *Press,* June 20, 1968.

Wintermantel, Ed. "History in the Making." Pittsburgh *Press,* June 8, 1969. An article on the Fort Pitt Museum.

Winters, Margaret M. "Primeval Planting for Point Park." *Carnegie Magazine,* April 1953, pp. 113–16.

Wright, Frank Lloyd. "For the Allegheny Conference— Cantilever Development in Automobile Scale of Point Park, Pittsburgh." 1947. Typescript.

Ziegler, Arthur P., Jr. "What's the Point?" *Charette,* September–October, 1970, p. 14.

Index

245